```
917      Brown, Ron, 1945-
.1304        Backroads of Ontario / Ron Brown.   Edmonton
Bro      : Hurtig, c1984.
             271 p. : ill., maps.



         1. Ontario — Description and travel — Tours.
         I. Title.
         088830238X  pb                    2149125 NLC
         0888302592                        2149109
```

6/he

BACKROADS
OF ONTARIO

BACKROADS
OF ONTARIO

RON BROWN

Hurtig Publishers
Edmonton

Hurtig Publishers Ltd.
10560–105 Street
Edmonton, Alberta
T5H 2W7

Canadian Cataloguing in Publication Data

Brown, Ron, 1945–
    Backroads of Ontario

Includes index.
ISBN 0-88830-259-2 (bound).—ISBN 0-88830-238-X (pbk.)

1. Ontario—Description and travel—1950– —Tours.*
I. Title.
FC3067.5.B769 1984   917.13'044   C84-091151-3
F1057.B769 1984

Design: David Shaw & Associates Ltd.
Cover illustration: J.A. Kraulis
Composition: Attic Typesetting Inc.

Printed and bound in Canada

Contents

The Story of Ontario's Backroads

*The road was scarcely passable; there were no longer cheerful farms
and clearings, but the dark pine forest and the rank swamp crossed
by those terrific corduroy paths (my bones ache at the mere
recollection), and deep holes and pools of rotted vegetable matter
mixed with water, black, bottomless sloughs of despond! The very
horses paused on the brink of some of these mud gulfs and trembled
ere they made the plunge downwards. I set my teeth, screwed myself
to my seat and commended myself to heaven.*

Backroading is a recent pastime and a far cry from 1837 when
traveller Anna Jameson wrote the above words. No doubt she
would wonder about the sanity of today's backroad adventurers.
Yet those who escape the hustle of high-speed freeways and seek
out the tranquility of another era have made backroad driving
North America's most popular outdoor activity.

This book leads you from Ontario's main highways onto the
backroads. The province had no expressways before 1939. That
was the year the Queen Elizabeth Way was opened. In 1929 there
was less than 2,000 km of hard surface, but before 1790 there
were no roads at all. European settlement of Ontario had just
begun with the arrival of the United Empire Loyalists from the
war-torn colonies that had become the United States of America.
The Loyalists settled the shorelines of the St. Lawrence River, of
Lake Ontario and Lake Erie, and they had no need of roads. But
the governor of the day, John Graves Simcoe, ever casting a wary
eye to the restless neighbour to the south, embarked upon the
building of military roads. In 1793 he ordered a road from
Montreal to Kingston—and Ontario had its first road. (You can
follow it today as County Road 18 through Glengarry County.)
This he followed with Yonge Street and Dundas Street, which also
survive and have retained their names.

7

Even though settlement was slow through the early years of the century, the pattern of Ontario's roads was taking shape. Surveyors made their way through the forests, designing townships and surveying each into a rigid grid of lots and concessions. Along each concession they set aside a road allowance, linked at intervals of 2 to 5 km by side roads. And so Ontario became a checkerboard that paid no heed to mountains, lakes, and swamps. Hence the difficulties that travellers like Anna Jameson had.

One of the first problems was that there was no one to build the roads. Although each settler was required to spend twelve days a year on road labour, settlers were few and far between at first. Not until the 1820s did roads begin to appear in any number. Some were designed to open the interior townships to settlers. Among these settlement roads were the Perth Road (from Perth to Kingston), the L'Orignal Road (along the Ottawa River), and the Napanee River Road. These are some of the backroads you can choose to drive along today.

Then there were the roads that led from the interior to the countless little wheat and lumber ports that appeared on the coves and river mouths of Lake Ontario and Lake Erie. They were useless in spring and little better in summer. Only in winter, when frost and snow combined to create a surface that was hard and smooth, did farmers haul their wheat to port.

In the 1840s the government turned road building over to private companies and to municipalities. Some of the companies tried such improvements as macadam and planks. But, rather than being grades of crushed stone, the macadam was often little more than scattered boulders. As for the planks, they rotted after a few years. Then things got even worse, for the railways burst upon the scene and the road companies turned their energies to railway building, as did many of the municipalities.

Meanwhile, the government had tried one more road-building venture, one that it would have preferred to forget—the colonization roads. This was in the 1850s when lumber companies were anxious to reap the pine forests that cloaked the highlands between the Ottawa River and Georgian Bay. Despite the fact that early surveyors had dismissed the agricultural potential of this upland of rock and swamp, the region was touted as a Utopia for land-hungry settlers. The government's main aim was to provide labour, horses, and food for the lumbermen. Once the forests were razed and the lumbermen had gone, the settlers who had moved to the area were left to starve. By 1890 most of them had left, and the roads in some cases were totally abandoned. Nevertheless, a few of them retain their pioneer appearance and pioneer buildings; they too have become some of the backroads in this book.

At the turn of the century, Ontario's road travellers had good news. In 1894 the Ontario Good Roads Association had been formed to lobby for better roads, and in 1901 the government passed the Highway Improvement Act to subsidize county roads. Finally, in 1915, the government got back into the business of road building and created the Department of Highways. The first 60 km of provincial road was assumed east of Toronto in 1917 and Ontario's highway system was born.

Meanwhile, northern Ontario was still railway country. Towns and villages north of the French River owed their existence to the railways, and what roads there were stabbed out from the railway lines to lumbering and mining areas. The only exceptions were colonization roads. Some had been built in the north to open up the Lake Timiskaming clay belt and the fertile lands of Rainy River, Dryden, and Thunder Bay. They were at first under the auspices of the Department of Public Works and the Department of Lands and Forests, but in 1937 they were taken over by the Department of Highways.

The years following the Second World War saw the great burgeoning of the auto era, and during the 1950s and 1960s Ontario embarked on a spate of road improvements unequalled in the entire previous two centuries. This activity continued apace. But however efficient the new roads were, they took with them much of Ontario's traditional landscape. Rows of maple and elm, cedar-rail fences and roadside buildings all fell before the bulldozer, and Ontario was suddenly left with a legacy of endless asphalt. Not one of Ontario's provincial roads was designed as a scenic road. It was not surprising, therefore, that motorists began to take to the backroads in increasing numbers.

It is impossible to assess the extent of Ontario's backroads. They fall under so many different jurisdictions: township roads, county roads, secondary highways, northern Local Road Board roads, public forest roads over Crown land, and even private forest roads that are open to the public. But the backroads in this book are special. Each has a story or a theme. Some follow the unhappy colonization roads, some the more prosperous settlement roads. Some explore rural areas that have retained their century-old townscapes and farmscapes. Others follow the shores of the Great Lakes. Some wind along quiet river valleys and over high plateaus. Others take you into northern Ontario to logging areas old and new, to once-booming silver fields, and to the fringe of the province's frontiers.

While the maps that guide you through each chapter contain basic information, you will also find it useful to refer to the Official Road Map of Ontario, which shows all provincial and county roads, and gives distances between towns. It is available free from most Ministry of Transportation and Communications offices.

You may also wish to obtain more detailed maps. For southern Ontario, there is the 1:250,000 series, available from the Ministry of Transportation and Communications, 1201 Wilson Avenue, Downsview, Ontario M3M 1J8. For northern Ontario, detailed maps can be obtained from the Ministry of Natural Resources, the Whitney Block, Queen's Park, Toronto, Ontario M7A 1W3. And don't overlook the driving and walking tours prepared by local counties and municipalities.

The routes in this book vary in length from 50 km to more than 300 km. All are passable in cars, though some of the side trips may be slippery in the spring. All have places where you can eat or fill a picnic basket, either at the start or along the route. Be prepared to pack a camera, a fishing rod, and perhaps hiking boots—as well, of course, as your curiosity about an Ontario that you will never see from those high-speed expressways. Even Anna Jameson would enjoy Ontario's backroads today.

BACKROADS OF ONTARIO

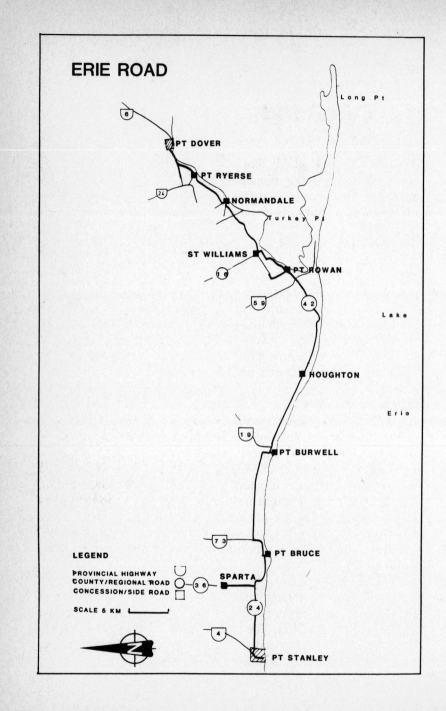

ERIE ROAD

Long Pt

6

PT DOVER

PT RYERSE

24

NORMANDALE

Turkey Pt

ST WILLIAMS

1 6

PT ROWAN

5 9

4 2

Lake

HOUGHTON

Erie

1 8

PT BURWELL

7 3

PT BRUCE

SPARTA

3 6

2 4

4

PT STANLEY

LEGEND

PROVINCIAL HIGHWAY
COUNTY/REGIONAL ROAD
CONCESSION/SIDE ROAD

SCALE 5 KM

N

1   Erie Road

This route winds along Ontario's most underrated shoreline, following a fascinating pioneer trail amongst Lake Erie's shores and bluffs. It begins at Port Dover, 60 km southwest of Hamilton on Highway 6, and runs on paved roads 95 km westward to Port Stanley.

This trip will be a special delight for the water lover. Public wharfs in most towns provide opportunities to cast for Lake Erie's popular yellow perch or to watch squat fishing tugs chug to their berths. Here too are bluff-top lookouts, and more public beaches than on any similar length of shoreline on the Great Lakes. There are marshes abounding in bird and plant life. And in between are some of Ontario's best-preserved early towns, including one ghost town. Most of the towns along the route have such facilities as restaurants, grocery stores, and gas stations.

A Bit of History

Lake Erie's first settlements were founded by Loyalists, refugees from America's post-revolutionary persecutions. But no sooner were they beginning to get established than a devastating American raid during the War of 1812 laid waste to farms, homes, and industries. However, settlement revived after the war, spurred on by Thomas Talbot, a retired army officer, who sold his land grants to any settler who met his stringent standards. Busy villages developed around mills and small harbours, and as the homesteaders moved up the creeks and crude trails, the backlands began to fill.

The railway age brought a further impetus, causing some of the towns to boom (though others lost business) and by the turn of the century many of the ports were thriving and the commercial fishery was flourishing. The introduction of tobacco farming in the 1920s gave a much-needed boost to agriculture. Today, fishing and tobacco growing still predominate in this region.

Port Dover

Port Dover, the first town on this route, is Ontario's fishing capital and the home of the world's largest freshwater fishing fleet. It began as a mill town called Dover Mills; but in 1812, as the American invaders left their fiery trail across the countryside, Dover Mills was reduced to ashes. To take advantage of the growing trade in lumber and grain, the townspeople rebuilt by the lake. Later, after the coming of the railway, commercial fishing boomed and Port Dover grew quickly. Most of the town's historic buildings date from those heady days in the latter part of the nineteenth century.

There are several points of interest in the town, including the Port Dover Harbour Museum. If you enter Port Dover on Highway 6 from Hamilton, turn left onto St. Andrews Street immediately after crossing the bridge and proceed to Harbour Street. Here you will find the museum, housed in a restored fisherman's shanty, which was built around 1890. Look especially for old-time fishing equipment and for the story of fishing on Lake Erie.

More fishing tugs glide into Port Dover than into any other freshwater harbour.

Fish nets drying at Port Dover.

On the west side of the harbour is the old fishermen's quarter. Net sheds and shanties, wooden and weathered, cast their reflections in the waters of the harbour. Farther south on Harbour Street are homes and shops dating from the turn of the century, and at the foot of Harbour Street is the Sandalmaker's Shanty, now a craft shop. Stretching beyond the streets out into the waters of Lake Erie is the public wharf. No matter when you visit, you will encounter local residents with a line in the water and a friendly word about the weather. If you visit the wharf in the evening, you can watch the squat fishing tugs glide behind the breakwater and manoeuvre for space in the new harbour on the east side.

If you need to stock up with a box lunch or simply to enjoy a snack, Port Dover's commercial core is focused on Highway 6 west of the bridge. Grocery stores, drug stores, and fast-food restaurants are all located here.

Port Dover to Normandale

To leave Port Dover, turn left from Highway 6 onto Nelson Street at the end of the commercial core. This part of the route is marked by brown and white signs proclaiming the Talbot Trail. For the

15

first 2 km the route treats you to bluff-top views over Lake Erie, and then it heads inland across a flat farmland of pastures, orchards, and a few commercial greenhouses. After 6 km, turn left at a crossroads, and 2 km farther on you will come to Port Ryerse.

Named for Colonel Sam Ryerse, an early mill owner, this wooded narrow gully has gone from busy shipping centre to quiet cottage community, and it has some of the oldest buildings on Lake Erie. Atop the east side of the gully stands the picturesque white-frame Memorial Anglican Church. Since 1869, the church has witnessed many changes, as has a large brick hilltop mansion nearby.

Your next stop after Port Ryerse will be another one-time centre of activity, Normandale. To get there, continue 1 km west on the Talbot Trail until you come to a fork in the road. Take the left branch, a winding farm road, and after 5 km you will come to a T-intersection. Turn left and after about half a kilometre you will be in the cottage community of Fishers Glen. In this wooded gully turn right, drive 2 km to a T-intersection; turn left at the intersection and drive 1 km to Normandale.

Normandale

As you descend the hill into this quiet valley, you may find it hard to call it "yesterday's Hamilton." Yet for three decades in the nineteenth century, Normandale was Ontario's foremost iron producer, thanks to one Joseph Van Norman. The production of iron had been begun here in 1815 by John Mason, who simply burned a mixture of charcoal and bog ore from the local swamps. Van Norman acquired the operation in 1828 and turned it into a major industry.

A town plot of 5 streets and 42 lots was laid out, and by 1846 the town had a population of 300, a grist mill, and a main street full of businesses. However, by 1848 the timber and ore were gone. So Van Norman moved on, and Normandale became a ghost town. Today it has revived as a cottage community.

Yet the evidence of Van Norman's day lingers on. At the foot of the hill is a T-intersection, on the southeast corner of which you will see an abandoned store and a two-storey frame building with a front gable. This is the Union Hotel, which was built by Van Norman and his business colleagues, who named it in commemoration of their collective effort. It has been partly restored and now contains a tearoom and a craft shop. Near the lake is the site of Van Norman's foundry, commemorated by a federal government plaque. So thoroughly was the industry abandoned that Van Norman's blast furnaces lay buried and forgotten until their rediscovery by Royal Ontario Museum archaeologists in 1968. One of the furnaces is now in Upper Canada Village in eastern Ontario, the other in the Eva Brook Donly Museum in Simcoe, just 17 km north of Normandale on Highway 24.

Normandale to St. Williams

To continue on the pioneer trail, drive west from the Union Hotel up the wall of the gully, and after 1 km look for a side road that branches left. This scenic section of the route winds through woods and fields for 1 km to a stop sign at Regional Road 10. About 3 km south of the intersection, at the foot of Lake Erie's cliffs, lies Turkey Point. Atop the bluff is Turkey Point Provincial Park and campground.

Beside the park, a golf course covers the site of Fort Norfolk and also of Charlotteville, which was built as an administrative centre. Both were instigated by Governor Simcoe during the last decade of the eighteenth century, when the threat of an American invasion was ever-present. But the fort was never completed, and the district capital was re-established at Vittoria, a safer inland location. Charlotteville and Fort Norfolk quickly vanished from the landscape. Only a historical plaque marks the spot. Turkey Point itself is a spit of shifting sand which extends 5 km into Lake Erie and encloses a vast marsh and a wide public beach.

As you drive west from Regional Road 10, the trees of a government forestry station loom overhead. About 3 km from Regional Road 10, the road skirts a high bluff with several viewing points across the grassy Turkey Point marsh to the wooded spit. Here you will begin to notice that the fields are flat and sandy, cultivated in long rows of a leafy crop, and that beside each field is a line of wooden shacks painted green or red, with large wooden louvres on the sides. This is Ontario's tobacco country and one of Canada's richest agricultural communities. Yet a little over half a century ago it was a wasteland.

Originally, Norfolk's sand plains, as they are called, were a parklike savannah of oaks and grasses. The first settlers, attracted by the light stone-free soils, quickly cleared the area of its sparse forest. However, a few bountiful crops depleted the soil, and one by one the farms were abandoned, leaving Norfolk a desert of blowing sand, good for little other than pine plantations. Then, in 1923, H. A. Freeman and W. L. Peltn carefully studied the soils and decided to introduce tobacco. Their foresight paid off and Norfolk has become Canada's leading tobacco region.

St. Williams

From the clifftop, the road ventures inland through the periphery of the tobacco country and after 3 km stops at the farm village of St. Williams. This community was originally called Neals Corner, but the name was changed to honour William Gellassy, a local landowner and religious leader. Located just 1 km from the lake, St. Williams was in its early years a shipping and milling centre. But with the demise of shipping and the growth of the tobacco industry it became a busy farm-service town of about 200. Although it is quieter now and many of its businesses have folded, you can find a gas station and a small grocery store if you require either.

St. Williams to Port Rowan

From the stop sign, turn left and drive a few metres to an unmarked road on the right. For 5 km this road winds through the tobacco fields and along the shore cliff to the busy resort town of Port Rowan. From the stop sign at the main street of Port Rowan, which is also Regional Road 42, the commercial core is to your immediate right. It is a small business area but offers the basics— groceries and a restaurant and gas station. There are few buildings of historical note, since most of the business district was burnt to the ground in 1919. At the north end, however, the blaze stopped short of the Baptist Church, which stands as it has since 1856, with its white steeple rising above its brick walls.

The main attraction of Port Rowan is its shoreline. Turn left and descend the hill to the Lions Club Park, a small, treed picnic area wedged between the harbour and a curving beach. Once a bustling lumber-shipping and fishing centre, the harbour is now a picturesque tumble of sagging wooden boathouses and rickety docks. Here and there are empty net sheds, drying reels, and

The Backus Mill is Ontario's oldest mill.

rotting hulls—the only evidence that a commercial fishing fleet once operated here.

From Port Rowan, you can take a side trip to see Ontario's oldest mill. Follow Regional Road 42 north through the town for 3.5 km and follow the signs to Backus Conservation Area. Here, the wooden mill grinds grain each day (from 10:30 to 2:30) just as it has done since it was completed in 1794. It was the only mill to survive the American invasion of 1812. The park also has trails and camping facilities.

Port Rowan to Port Burwell

Return to Port Rowan, follow Regional Road 42 through town, and then carry on for 2 km until you arrive at a stop sign for Highway 59. To the left lies Lake Erie's most conspicuous landform, Long Point, a 32-km finger of shifting sands and swampy channels that stabs into Lake Erie. Incredibly, half the point is owned by an American hunt club and is out of bounds to Canadians, a denial of national rights that is severely enforced by a private security force. The Ontario government did, however, manage to hang on to a small section and have it made into the Long Point Provincial Park, while the hunt club donated a sizable chunk to the federal government as a wildlife sanctuary.

Unless you decide to visit Long Point, continue straight through the intersection. After 2 km you will come to a wide, swampy inlet and a small string of old frame houses, the mysterious village of Port Royal. So little is known of its origins that even a century-old history simply called it a "very old village."

From Port Royal, Regional Road 42 abandons the shore and barges straight through the farmlands. You will have few glimpses of the lake until, after 8 km, you reach a handful of old buildings that are called Clear Creek. Another of Lake Erie's busy lumber-shipping points, Clear Creek lost its unprotected wharf to Erie's waves after just a few decades. A store and one-time hotel still stand at the corner, and a few houses line the side street that once led to the wharf. There is no longer any public access to the lake.

Continue along Regional Road 42. After 4 km, a small range of hills will loom up on the left. Known as the Sand Hills, this ridge marks the sudden appearance of a string of shoreline sand dunes. A private park, the Sand Hills have camping and picnic facilities, as well as a beach. For the next 2 km smaller dunes follow the road, and the tobacco fields reappear. Then, on the left at an intersection, stands an empty white building. This was once a hotel and store, and it is one of the few surviving buildings of a ghost town called Houghton. Like Clear Creek, Houghton grew as a busy lumber port, but as it had no natural harbour, the exposed wharf soon crumbled in the waves. Even though Houghton was also the township administrative centre, all that now remains is the old hotel and a red brick Baptist Church.

From Houghton continue west on Regional Road 42. Although the road is less than 1 km from the water, it does not swing close enough to offer any views. Instead, it continues in a straight line through tobacco fields for 12 km to Port Burwell.

Port Burwell

Once a busy coal-shipping and commercial-fishing port, this village of 700 is quiet now, most popular for its beaches. From a

20

T-intersection in the heart of the village, Regional Road 42 (here called County Road 42) continues to the right. Follow this road across the bridge. On the river below, a few fishing tugs still tie up and offer fresh fish for sale. If you wish to swim, you can follow the signs to the Iroquois Beach Provincial Park, one of Lake Erie's longest beaches.

Port Burwell to Port Bruce

Continue west along County Road 42. Thanks to Ontario's moderate climate, this is not only prime tobacco country but also greenhouse and orchard territory. Some of the peach and cherry orchards offer the opportunity to pick your own fruit; others sell by the roadside.

For the next 15 km the road follows a straight line about 2 km inland. The farmland is flat and prairielike. Prosperous rural communities, such as Lakeview and Grovesend, dot the route. Then, at Provincial Highway 73, County Road 42 ends. Turn left here and follow the highway 3 km through a series of deep, wooded gullies to the once-busy Port Bruce.

Port Bruce

In an unusual setting, the gully breaks into three channels before entering Lake Erie. The effects of erosion have left a series of hills, which were once the shore bluff, and it was around these hills that the village grew. It, too, started as a lumber port and then boomed with the growth of commercial shipping. But Port Bruce never attracted a railway, and the fishermen soon moved off to ports that did. The cliffs and valleys, however, did not go unnoticed, and Port Bruce has become a popular cottage and recreation centre. Beside the river mouth is a small, treed park, and the long, sandy beach is a provincial park. However, not all the fishermen have gone. In a shanty called Duffy's Place, the last of the Port Bruce fishermen sells fresh and smoked fish.

Port Bruce to Sparta

To leave Port Bruce, follow Highway 73 back to the bridge and turn left onto County Road 24. For 2 km this road carries you past clifftop views before it swings inland. After 4.5 km, watch for the intersection with County Road 36 and turn right. Carry on along this road for 3.5 km and you will arrive in Sparta, Ontario's oldest and best-preserved Quaker village.

This one-time hotel in the early Quaker village of Sparta has been partly restored as a tearoom.

Sparta

Although new homes have been built around Sparta, the original village core surrounding the main intersection has survived almost intact. On the southeast corner is the general store (now a craft shop) which was built in 1842 of hand-made bricks. On the northwest corner stands the Ontario House Hotel, with its long wooden porch still in place. It, too, was constructed in 1842, and it stood empty for several years before receiving new life as a tearoom. Next to it is an antique store, the Olde Anvil and Forge, which was the village smithy and was constructed of adobe brick more than a century and a half ago. Opposite the forge is a ramshackle board-and-batten building which once housed the village's tinsmith. On the southwest corner stands the Haight Zavitz House, built in 1820, one of the province's oldest and best examples of Quaker architecture. Many other frame homes along the main street predate 1850 and have been carefully preserved.

Sparta to Port Stanley

Return south along County Road 36 to County Road 24 and turn right. The flat, prosperous farmlands here seem endless. Farm homes, which might more appropriately be termed mansions, testify to the bounty. One outstanding example is just 2 km south of Sparta on the east side of the road.

After 9 km on County Road 24, you will come to Highway 4. Turn left down the highway and drive the 2 km to Port Stanley—a town of 2,000 which still lives off shipping and the lake.

Port Stanley

This area was first settled in 1818, several years after the shore-line farther east was opened. The harbour at Port Stanley was not ready until 1823, and the place remained a small shipping port until 1857, when the railway reached town. Built jointly by the counties of Middlesex and Elgin, the London, St. Thomas, and Port Stanley was Ontario's shortest railway.

Port Stanley is an appropriate finale to the Erie Road—a busy modern community that retains a rich repertory of historical buildings. Highway 4 leads to the junction of Bridge and Main streets. Here you will find downtown Port Stanley, with its shops, taverns, and restaurants. Main Street follows the east bank of the harbour, and along it are Port Stanley's oldest buildings. No. 211 is the Russell House, a brick inn constructed in the 1850s and later recycled as a bank, a butcher's shop, and offices. No. 207 is unarguably Port Stanley's most historic building, for it was built in 1822 by the town's founder, Colonel John Bostwick. Originally a warehouse, it is now a private home. Next to it stands a yellow brick house, considered by many to be the port's most handsome structure. It was built in 1873 by Manuel Payne, who served variously as postmaster, telephone operator, and custom's officer. Farther along is the Cork Kiln, which was built in 1900 to serve the fishing industry. Here, too, are net sheds, ice houses, and other buildings from the early days of fishing. Bobbing in the water beside them is a string of modern fishing tugs.

The Ontario Ministry of Citizenship and Culture has prepared a walking-tour brochure of Port Stanley's attractive old buildings. It is available in local stores. Port Stanley also has a large sandy beach, which can be reached by following William Street to Edith Cavell Boulevard.

To reach Highway 401, your most likely route home, follow William, George, and Bridge streets to Highway 4 and drive north for about 30 km through St. Thomas to Highway 401. St. Thomas has a wide range of restaurants and overnight accommodation if you wish to linger in the area.

23

GRAND RIVER ROAD

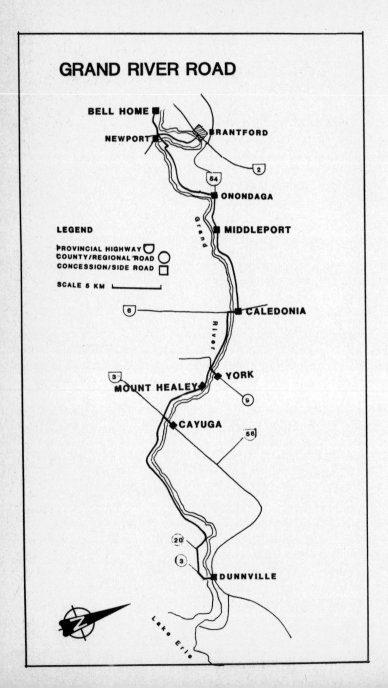

BELL HOME ■

NEWPORT ■   BRANTFORD

2

54

■ ONONDAGA

Grand

■ MIDDLEPORT

LEGEND

PROVINCIAL HIGHWAY ⬭
COUNTY/REGIONAL ROAD ◯
CONCESSION/SIDE ROAD ▢

SCALE 5 KM

River

6   ■ CALEDONIA

3   ◆ YORK

MOUNT HEALEY ◆   9

◆ CAYUGA   56

20

3   ■ DUNNVILLE

Lake Erie

2   Grand River Road

The Grand River lives up to its name. On its way to Lake Erie, it has carved a valley that is wide and deep as it tumbles and boils past mill towns and dark, wooded river banks.

This backroads route follows the river bank and leads to striking vistas, quiet lanes, a long-forgotten canal, and such historic sites as the Bell Homestead and Chiefswood, the home of the poet Pauline Johnson. The route is relatively short, starting on Highway 2 in Brantford and following the Grand River downstream for 50 km. It requires roughly half a day. There are gas stations, lunch bars, grocery stores, and riverside parks along the route, so there is no need to make elaborate preparations before setting out.

This trip should appeal to almost everyone. It has history and Indian lore, handsome nineteenth-century homes, hotels and mills, and opportunities to fish, photograph, or just relax in a riverside park. The roads are paved, at least for most of their length, and although the area is heavily populated, traffic is light.

A Bit of History

The story of the Grand River delves into the annals of Ontario's Indian history. In 1784 the Mohawk chief, Joseph Brant, and his Six Nations followers from New York State were granted all the lands along the river as a reward for having helped the British to several hard-fought victories in the American Revolutionary War. But the British began to reduce Brant's holdings when settlers made their way up the Grand, clamouring for land.

Settlement remained light until in 1829 William Merritt and Absalom Shade decided to construct a canal along the Grand and pressured for more of the Indian lands. The first ships passed through the canal in 1835, and lockside towns soon burst into life. Sawmills and grist mills flourished. But the river traffic dwindled during the 1850s as railways began to snake their way across the countryside. The last vessel passed through the locks in 1890, only 55 years after the canal was first opened. An era was over.

It was an era that was soon forgotten. Some of the riverside towns dwindled to hamlets. Others vanished entirely. Only Caledonia and Cayuga, which had railway stations, remained stable.

Eventually, the recreation boom brought new life to the banks of the Grand. The river sprouted cottages and buzzed with motorboats. Parks replaced lock stations, new dams replaced old ones. Today, virtually no trace remains of the original canal, yet its banks are steeped in history and lined with farms and forests, providing an unusual backroads drive.

Brantford to Newport

The first portion of the trip leads to two historic sites and takes you along the high, scenic banks of the river. From Highway 2 in Brantford, turn south onto Lockes Road and follow the yellow and blue directional signs to the Mohawk Chapel, about 1.5 km distant. Sitting in a grove of trees that shade an ancient cemetery, this chapel is Ontario's oldest Protestant church.

It was on this site that Chief Joseph Brant in 1784 settled his band. They built a school, 24 houses, and a small log chapel, and

It was in this house that Alexander Graham Bell worked on the invention of the telephone.

the following year added St. Paul's Chapel, the gleaming white-frame building that you see here. Although there are two historical plaques, the site is not a park, so don't expect to find facilities or a place to picnic. These are available at the next and equally historic site on this route, the birthplace of the telephone.

To get there, drive to nearby Birkett Lane and turn left. Continue for 2 km and turn left again onto Erie Avenue, which becomes County Road 4. After 1 km, you will cross the Grand River, which meanders across a wide flood plain. Atop the far bank, turn right onto Tutela Heights Road. The yellow and blue signs there will direct you to the home of Alexander Graham Bell.

It was to this home that Alexander Graham Bell moved with his parents in 1870. Here Bell carried out some of the early experiments which led to his great breakthrough in Boston in 1876, when he spoke the first words ever heard through a telephone. It was also from this homestead that, later in 1876, Bell placed the world's first long-distance telephone call to the town of Paris, 14 km away.

There is ample parking space, washrooms and picnic tables, landscaped grounds for strolling, and superb views over the Grand valley. In the white-framed homestead, the rooms are furnished as in Bell's day and some of his personal effects are on display. Beside the Bell Homestead is the Henderson Building. Originally located in Brantford, it was Canada's first telephone exchange and it houses a display of interesting and odd early telephones.

On leaving the Bell Homestead, return east to the intersection with County Road 4 and cross it. Here the road lurches down into the valley and follows the river for 2 km to the scattered hamlet of Newport. Newport began life as Burtche's Landing, a riverside shipping point for pine and then grain. But as the canal declined, so did Newport. Today, a few old houses and a yellow brick community centre with a view across the river are all that survive.

Newport to Middleport

This stretch of the route takes in the home of Pauline Johnson, the celebrated Indian poet. At the intersection in Newport, turn right. Drive 1 km to a stop sign at County Road 4 and turn right again. Follow this road for 1 km to County Road 18 and turn right once more. Here you cross the river and enter its flood plain. About

2 km from the bridge, look for a dirt road that leads right, and follow it. The road wanders along the north bank of the river, through quiet fields and past prosperous riverside farms, many of them dating from the time of the earliest settlements.

After 8 km you will come to a stop sign at Highway 54. Turn right here, passing the homes of Onondaga Indians (the descendants of the Onondaga who accompanied Brant to the Grand). About 3 km farther on, you will come to a shady riverside park. This is Chiefswood, the birthplace of Pauline Johnson. In 1845 Emily Howells, a young English immigrant, met Six Nations chief George Johnson, who was then working as a government interpreter. In 1853 they were married and Johnson built her this Georgian mansion called Chiefswood, a home that entertained such dignitaries as the Prince of Wales. Their daughter, Pauline Johnson, became an internationally celebrated poet and performer. Today, her birthplace is a museum, open daily in the summer and devoted primarily to Pauline Johnson and her works.

Middleport, the next village on your route, lies 2 km eastward on Highway 54.

Middleport

This small and picturesque village began, as the name suggests, as a landing on the Grand River Canal. For a time, it shipped timber

The Middleport church dates from the days of the canal.

The general store in Middleport still carries on in the country store tradition.

and grain, and eventually a town plot was laid out. But once the canal traffic began to decline and the railways had passed Middleport by, the community rapidly dwindled. Two of the more picturesque buildings of this trip can be seen in Middleport amid the few new homes of commuters to Brantford. On the tiny main street, shaded by the trees of the river bank, is an early board-and-batten church. Surrounded by a white picket fence and a spacious cemetery, it dates from the days of the canal. Across the road is the old general store. Built in the closing days of the canal, it has managed to retain its original façade, a two-storey verandah, and even a wooden bench. To this day, it remains a general store in the country tradition.

Middleport to Caledonia

From Middleport, your route continues southeast along Highway 54. In this area, the river banks recede and become gentle hills, among which are several handsome riverside homes dating back more than a century. Then, after 10 km, around a bend appears a string of buildings, those of Caledonia.

Caledonia

Few towns of 2,500 can claim as many nineteenth-century buildings as Caledonia. Most of these buildings are within a few blocks of the main intersection. The town hall stands two blocks east of the intersection on Highway 54 (Caithness Street East). This tall brick structure with embedded columns was built in 1857 and has appeared in books featuring Ontario's architectural highlights. When the creation of a government at a regional level eliminated the need for a town council, the hall became redundant, and it is now a museum.

A few paces from the town hall is 46 Caithness Street. This 1847 building was the home of Dr. William McPherson, one of the town's first physicians, and it still retains its two-storey balcony. Dumfries Street runs beside the town hall. Look there for No. 7, a small frame building now covered with stucco. Originally the Ryan Hotel, it was built in 1854 and is one of the few frame buildings of that period to survive. Even more remarkable is 22 Dumfries Street, which was at one time a stagecoach inn. It was built in 1836 and is the oldest building in Caledonia.

The year 1852 marked the coming of the railway, and Caledonia entered a boom period. Many of the buildings in the down-

The former tollkeeper's house at Caledonia is more than a century old.

town core date from those heady days, including the old Opera House on the northeast corner and the tollkeeper's house at the eastern end of the bridge. The latter is a solid two-storey brick house with elaborate yellow and red brickwork and high ornate chimneys. It was built in 1857, during a period when toll roads were common, though unpopular.

If you have worked up an appetite while walking Caledonia's streets, there are restaurants downtown that offer a simple meal or a cold drink. Or you may wish to relax in a riverside park. A few blocks north, on Highway 54 by the railway bridge, is a treed park with picnic tables and washrooms. The park occupies the site of the town's first mills and a canal lock station. The ditch that cuts through the grounds traces the route of the old lock.

Before you leave Caledonia, there is one more site that is well worth a visit. Drive back to the junction of Highways 6 and 54, and turn right. Cross the arched concrete bridge and again turn right. Just upstream lies the oldest mill on the Grand River. Built in 1863 on land owned by James Little, this four-storey frame grist mill has become a popular subject for photographers with its weathered exterior and the river swirling past.

Caledonia to York

To continue on your route, return to Highway 6 and turn right. After 1 km, turn left onto the South River Road. Here, by the water's edge, are farms that date back more than a century. The road follows a high bank about 1 km from the river, offering a splendid view of the wide, gentle valley of the Grand. After 6 km the road stops at a T-intersection. About 1 km to the left, across the river, lies the sleepy one-time lock village of York.

Although York is small, it is rich in buildings dating from the canal period. It was located at the site of the second lock on the Grand River Canal. Consequently, the village developed quickly and at its peak had 450 residents, along with several hotels, stores, and mills. But then the canal closed and the railways passed York by. Its population plummeted to 175 and it became the quiet residential hamlet that you see today.

Cross the bridge and turn right onto Highway 54, which is the main street through the village. Beside the road at the site of the lock and mill, you will find a small riverside park. Across the road from the park, look for the red brick Mason's Lodge.

Another interesting building is the Barber Hotel, built in 1862; it has been designated by the municipality as a historical and architectural site.

York to Cayuga

To leave York, return to the west bank and branch left onto the river road. Shaded by the trees on the bank, the road hugs the wide river. This is a long-settled shoreline of old farmsteads and attractive vistas, and it includes a ghost town. As the road swings back from the bank 2.5 km from the bridge, a large brick building looms on your left. Two storeys high and six bays square, this is the Dochstader Hotel, the sole survivor of a mill town called Mount Healey.

When John Donaldson arrived here in the 1840s, he built a sawmill, a grist mill, and then (with the discovery of gypsum in the river bank) a plaster mill. By 1850 the little industrial village could boast a church, a school, a store, a blacksmith's shop, and 150 residents. Many of the inhabitants lived in a row of cabins, others in the Dochstader Hotel. But with the closing of the canal and the depletion of gypsum and timber, Mount Healey suffered more than most. It didn't just decline, it disappeared. The old Dochstader alone survives.

The hotel has been converted into a residence, and the present entrance is through what was the rear of the building. Although the village road is scarcely traceable, you may yet discern, in the field south of the hotel, a few foundations that were once the site of the busy community.

The river road carries on for another 3 km, meeting Highway 3 just after crossing the Michigan Central Railway. A left turn on Highway 3 will take you into Cayuga.

Cayuga

Another of the canal villages, Cayuga boomed when the railways reached town, but then it stagnated. Although it was named the county seat in 1850, it remained smaller than its rival, Caledonia, and its current population of 900 is an increase of only 200 over its peak in the last century.

After you cross the bridge, turn left onto Cayuga Street, the once-bustling main street. On the right, a tall, red brick building houses the post office. Next to the old county courthouse, this is

A view of the Grand River and its flood plain.

the town's most elaborate structure. Continue to the courthouse, where on the grounds of the museum you can explore an old log cabin, which was moved onto the site from a nearby farm. The courthouse itself is a domed limestone structure, built in 1851.

About 5 km from Cayuga stands the stone Chrysler home. To reach it, go back across the bridge, drive to the river road, and turn left. The Chryslers were among the earliest settlers on the lower Grand, and they purchased the estate in 1808. The family owns it to this day.

South of the Chrysler house, the river banks disappear and the backshore becomes low, in places swampy. Riverside farms mingle with country homes and with rows of cottages. Wide and sluggish, the river is suddenly alive with motorboats and fishermen. After 10 km the road bends away from the river to Regional Road 20. Turn left here. For the last 7 km, the land is swampy and the views of the river few. The road and the trip end at a stop sign marking Regional Road 3.

To return home, drive left to Dunnville. Here you can follow Highway 3 northwest, either to Highway 56 (the road that leads you back towards Hamilton and Toronto) or to Highway 54 (which leads back to Kitchener). To return to western Ontario, simply stay on Highway 3.

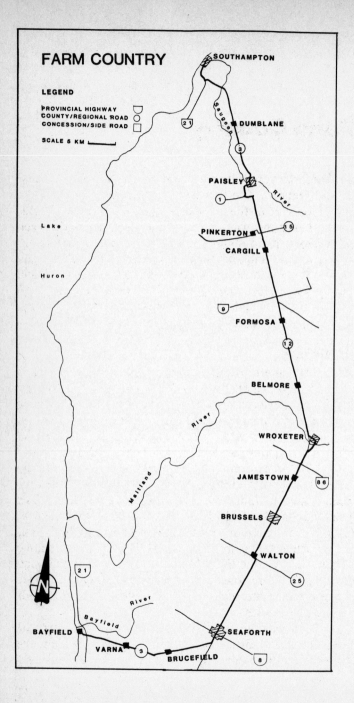

FARM COUNTRY

LEGEND

PROVINCIAL HIGHWAY
COUNTY/REGIONAL ROAD
CONCESSION/SIDE ROAD

SCALE 5 KM

SOUTHAMPTON

DUMBLANE

PAISLEY

Saugeen River

PINKERTON

CARGILL

FORMOSA

BELMORE

WROXETER

JAMESTOWN

BRUSSELS

WALTON

Maitland River

SEAFORTH

BAYFIELD

VARNA

BRUCEFIELD

Bayfield River

Lake

Huron

3 Farm Country

This is a route for anyone with a yearning for rolling pastures and a view of old Ontario. The trip starts at Southampton on Lake Huron and follows the fertile farmlands 120 km south to Bayfield. In the towns along the way, some of Ontario's best-preserved nineteenth-century main streets can be seen. There are farmscapes, riverscapes, and old buildings enough to delight any photographer; and for those who wish to swim, the trip starts and ends on sandy Lake Huron beaches. The towns on the route can provide most of the amenities you will require; they have gas stations, drug stores, grocery stores, and restaurants.

A Bit of History

There are two chapters to the settlement of Bruce and Huron counties. The first is that of an energetic entrepreneur named John Galt. In 1824 he chartered the Canada Company and advertised extensively in the United Kingdom the bounties of the Huron Tract, the territory that would become Huron County. Most of the land was level and stone-free, and it quickly attracted settlers.

By 1850 most of Huron County's farms were taken and the government looked north to Bruce County, which was at the time a dark and mysterious Indian land known as Queen's Bush. The government purchased it from the Indians and brought in surveyors. To help settlers move in, roads were cut through the forest, the most important being the Huron Road from Galt to Lake Huron. Then, in 1851, the Elora Road was laid out from Guelph to Southampton. Before long, other roads were built. Villages grew up at important intersections and at places where the roads crossed water-power sites.

The next step was the coming of the railways. In 1864 the Wellington, Grey, and Bruce Railway came through from the south, followed by three other lines from the south and east. As

35

usual, towns lucky enough to lie on their path burgeoned into important manufacturing centres, while those that were bypassed stagnated. Even though most of the towns and villages eventually lost their industries, they continued to serve the farmers, and today they retain their nineteenth-century streetscapes of brick stores and shady residential lanes.

Southampton

The trip starts in the tree-lined streets of Southampton, on Highway 21 (which can be reached from Highway 9 or 10). Southampton began as a fishing village and became a busy port when the Elora Road was opened in 1851. But its real boomtime began with the arrival of the Wellington, Grey, and Bruce Railway in 1871 and with the growth of several furniture factories. Most of Southampton's buildings date from those years.

The main street, only two blocks long, runs west from Highway 21 and ends pleasantly at a long sandy beach. Here, the municipality has developed a small, landscaped rock garden. At the corner of the main street and Highway 21 is the Southampton Hotel. With its yellow brickwork and wrought-iron balconies, it rates as the most handsome of the business buildings.

On an island about 2 km southwest of the harbour is Chantry Island Lighthouse. This 30-m stone tower was built in 1859 and is one of the oldest on Lake Huron. The harbour is located a few blocks north of the business district and here you can launch or rent a boat to visit the historic tower.

On Highway 21, at the north end of the town, is the museum. Large for a town this size, it contains 11 rooms of artifacts, documents, and photographs. Visit in particular the Indian Room, the Fishing Room, and the Pioneer Room. On the grounds you will find a log cabin and log school, which were brought here from surrounding townships.

Southampton to Paisley

This portion of your route follows the broad, fertile Saugeen River Valley. Drive out of Southampton south on Highway 21 and measure 2 km from the railway crossing, which was the terminus of the old Wellington, Grey, and Bruce Railway. Then turn left onto County Road 3 (the alignment of the old Elora Settlement Road) and at 3 km from the turn, cross the Saugeen River where it

The country school at Dumblane no longer echoes to the sound of children's voices.

has carved a rugged gorge into the clay cliffs. The road then bends south and follows a straight course for 14 km. After 2 km, you will pass the old road village of Burgoyne, and after a further 6 km the one-time hamlet of Dumblane. Here, set in a grove of willows, is the Dumblane School. With its yellow brick and its bell tower, it has changed little since the area farm children fidgeted through eight grades of education. It is the most photogenic school on this trip.

Continue for 4 km beyond the school to the turnoff to the Saugeen Bluffs Conservation Area. Its 200 ha offer camping, fishing, hunting in season, and a few short hiking trails; 4 km farther on, in a shallow valley where the Teeswater River flows into the Saugeen, is a village in which you will want to linger—the village of Paisley.

37

Paisley

Although Paisley dates from 1851, its boomtime began 20 years later, with the arrival of the Wellington, Grey, and Bruce Railway. By 1890, Paisley had a population of 1,500 and several factories and mills. Today, it claims only two-thirds of that population, while the industries have all vanished.

Thanks to the efforts of interested citizens and a Province of Ontario grant, the main buildings of this attractive village have been preserved and its streets beautified. In the middle of town, on the south side of the bridge, stands the town hall with its delicate bell tower and its sidewalks redone in interlocking brick. Built in 1876, it remains the focus of the community. Beside it is the green hose tower of the 1891 fire hall, and across the road looms the 1885 Fisher woollen mill. Behind the woollen mill, and still operating on water power as it has since 1855, is the Fisher grist mill. South of the town hall, a string of commercial buildings climb the hillside, most of them dating from 1880-1910.

If you wish to spend more time in the village, drop into the town hall and ask for the walking-tour brochure. It guides you along the main street and through some quiet residential lanes, and explains the history of the main buildings.

The Saugeen River at Paisley.

To leave the village and continue the trip, turn west at the town hall and follow Mill Street (County Road 1). You will soon come to one of Ontario's most picturesque mills. Now disused, the Stark grist mill was built in 1884; it is Ontario's only surviving five-storey mill constructed entirely of wood.

Paisley to Cargill

From the mill, the road crosses the bridge and climbs up the wall of the Teeswater River Valley. Stay on this road for 1 km and then turn left onto a dirt road. Drive another 2 km, turn left again, and 1 km farther on turn right. Here you are on a quiet country road that parallels the busier County Road 3, which lies 2 km to the east. This dirt road is the original alignment of the Elora Settlement Road. That is why the old villages are found on this backroad, rather than on the busy county road. The road takes you south through Ontario's prime beef country. Green pastures and blowing cornfields are level and stone-free; many of the old wooden barns now sport gleaming aluminum silos.

After 7 km you will meet County Road 15. To follow it on a side trip to the small valley village of Pinkerton, turn right. After 1 km, the road winds into the valley of the Teeswater River and passes the feed mill, general store, blacksmith's, and church buildings that still serve the farm community as they have for more than a century.

Cargill

From Pinkerton, return to the Elora Road, turn right, and drive 2 km to Cargill. This was another, and larger, mill town. It dates from 1879, when Henry Cargill bought 1,600 ha of timber and built a sawmill, a grist mill, a planing mill, and a store. Today, although most of the industries have vanished, the village has retained its collection of solid yellow brick buildings and has a population of about 100. As you enter Cargill, turn right and cross the bridge. Here you will find the planing mill, a brick store that is a block deep, a crescent of identical yellow brick houses, and the Village Inn. Located in the old Cargill Hotel, the Village Inn offers licensed dining and still displays its century-old façade.

A modern addition to the village is its community park. To reach it, return to the Elora Road and turn right. Here, beside Henry Cargill's millpond, you can picnic or fish. On the far

Some of Ontario's most prosperous farms lie along this backroads route.

shore, Howson and Howson have enlarged and still operate the mill which first spawned the village.

Cargill to Formosa

Continue south on the Elora Road. For 10 km the road takes you through prosperous farm country. Beef cattle graze lazily in rolling pastures, hay and oats waft in the wind. Most farmhouses are large and constructed of yellow or red brick, some elaborately mixing the two colours.

Cross Highway 9 and carry on south. After 1 km, the old Elora Road leaves your route and angles southeast. Drive straight ahead onto County Road 12, the old Wroxeter Stage Road, which was built to link Wroxeter with the Elora Road.

Formosa

At 3 km from the intersection, nestled in the wide valley of Formosa Creek, lies the little town of Formosa, which was settled by a colony of Roman Catholic Germans. The location not only spawned the usual mills, but also the trademark of any good

German town—a brewery. Formosa's present population of 200 is a slight drop from the 350 of its peak years but it still retains the stores, hotels, and even a descendant of the original brewery.

Although the creek is small, the valley is steep and wide. From the shoulder of the valley, you have a striking view of the village rooftops below. To your left, the church with its soaring steeple has been a landmark since 1885. Drive down the hill and follow the main street past the taverns and stores. At the south end of the village stands the empty brewery. Until 1970, it was known as the Formosa Spring Brewery and was the last of Ontario's traditional small-town beermakers. In 1968 it gained national fame as the only such establishment in southern Ontario to defy a long beer strike and stay open. Thirsty customers drove from all parts of central Ontario to line up, some for an entire day, to buy their favourite drink. Today, the brewery is closed.

Formosa to Wroxeter

Continue south through the village on County Road 12, which climbs out of the valley onto the rolling plain above. For 20 km the road takes you through fertile farmlands and forgotten cross-road hamlets with names like Ambleside and Belmore. After crossing Highway 87, you will come to Wroxeter, a town with one of the most remarkable main streets in Ontario.

Wroxeter

As you cross the bridge and enter the silent downtown area, you may wonder if you have entered a ghost town. Of the dozen and a half stores that line the main street, more than two-thirds are boarded up.

Wroxeter dates from 1854, when the Gibson family arrived from Scotland and bought a large tract of land around a water-power site on the Maitland River. Within ten years Wroxeter had three stores; and within twenty years, when the Toronto, Grey, and Bruce Railway arrived, it had five hotels and five stores, with mills and factories along the Maitland River. But after the turn of the century, the large factories in the cities to the south became too keen competition for the smalltown factories, and many of Wroxeter's industries closed. Then, after the First World War, rural depopulation began. Those people who remained soon had cars to carry them to larger towns, and one by one Wroxeter's stores closed.

Along the wooded river banks, you will find no trace of the old industries that marked Wroxeter's heyday. But across the bridge is a startling sight. For two blocks stand handsome brick commercial buildings with upper windows that are arching and attractively corniced; but at street level the one-time shops are closed and boarded. Fading signs advertise former occupants.

At the south end of the business section, at the corner of Centre Street and Ann, five roads converge. To continue on your route, cross Ann and then immediately fork right. This will take you through another small neighbourhood and out of the faded village.

Wroxeter to Brussels

Drive 1 km to the T-intersection with County Road 12 and turn left. After 2 km, you will come to Highway 86. Cross it, remaining on County Road 12. (Although you are now in a different county, Huron, the road number remains the same.) At 2 km from Highway 86 you will encounter the lonely and picturesque Jamestown country store. Jamestown itself is a nondescript collection of houses, and the general store stands alone in a field. Now closed, it retains most of its original features—a wooden porch, an enclosed balcony, and a modified boomtown front. Beside it is a later addition, a small gas station, which is also closed.

For the next 8 km you cross farmlands that are flat and so clear of trees that they are almost prairielike in appearance. Most of the farms front onto the roads which branch east and west from County Road 12, so if you want to see any of these handsome homes, you will need to take a side trip down one of the side roads.

Brussels

Brussels lies 8 km beyond Jamestown. It is another town that shows the scars of decline. It began in 1852 when William Ainley arrived and laid out a town plot, and William Vanstone erected mills on the Maitland River. The arrival of the Wellington, Grey, and Bruce Railway in 1864 turned it into a busy factory and shipping town. But the early years of the twentieth century were unkind to Brussels, and its population plummeted from 1,880 to today's 1,000. Were it not for the prosperity of the surrounding farmlands, it too would be a ghost town.

Brussels offers a pleasant break in your journey. Here you have the opportunity to relax beside the river, to photograph the commercial buildings, or to replenish your gas tank and lunch basket. The bridge over the Maitland River marks the northern limit of the business section, and beside it is a small, treed picnic park maintained by the town. In addition, a conservation area with picnic facilities and a picturesque wooden grist mill lies along Mill Street, two blocks east of Turnberry Street, the main thorough-fare.

The best example of a well-preserved commercial building is the Graham Block, situated on the southeast corner of Market and Turnberry streets. It is three storeys high and has retained its nineteenth-century façade.

Brussels to Seaforth

Continuing on your journey, a drive of 7 km from Brussels brings you to Walton, a one-time stopover village at the intersection of County Road 25. One of its two original hotels is now a restaurant. Drive left on County Road 25 for a few metres, then turn right and resume your route along County Road 12. Many farms here have large Georgian-style homes, built during the 1830s and 1840s. Again, the lands are flat and are used mainly for the grazing of beef cattle. However, as you proceed south, the climate becomes milder and you will begin to see a greater range of crops, such as beans and flax. At 15 km from Walton you will come to Seaforth. Although it remains a busy town, the largest on this route, its streetscapes are pure nineteenth century, and they contain many mansions and commercial buildings worth photo-graphing. So plan for a prolonged stop here.

Seaforth

Ironically, Seaforth is younger than its two suburbs, Egmondville and Harphurey. Egmondville was named for Constant Van Egmond, one of the builders of the Huron Road. On the banks of Silver Creek, 2 km south of the heart of modern Seaforth, he built a sawmill and a grist mill. On the Bayfield Road, this community became a busy mill village with taverns, shops, and three general stores. Meanwhile, 3 km northwest of Egmondville, on the Huron Road, landowner Dr. William Chalk had opened a post office in 1839 and had surveyed a townsite. Since the Huron Road was bustling with traffic to the newly opened Huron Tract lands, this site was ideal for a village. Harphurey soon contained two hotels and three blacksmith shops, plus a store and several other shops. Meanwhile, the intersection of the Bayfield Road and the Huron Road itself, where Seaforth would later grow, remained a lonely intersection known ignominiously as Guidepost Swamp.

The event that turned the tide was the extension of the Bayfield Road north of the Huron Road to Brussels. Suddenly the intersection sprang to life, with farmers urging their nags to drag wagons full of grain just a little faster. Grain agents and other farm businesses moved to the intersection from both Harphurey and Egmondville. Following the boom brought by the Lake Huron and Buffalo Railway in 1870, Seaforth grew west and south to absorb both old Egmondville and Harphurey. By 1900, Seaforth's population had peaked at 2,500, and it has declined only slightly since. Although most of the town's early factories have long since gone, Seaforth remains a major regional shopping town. Its commercial sector covers about four blocks and is one of the most striking streetscapes in western Ontario.

The tower of the Cardno Opera House dominates Seaforth's downtown streetscape.

You will enter Seaforth on County Road 12 (Main Street). After you stop for Highway 8 (the old Huron Road), proceed south into the commercial core. Even from a distance it is an imposing sight. Guarding the street like sentries are three towers. On the east are the towers of the town hall (built in 1893) and the post office. On the west side, the tower of the Cardno Opera House (built in 1877), now Stedmans Department Store, soars above the others. Here too are restaurants and stores where you can freshen your film supply, refill your picnic basket, or simply relax over a coffee.

On the back streets behind the commercial core are several nineteenth-century mansions, such as 99 Goderich Street West, built within the first half-decade of Seaforth's existence; 38 Louisa Street, at John, another of Seaforth's oldest homes; and 88 Goderich Street East, which dates from the 1860s and was built by Dr. T. Coleman, the village's first reeve.

Seaforth's most historic building can be seen on your way out of town. Drive south on Main Street and cross the tracks, and after 1.5 km you will come to the brick mansion which Constant Van Egmond built in 1846. Preserved and restored by the Van Egmond Foundation, it is open to the public during the summer months. South of the mansion, County Road 3 (the old Bayfield Road) forks right from County Road 12 and leads west towards the Lake Huron port of Bayfield, the oldest village on this trip.

Seaforth to Bayfield

Follow County Road 3 for 8 km across Huron's flat clay plains. A stop sign marks Highway 4, and here you pass through the tiny village of Brucefield. Sadly, insensitive highway widening has removed many of Brucefield's early crossroads buildings. After a further 6 km on County Road 3, you will come to another small crossroads hamlet, Varna. Here an old general store and small feed mill hug the intersection and perpetuate the hamlet's traditional role as a farm-service village. A further 9 km brings you to the end of your trip and to the remarkable town of Bayfield.

Bayfield

Through a gap in the high clay cliffs, the Bayfield River swirls into Lake Huron and forms a small but protected harbour. Bayfield is remarkable in many ways. It is one of Lake Huron's earliest towns; its street pattern is radial rather than grid; and its tree-lined main street is one of the best preserved in the province for a town of its size.

As early as 1836, Bayfield was a busy port, for settlers departed regularly along the Bayfield Road to their lands in the interior. But the railways went elsewhere, and by the end of the century Bayfield was in decline. Although a small fishing fleet and the productive farmlands of Bayfield's hinterland prevented it from becoming a ghost town, it was not until Lake Huron's shores became a popular recreation mecca that the town revived.

On the outskirts of Bayfield, County Road 3 ends at Highway 21. Turn right here and drive 1 km to Clan Gregor Park, the main square, where the town's streets converge. Turn left at the park and follow its perimeter to Main Street.

Bayfield is a town to be enjoyed on foot, its Main Street a wide avenue two blocks long. Rather than the large commercial blocks of other towns, each store and business is a separate building surrounded by lawns and cooled by shade trees. As you walk from the park, the first building on the left is the Albion Hotel, which still provides food and drink. It was built in 1840, though the two-storey verandah was added later. Across from the hotel, on the right side, is a trio of early buildings. The Westlake residence is near the corner; beside it, with its verandah, is the Village Store; and then there is the Roger's House (1834), one of the town's earliest buildings.

Over the next two blocks, nearly every building has been lovingly preserved to retain its nineteenth-century features. Two are of particular interest. One of these is the library, on the right in the middle of the second block; it is housed in a small, early shop with delicate curving windows. The other, the Little Inn, is at the end of the same block; it was built in 1847 and is surmounted by a cupola. The Little Inn's large wraparound porch has recently been reconstructed so that the building can once more display its original façade. Inside, the rooms have been refurnished in the style of the last century, including the dining room, which serves licensed meals.

After you have strolled Main Street at your leisure, you may wish to visit the harbour and the beach. In this case, follow Main Street to Bayfield Street and turn right. Then turn left onto Long Street, which drops down the wall of the steep ravine that forms

Bayfield Harbour. The harbour is now a haven for pleasure craft, their slender masts forming a thick forest. At the end of the street is a parking lot and the beach. Although the beach is stony, it offers a pleasant view south along the steep shore bluffs of Lake Huron. On the opposite side of the harbour you may see the squat white tugs of the Bayfield fishing fleet, and behind them the drying racks, net sheds, and ice houses that make any fishing port a ramshackle but picturesque subject for the photographer.

If you are returning to central or eastern Ontario, retrace your steps to Seaforth and follow Highway 8 east. It leads to Kitchener, where you can pick up Highway 401. If you are heading to the London area, drive back along County Road 3 to Brucefield, where you can join Highway 4. For the Windsor area, take Highway 21 south from Bayfield.

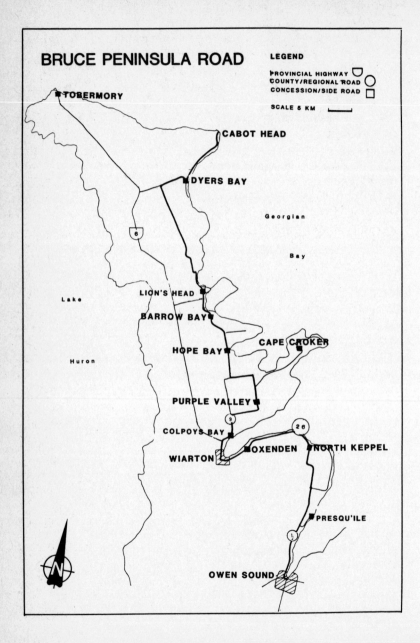

BRUCE PENINSULA ROAD

LEGEND

PROVINCIAL HIGHWAY
COUNTY/REGIONAL ROAD
CONCESSION/SIDE ROAD

SCALE 5 KM

TOBERMORY

CABOT HEAD

DYERS BAY

Georgian

Bay

6

Lake

LION'S HEAD

BARROW BAY

CAPE CROKER

Huron

HOPE BAY

PURPLE VALLEY

9

COLPOYS BAY

2 6

WIARTON

OXENDEN

NORTH KEPPEL

PRESQU'ILE

1

N

OWEN SOUND

4 Bruce Peninsula Road

This is a road that winds beneath brooding limestone cliffs and past the remains of once-busy pioneer farms and lumber camps in what is probably Ontario's best-known geographic region, the Bruce Peninsula. The route starts in the town of Owen Sound, at the end of Provincial Highway 10, and twists and bumps along 130 km of dirt backroads up the east side of the Bruce Peninsula, ending at a remote point of rock called Cabot Head.

If you are coming from the Toronto or Kitchener area, or from farther away, you may wish to consider spending the night. Owen Sound abounds in good motels and campgrounds, though there are few at the other end of the route. Wherever you stay, reserve ahead. During the summer, the morning ferry to Manitoulin Island from Tobermory is so popular that motels are usually full. Before you start, you can stock up with a picnic lunch from Owen Sound's grocery stores. There are few restaurants along the route, though you will find snack bars and sufficient gas stations.

A long, limestone finger, the Bruce Peninsula divides Lake Huron from Georgian Bay. On its eastern side, the high cliffs of the Niagara Escarpment plunge into Georgian Bay's clear waters. The west side of the peninsula is a marked contrast. Amid a shoreline of swampy coves, the limestone plain slips quietly beneath Lake Huron.

This is a trip for every outdoors person. For spelunkers and geologists, there are caves and the strange rock pillars known as flowerpots. Plant lovers can rummage around the swamps for the rare calypso orchid and other unusual flowers and plants, while hikers can clamber over some of the roughest portions of the famous Bruce Trail. And for divers, there is Ontario's only underwater park, Fathom Five, with its treasure trove of wrecks.

A Bit of History

Settlement on the Bruce has always been sparse. Archaeologists claim that despite a few small fur posts, the Indian population was light. When the townships of the Bruce were bought from the Indians and surveyed into farm lots in the 1850s, the few settlers were more interested in selling the timber than in farming.

Sawmilling was the primary industry of the peninsula throughout its early years. At one time or another, most of the protected west coast coves housed a mill and a small community, but there were few settlements on the exposed shoreline of the east coast. Inland from the coasts, the bedrock and boulders discouraged the few pioneer farming communities that did start up, and today only two remain.

Tourists have now replaced the farmers and lumbermen; and campers, hikers, divers, naturalists, and cottagers crowd the peninsula.

Owen Sound to Wiarton

Owen Sound sits at the head of a deep bay bordered by the cliffs of the Niagara Escarpment. It contains a full range of shops, most of them downtown, on or near 16th Street, the street that the highways follow. To begin the route, drive west on 16th Street across the bridge to 4th Avenue and turn right. As the houses and shops begin to thin, the road becomes County Road 1 and follows the shoreline of the bay.

At 6 km from the downtown core is the Indian Falls Conservation Area. In late spring and early summer, the Indian River falls veil-like into a 20-m gorge. An easy 1-km wooded walking trail follows the gorge to the falls. Unfortunately, unless the weather has been rainy, the river is usually dry by midsummer.

North of the falls, the route passes farms and pastures. Small hamlets, which once catered to the needs of the local farmers, cluster about most crossroads. East Linton, 5 km from the park, still has a 100-year-old brick United Church, while 2 km farther on, at the next crossroads, the hamlet of Hogg contains a stone one-room school, now a private residence. In this area, the escarpment lies about 4 km from the water's edge, and the road itself about 1 km, while the plain between is a fertile and prosperous farming area.

On the shore is the site of a vanished village, Presqu'ile,

50

which has lost most of its buildings but still has a photogenic wooden lighthouse. Turn right at Hogg, descend the hill to the shore, and follow the cottage road for 2 km to the lighthouse. Now a residence for a boys' camp, it was built in 1900 when Presqu'ile was a busy shipping village. Today, however, the mill, docks, and most of the houses have disappeared. Only the village store, now a tuckshop for the camp, and a couple of old houses survive.

Return to Hogg and continue on County Road 1. Another 5 km brings you to the larger crossroads village of Kemble, where the brick Methodist Church is now a senior citizens' home.

From Kemble drive north. After 2 km the road grinds up a wooded outlier of the Niagara Escarpment, where, to the right, the view extends across the waters of Owen Sound bay. Continue 2 km, follow the road left for another 1 km, and turn right at the side road. The view that greets you is sudden and panoramic. Here, at the brink of the cliffs, the ground drops to a flat pastoral plain that stretches 2 km to the blue waters of Colpoys Bay and its green, wooded islands. Extending out of sight on the horizon is the long white cliffline of the Bruce Peninsula.

Views along the Bruce Peninsula encompass both field and water.

Drive down the hill and cross the plain. On the shoreline sits the hamlet of North Keppel, a one-time shipping village that still contains its general store and several original houses. Turn left and follow the shore road for 5 km. Numbered as County Road 26, this road skirts the water where a handful of cottages are squeezed against the shore. Then, as the road swings inland, it climbs a shore cliff. Continue for a few metres and look for a small park and lookout, where you can pause and enjoy the view across Colpoys Bay, or have a picnic. Here the escarpment consists of two bluffs—the 50-m shore cliff in front of you, and behind you Skinner Bluff. On the narrow plain, early settlers tried to farm, but the soil was shallow and rocky, and most farms failed. As you follow the plain, you can see the remains of these farms. Although many of the houses are still occupied, the barns have crumbled in ruins.

Another 4 km from the little park, the road eases inland and up the second cliff to a yawning limestone cave. At the brow of the hill, watch for the sign to Bruce's Cave Conservation Area. There is neither a gate fee nor any facilities. But, from the dirt parking lot, you can follow the trail through the woods for half a kilometre to the cave. It has no passages, but is a deep ballroomlike cavern in the rock wall, its opening divided by a high rock pillar. A second, smaller cave lies a few metres away.

From the inside, Bruce's Cave seems to provide good shelter.

From the conservation area, resume your route along County Road 26. After 1 km you will cross a small bridge over a tumbling stream and enter the hamlet of Oxenden. There are two buildings of historic note here. One lies beside the stream and is the grist mill, built in 1866 when Oxenden was a busy landing and farm-service village. The mill is now covered with stucco and has been converted to a private dwelling. The other building of note is the village store at the northwest corner of the intersection. Although the store is no longer in business, it retains many of the century-old architectural features and signs that typified the general store of a century ago.

Your next stop, Wiarton, lies 5 km farther along the road.

Wiarton

Wiarton offers a combination of interesting buildings and water-side recreation. Located at the head of Colpoys Bay and nestled beneath the cliffs of the escarpment, the town is a relative latecomer to southern Ontario's urban scene. It began around 1870 on the lucrative lumbering trade and only ten years later had eight sawmills. When the railway arrived, not only did the fishing industry boom, but furniture factories became Wiarton's main industry. Meanwhile, the town's population swelled to over 2,000. Today, sleek yachts have replaced the fishing tugs, and a campground and park have replaced the factories.

The road from Oxenden enters Wiarton from the east on Frank Street. Follow it to Highway 6 (Berford Street) and turn right. This is the main street and it takes you to the commercial core, where you will find a few small restaurants; and if you need to replenish your picnic supplies, there are grocery and variety stores.

There are a few historical buildings in Wiarton that are worth a look. Among these are the two hotels in the downtown area, which were built before the turn of the century, and the three-storey stone feed mill, which still supplies local farmers as it has since 1903.

If you turn right at the feed mill and follow Bay Street to its end, you will pass the yacht basin and come to the government fish hatchery. The two buildings, one frame, the other stone, were built in 1909 and were a government effort to arrest the decline in fish. But the battle against overfishing, pollution, and, finally, the sea lamprey was a losing one, and the commercial fleet today is a fraction of its former size; the sport fishery is negligible.

Wiarton to Hope Bay

Leave Wiarton north on Highway 6, and after 3 km turn right onto County Road 9. This road soon descends the escarpment to the shore and enters the village of Colpoys Bay, an early sawmill village which predated Wiarton by two decades.

From Colpoys Bay, the route follows a network of pioneer concession roads, which crisscross the flat, tablelike top of the escarpment, sometimes swooping down to hug the shore and at other times soaring to the brink of the cliff, giving views of distant headlands and sparkling bays. Short side trips lead to caves, coves, and quiet beaches.

Stay on County Road 9 as it swings inland from Colpoys Bay. Drive north for 4 km and then turn right onto an unmarked dirt road. Continue for 5 km through a few pockets of pastureland to a crossroads and turn left. Here you will come upon a small collection of buildings in the colourfully named Purple Valley. This was an important centre for early pioneers. Today, Purple Valley is an area of abandoned farmsteads, a few hay farms, and a maple syrup industry. Beside the former community centre and church is the country store, looking much as it has for nearly 100 years, and remaining in the same family for 70 of them.

Continue north for another 5 km. The second crossroad from the store leads to the Cape Croker Indian Reserve, with its campground, its Indian village, and one of the peninsula's oldest churches. This makes an interesting side trip.

To continue on your route, carry on north from the intersection. Then, after 3 km, turn right onto an unmarked road and drive 3.5 km to the turnoff to Hope Bay. The side road to Hope Bay is only 1 km long, but as it descends the escarpment it provides you with a picturesque vista over the bay, which is walled on both sides by limestone bluffs. A century ago, Hope Bay was a busy log-shipping centre, but today cottages have replaced the workers' homes on the narrow streets, and a public beach and campground have replaced the docks and the piling area. Here, along a public beach, you can stretch your legs or have a picnic before resuming your trip.

Hope Bay to Lion's Head

From Hope Bay, drive back to the turnoff and continue north. This dirt road, which runs as straight as the terrain permits, was surveyed as a farm road, part of a system of concession roads that enabled settlers to travel to their farm lots. But in this area, as through much of the Bruce, the soils were rocky and the farms short-lived. You will pass fields that are overgrown, many reclaimed entirely by the forest, and the gaunt shells of cabins and barns that peer from the bush.

About 4 km from the Hope Bay turnoff, watch for signs pointing to the Scenic Caves. A dirt road on the right leads you 3 km to the site. The caves are on private property, and there is a charge of $3 for a guided tour. These are the caves which were home to prehistoric cave dwellers in the movie *Quest of Fire*. Shortly after the movie was filmed, one unsuspecting stroller discovered to his horror a fur-clad body lying on the ground. Not until he learned that it was a discarded dummy used during a fight scene did he breathe a heavy sigh of relief.

From the Scenic Caves turnoff, the road twists northward through a rocky woodland for 2 km and suddenly emerges onto a wide plain. Originally a dank, repelling swamp, the Eastnor Plain was drained to produce the most prosperous farming community on the peninsula. It is now a treeless landscape of green fields, grazing cattle, and blowing hay.

In any large farming area, it is natural to expect to find a mill town, and the one here is Barrow Bay. After travelling 1 km over the plain and across a bridge, you will see a pair of unusual old buildings on the left side of the road. The first one, a simple board-and-batten affair, is the former office of the Barrow Bay Lumber Company and it dates back nearly 100 years. Beside it is the still-active general store. If you look downstream from the bridge, you will see a stone wall. This is all that remains of Barrow Bay's mill dam. The foundations of the mill (which burned in 1947) now support a new cottage.

Continue north across the plain for a further 4 km and you will come to Lion's Head, the largest town north of Wiarton.

Lion's Head

This town of 600, located on a small, sheltered harbour, began as a shipping and fishing centre. The prosperity of the farming community elevated it to a busy commercial centre at the turn of the century, and tourism has helped to keep it that way.

You enter the town on the main street, where there are shops, restaurants, and a bank. If you turn right at the bank and drive two blocks, you will come to the municipal beach, which offers camping, picnicking, bathing, and also access to the Bruce Trail. Extending into the harbour is a long public wharf, where you can see everything from luxury yachts to simple runabouts and the stout white tugs of the remaining village fishermen. Looming over the harbour, the great wall of the Niagara Escarpment reaches out to a craggy headland. Before it was eroded, the rocky profile resembled the head of a lion, thus giving the village the name it retains today.

Lion's Head to Cabot Head

This last section of the route traces little-used concession roads through some of the emptiest part of the peninsula and then follows a rocky shoreline beneath looming limestone cliffs to a remote headland.

Leave Lion's Head by driving north on the main street, which before long swerves down to the water and to the wide expanse of Whippoorwill Bay. During the next 2 km, after passing a string of cottages, you will find several opportunities to pull over to the roadside and wander along the rocky shore, or to cast a line into the surf. From the northern head of the bay, the road bends inland and enters the Forty Hills. This rugged limestone ridge continues to defy road building and forces the gravel road to snake precariously around each outcropping. The bends are sharp, so be on the lookout for oncoming traffic.

After 3 km the road emerges from the hills into the one-time farming community of Cape Chin. Most of the farms here have been abandoned, and as you start along the straight stretch of road you will see on your right the vacant log cabin of an early settler. Because the square pine logs are in high demand, such cabins are becoming rare.

At the next intersection, 1 km from the cabin, continue straight on. A little more than 1 km from the intersection, look for a stone church standing alone in an empty field. This is the widely known and much-photographed St. Margaret's Chapel, which was completed in the 1930s. It took three years for the area's

St. Margaret's Chapel at Cape Chin was built by the local farmers.

determined farmers to haul stone from fields and little quarries, and to erect the solid church. The windows are glazed, the pews made of oak, and the building is open to the public.

North of the church, the road bends sharply right and then forks left. The next 9 km follow another old concession road through swamps and around rock outcrops. A few pioneer farmers tried to carve out farms here, but the overgrown fields and derelict barns testify to the futility of their efforts. After 10 km the road ends abruptly at a T-intersection. Turn right and travel 4 km to another T-intersection. Turn right again and descend the hill into the little waterside village of Dyers Bay—and to a vista that you will be unlikely to forget.

Once a thriving lumber town, Dyers Bay now consists of a store, a gift shop, a restaurant, and a string of cottages. Here you start the last and the most scenic portion of the route. From the village, the road winds along the narrow beach 10 km to Cabot Head. After 3 km the cottages begin to thin out until there is just no more room at the base of the huge cliff.

Roughly 2.5 km from the last cottage, the road crosses a small culvert. If you are a hiker, stop here and explore the remains of one of Ontario's more ingenious sawmill efforts. In 1881 Horace and Robert Lymburner acquired rights to the timber which covered the mesa atop the bluffs. There, Gillies Lake empties down a cascading stream into Georgian Bay 100 m below. Down on the beach, where tugs could haul the lumber off to the south shore and the railways, the Lymburners built a mill and a town. At first the logs were simply hurled down the cliff into a small pond on the beach. But the damage to the logs was enormous, so the Lymburners decided to build a log slide. By damming the outlet from Gillies Lake and periodically allowing great gushes of water and rock to plummet down the steep gully, erosion soon carved a natural flume, which was then lined with planks. But by 1905 the timber was gone and the Lymburner mill fell silent.

Today, you can hike up the steep gully to the remains of the wooden flume and the dam on Gillies Lake. The trail is clear and well worn. But be careful during wet weather, for the rocks can become dangerously slick and it's a long tumble to the bottom. Also, be sure to wear long pants and thick shoes, for the poison ivy in places forms an unbroken mat.

Whippoorwill Bay—a quiet spot where you can "get away from it all."

Cabot Head

From the mill site, a drive of 5 km brings you to Cabot Head, one of the most placid points of land in Ontario. Cabot Head is a small swampy plain at the foot of the escarpment, enclosing the small harbour of Wingfield Basin. Here, at the northeasterly point of the peninsula, a lonely lighthouse is the sole remaining building of what was once a bustling sawmilling and fishing village. Built in 1895, the squat wooden lighthouse is no longer in use. It has been superseded by the modern beacon which stands beside it.

This is the end of the road. Here the escarpment changes direction and runs westward in a wild, rocky, and unsettled shoreline. There is little to break the tranquility of Cabot Head. You can swim, picnic, fish, or simply let Georgian Bay's breezes waft through your hair, with probably no more company than a small swarm of raucous seagulls.

As regards your return journey, Highway 6 is the only highway that extends the length of the peninsula. To reach it, drive back to Dyers Bay village and follow the route west for about 6 km to Highway 6. To the right lies Tobermory. While it is not part of this backroads route, it is worth a visit. It is from Tobermory that the 115-car ferry, *Chi-Cheemaun*, departs four times daily to Manitoulin Island. Here, too, you can charter a boat to the internationally famous Flowerpot Island, where you can camp and hike. Or you can voyage to the province's only underwater park, Fathom Five, which has the greatest concentration of sunken vessels in the fresh waters of North America. Check in with the park office located at the Tobermory Harbour.

Tobermory developed around two picturesque harbours, the Little Tub and the Big Tub. Most of today's village rings the former. Amid the pleasure craft and charter boats, you can spot the squat tugs of the few remaining commercial fishermen. The Tub, as Tobermory is called, has a small selection of restaurants, shops, and motels. If you wish to stay overnight, you should reserve ahead, for the popularity of the Manitoulin ferry usually means full rooms. You may well wish to stay the night, for it is a 100-km journey just back to the base of the peninsula. There, at Wiarton on Highway 6, several other provincial highways fan out to the rest of the province.

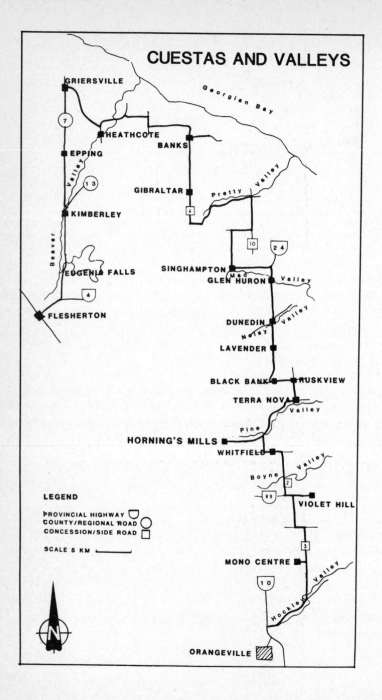

CUESTAS AND VALLEYS

Georgian Bay

GRIERSVILLE

(7)

HEATHCOTE

BANKS

EPPING

Valley

(13)

GIBRALTAR

Pretty Valley

(6)

KIMBERLEY

Beaver

(10)

(24)

EUGENIA FALLS

SINGHAMPTON

GLEN HURON

Mad Valley

(4)

FLESHERTON

DUNEDIN

Noisy Valley

LAVENDER

BLACK BANK

RUSKVIEW

TERRA NOVA

Valley

Pine

HORNING'S MILLS

WHITFIELD

Boyne Valley

(2)

(89)

VIOLET HILL

LEGEND

PROVINCIAL HIGHWAY

COUNTY/REGIONAL ROAD

CONCESSION/SIDE ROAD

(3)

SCALE 5 KM

MONO CENTRE

(10)

Hockley Valley

N

ORANGEVILLE

5   Cuestas and Valleys

This route takes you among the gaping valleys and breath-taking vistas of Ontario's most unusual and scenic geological feature, the Niagara Escarpment. The route begins at Orangeville, 60 km northwest of Toronto, and for 80 km it zigzags northward over century-old concession roads, plunges into wide valleys, and soars onto rocky cuestas. It ends in Beaver Valley, one of the province's most beautiful valleys.

With its windswept lookouts, pastoral valleys, and tumbling streams, this trail is most likely to appeal to the recreational driver. Fishermen, however, will be able to drop a line in Ontario's best trout streams, while the hiker, at several points along the route, can gain access to the Bruce Trail; and the aficionado of Ontario's rural vernacular architecture will discover outstanding nineteenth-century farm homes, churches, schools, and even Orange Lodges.

The villages along the route are small, and few contain gas stations or restaurants, so you would be advised to stock up at Orangeville before starting out.

A Bit of History

Before 1850 the area between Orangeville and Georgian Bay was still a land of silent pine forests. The lack of roads and navigable rivers held settlement at bay. Even so, some hardy settlers forged their own trails, and by 1830 they had built sawmills on the tumbling brooks. But these were the exception. It was not until 1850 that three roads finally breached the wilderness: Hurontario Street, from Port Credit on Lake Ontario to Collingwood on Georgian Bay; the Mail Road, from Barrie on Lake Simcoe to Meaford on Georgian Bay; and the Garafraxa Road, Ontario's first colonization road, from Shelburne to Owen Sound.

61

Once the roads were open, settlement took off. By 1860 all the townships over this roof of land had been surveyed into concession roads and farm lots. Land-hungry settlers quickly gobbled up the lots and cut away the forest. Along the rivers and streams, mill sites grew into towns which provided basic services for area farmers.

Then the growth slowed. Although the 1870s and 1880s were the years of Ontario's railway boom, the railway builders found the escarpment an obstacle that they could not surmount. There was another difficulty too. Many farmers moved away, discouraged by the steep, stony soils of the river valleys.

During the past two decades, a new wave of development has swept over the crest of the escarpment. As growth from Toronto pushed northwest and as better roads increased commuting distances, wealthy commuters grabbed scenic escarpment land for their country homes. In the past, gentlemen's agreements between the farmer-owners and the Bruce Trail Association had allowed the hiking trail to follow the escarpment crest from Tobermory to Queenston. But when city-dwellers bought country lots from the original farm owners, many of them did not respect the gentlemen's agreement and hikers were forced onto hot, dusty roads. The Ontario government then established the Niagara Escarpment Commission in order to protect the natural environment and to guarantee Bruce Trail hikers the best possible route. But after ten years it has done neither, and the future of the escarpment remains uncertain.

Hockley Valley

Orangeville, the starting point of this trip, lies at the junction of Provincial Highways 9 and 10. At the stoplights in the centre of the business district, turn north up First Street to the stoplights at Highway 10 and turn left. Drive 5 km to the Hockley Valley Road and turn right.

The Hockley Valley is the southernmost of the great gorges you will pass through on this route. Measuring 15 km from head to mouth, it is one of the shallower valleys of the trip. Its beauty lies in its tumbling stream and gentle, forested slopes.

The Hockley Valley Road follows an ancient Indian trail, one used by the early settlers to reach their new farm lots. Today, the road is paved, and it enters the valley at the head, a mere gully. As the valley widens and deepens, woodlands of maple and oak cling to the hillsides. Down on the valley floor, a small creek called the Nottawasaga River begins its 100-km journey to Georgian Bay.

After 5 km, turn left onto Mono Road 3. Within a few metres you will cross the river, which is here a busy brook shaded by cedar forests. From the river, the road twists and struggles up the steep valley side. After a kilometre, it emerges onto the crest— and suddenly, to your left, lies a panoramic vista. The viewpoint, however, has not been developed, and to photograph it or just contemplate, you must pull onto the shoulder and park. From this vantage point, you can see south across the wide, forested valley and west towards the head. A few metres beyond the viewpoint the road straightens out, and here on the left, marked by two white paint slashes you will find access to the Bruce Trail. The attractive hiking trail leads across fields, down to the wooded valley floor, and along the river onto the main valley road where, sadly, private owners have refused Bruce Trail hikers permission to use their land.

Mono Hills

"Mono" is from the Scottish "monadh," meaning "hill," and that is what you will find along this section of the route. Within 2 km from the Hockley lookout, the escarpment falls away to the east

A road in the Mono Hills, north of the Hockley Valley.

into a tumble of foothills and then levels out into flat farmlands. Then, about 4 km from the lookout, the escarpment fractures into mesas, or outliers, separated by a wide, shady gulch, into which the road suddenly plunges.

At the 5-km mark, you will meet County Road 11. For a short side trip, turn left onto this road and drive 1 km into the little village of Mono Centre. A one-time mill village, it lies nestled beneath the rim of a limestone mesa. With its former general store, its Burns' United Church (built in 1837), and a collection of nineteenth-century homes, it is a quiet shadow of its busy days. To get back on your route, return the way you came and turn left at Mono Road 3.

The next stretch of road offers spectacular vistas on the right and a wooded ridge on the left. When you are 4 km from County Road 11, you will come to a crossroads. Turn left here and drive 1 km to a plaque. This sign was erected by the Niagara Escarpment Commission and it describes the evolution of the Mono Hills. Here, too, are 700 ha of public land. Although the lands are not yet developed, you can explore the limestone cliffs with their fractured caves.

From the plaque, follow the road west as it winds up a gully pinched between two rock mesas. After half a kilometre watch for a fork to the right, and take it. At this point you are above the escarpment and more than 1 km from its lip. Much of the rolling farmland has been converted to wealthy country estates. After 2 km the road plunges into the historic Sheldon Creek Valley. Although this valley is neither wide nor deep, it was once the scene of early pioneer mills, including Sheldon Mills. Until this building burned several years ago, it was the second oldest mill in the province. The oldest extant mill is the Backus Mill on the shores of Lake Erie (see Backroad 1, the Erie Road).

Continue a further 2 km to a stop sign at Provincial Highway 89. To the right is Violet Hill, a little hamlet with preserved buildings that are well worth the side trip. To make this side trip, turn right on Highway 89 and after 2 km look for buildings with the signs "Mrs. Mitchells" and "Granny Taught Us." The latter was a Loyal Orange Lodge built in 1898 (and renovated into a craft shop). The former was the village school and is now a popular restaurant named after one of the teachers. Both buildings have been sensitively restored by James and Maureen Baufeldt, who have made the 110-year-old Methodist Church their home. Their concern for history has spread to other residents of Violet Hill, who have preserved along the small village street some of the village's early homes.

Boyne River Valley

From Violet Hill, retrace your steps west on Highway 89 for 2.5 km until you come to the second crossroads. Turn right here down the concession road, Mulmur Road 2. After 1.5 km, you will descend into the dark, wooded valley of the Boyne River. At this point, although the river is but a trickle, the valley floor is wide and swampy. Here the Toronto Board of Education operates its Nature Science School and here the Ministry of Natural Resources owns several hundred hectares of land which, although public, have not been developed.

From the lip of the Boyne Valley, continue north for 3 km. Here the terrain becomes level and the farms prosperous. Then, at County Road 17, turn left. After 1.5 km, at the northwest corner of the first crossroads, you will see a red church. This is Christ Church, built in the 1850s. Together with a small white building, which was the Orange Lodge, it is all that remains of the once-bustling village of Whitfield. At its peak in the late 1880s, Whitfield contained stores, a blacksmith's shop, and several homes.

Pine River Valley

Drive 1.5 km west from Whitfield on County Road 17 and then turn right at a crossroads. Continue for 1 km down a forested gully and into the valley of the Pine River, one of the widest and deepest on the trip. At a stop sign, turn left onto the Pine Valley Road. Here, about halfway between the head and the mouth of the valley, the road is squeezed between the wall and the tumbling Pine River. After 1 km, look on the right for the Pine River Fish Sanctuary. On this artificial lake, you can cast for trout or sunfish. The area has a few picnic tables and offers some short hikes among its wooded hillsides.

From the fish sanctuary, turn right once more onto the Pine Valley Road and drive 3 km up an ever-narrowing valley to the historic mill town of Horning's Mills. Today's 150 residents are fewer than half the number who lived here a hundred years ago,

The hamlet of Horning's Mills on the way to Terra Nova.

and the town's businesses have diminished from two dozen to just two. Development began in the 1830s, when Lewis Horning opened a sawmill and later a grist mill. As settlement progressed, the village boomed. But the disappearance of the forest and the advent of the railways doomed the village and it suffered a decline from which it never recovered.

The Pine Valley Road ends at a stop sign in the heart of Horning's Mills, and here you can find the village's oldest buildings. On the southeast corner, a historical plaque tells the story of the town. On the west side of the road are two stores. One, constructed in board and batten, still operates. On the northeast corner stands one of the village's oldest structures, the Allen Hotel. Built in 1873, the fading yellow-frame hostelry is now a private home, yet it has changed little in appearance.

From Horning's Mills, follow the Pine Valley Road back down the valley. About 2 km after you pass the entrance to the fish sanctuary, the road bends left and passes scattered frame buildings and the site of the one-time mill village of Kilgorie. Here Hurontario Street, now little more than a bush trail, crosses the Pine River. Keep to the road you are on as it winds farther down the gully and emerges suddenly onto the floor of the lower valley. Here, early farmers established a prosperous agricultural community on the silty soils of the flood plain. Today, many of the pastures sprout modern country homes.

After driving 5 km from Kilgorie you will enter the crossroads village of Terra Nova. Although a general store still operates, this is primarily a residential community. At the main intersection, turn left. The road now begins to climb the wall of the valley and after 3 km reaches the crest of the north wall and the most sweeping vista of the trip. Stop the car and enjoy the view. Below you, the homes of Terra Nova are tiny specks; 5 km away are the forested slopes of the south valley wall. To the west you will see the narrow neck of the valley, and to the east the rolling quiltwork of farms that mark the valley's mouth. At the intersection are three buildings, all closed—a store, a school, and a blacksmith's shop—which mark the site of a hamlet called Ruskview.

From the Ruskview crossroads, drive west. After 2 km the road descends into the Black Bank Valley, a deep fissure in the bedrock which extends from the Pine Valley north to the Pretty River Valley. As you descend, look on the right for a stone farmhouse. Built in 1871, this is one of the few stone buildings in the area. At the bottom of the little valley there is a pair of cabins, the sole survivors of the one-time mill village of Black Bank.

As the road grinds up out of the valley, watch for a hidden intersection and then turn right. Here, on the surviving northern portion of Hurontario Street, you will emerge onto a high, level plateau, where healthy farms and cornfields stretch away on both sides.

At 3.5 km from the intersection, you will come to a hamlet with the delightful name of Lavender. Although small, Lavender played an important role as a stopping place on Hurontario Street, and as a farm-service village. The former hotel on the northwest corner is now a private residence, as is the former store on the northeast corner.

Noisy River Valley

As you continue north for the next 1.5 km, the land drops away, and before you spreads the valley of the Noisy River. Because this is not a developed lookout point, you must pull over to the side of the road to admire the view. From the lip, Hurontario Street winds to the valley bottom and enters the village of Dunedin. Here, where Hurontario Street crossed the Noisy River, Judah

Baverman built the area's first sawmill, which became the focus for a busy village. Today, its population has shrunk to about 100 and its businesses have vanished. On the single main street, the stone blacksmith's shop and the general store still stand, although closed, while on the old village lots newer residents have added modern homes. Halfway along the main street an early settlement road known as the River Road merges in from the left. Pass this and take the second road left, the continuation of Hurontario Street.

North of Dunedin you will drive over rolling hills, where many of the original farms have been replaced by hobby farms and country estates, and after 3.5 km you will enter the Mad River Valley.

Mad River Valley

As the road descends into the valley of the Mad River, the first views of Georgian Bay appear far to the right. On the banks of the Mad River is the bustling modern mill village of Glen Huron, a village that thrives today, as it has for 130 years, on its mills. James Cooper built the valley's first mills in the 1840s, but he had already departed when the Hamilton brothers opened their grist mill in 1874. Although Hamilton's new mill and company store are modern replacements, they continue a tradition that is as old as settlement in Ontario.

Pass the mill, follow Hurontario Street left and drive up the hill out of the village. Continue for about 1.5 km to a stop sign at Highway 24. Turn left along Highway 24 and after 1.5 km you will come to Devil's Glen Provincial Park. Perched on the side of the Mad Valley, which is here a narrow gorge, this park offers hiking, camping, and access to the Bruce Trail.

Continue westward on Highway 24 for another 2.5 km to the mill village of Singhampton. Near the main intersection sits the Hampton House dining lounge, a restored nineteenth-century hotel. It was built in 1865, as the Exchange Hotel, to provide room and board for stagecoach travellers. Not only has the attractive red and yellow brick exterior been cleaned, but the interior has been restored to a nineteenth-century style. If your gas tank or lunch bag need filling, you can call in at the gas station or at the general store just across the street.

Pretty River Valley

From Singhampton's main intersection, drive north up the Nottawasaga townline road. After 5 km turn right and drive another 2 km to the Nottawasaga 10th Concession. At the northwest corner of this intersection sits another rare fieldstone house, this one constructed in the 1850s during the earliest days of settlement. Turn left and follow Nottawasaga Road 10 for 4.5 km to the second crossroads, the road to the Pretty River Valley, and turn left again. Here, a looming rock wall hides the entrance to the valley. However, as you proceed west, the walls part and the road passes through a narrow defile into a wide pastoral valley. Surrounded by high, wooded hills, this valley is nearly circular and is about 3 km in diameter. More than a dozen farms nestle on its floor, protected from the raging winds that howl over the plateau.

The scenic road winds through pastures and woods to the head of the valley, where it again seems blocked by a wall of rock. Measure 6 km from your last turnoff and then look for a narrow dirt road leading to the right. Follow this road up the steep valley wall. As the valley drops away behind you, you will emerge onto a high plateau, known as the Roof of Ontario. This is southern Ontario's highest point of land.

The Roof of Ontario

From the wide expanse of Georgian Bay 10 km to the north, the winds sweep unhindered over this tabletop of land, bringing fierce storms both winter and summer. Yet, from its lofty summits, you can gaze over the most extensive vistas in southern Ontario.

Just after you surmount the crest from the Pretty River Valley, you will come to a stop sign at Collingwood Township Concession Road 4. Turn right. Along this stretch of road is a land of fractured rocks and abandoned farms. To reach the first of the lookout points, drive north for 3 km and turn right down a dead-end road. This road leads to the top of Osler Bluff, a soaring limestone promontory of the escarpment that offers a remarkable view of the flat farmlands at your feet, with the Simcoe Highlands shimmering blue in the haze of the distant horizon. Here, too, you can gain access to the Bruce Trail. Even a short stroll will reward you with more views, and the trail is tame, so your sneakers will do.

Return to Concession Road 4, turn right, and drive 5 km to a crossroads and a hamlet called Banks. Turn right here, follow the road for 2 km as it descends a small cliff, and 1 km farther on you will come to the highest lookout in southern Ontario. Ignored by the local municipality and by the Niagara Escarpment Commission, this lookout has no facilities whatever, and the parking area is a rutted turnoff beside the road. Yet this view encompasses so much that you may wish to pause a while here. Below lies a patchwork of fields, and beyond them the streets and white grain elevator that mark the port of Collingwood. As a backdrop, there are the blue waters of Georgian Bay, its shoreline curving gently until it disappears on the horizon.

Before continuing your road trip, you may wish to explore southern Ontario's most extensive cave system. Privately owned as they have been since 1934, the Scenic Caves are located another kilometre along the road you have been following. In these caves, linked by ladders and bridges, lie more than half a dozen chambers, bearing such descriptive names as Fat Man's Misery and the Ice Cave, where ice persists even during the summer. The Scenic Caves are a commercial operation and there is an admission charge.

The Beaver Valley

To resume your journey, retrace your route to Banks. Turn right and again follow Collingwood Concession Road 4. This, the last segment of the trip, takes you into what many consider to be the most beautiful of Ontario's valleys, the Beaver Valley. Certainly, it is one of the widest and longest. Several lookouts ring its rocky walls, and a rushing river winds across its wooded floor. Protected by its walls and moderated by the waters of nearby Georgian Bay, the valley's singular microclimate has produced extensive, lush orchards that grow the now-famous Northern Spye apple.

From Banks, the road continues north for 2.5 km and then bends sharply west, following the escarpment. After another 1 km, the panorama of the Beaver Valley unfolds before you. Here, at its mouth, the valley is wide and gentle, quilted with orchards and pastures; 7 km away is the floor of the valley, and 11 km away the western wall. There is no single place that can be called a lookout. Rather, this is a vista that changes as you ease down the valley slope.

At 1 km from the crest, a side road leads right, and 1 km down this road you will find one of Ontario's rarest barn styles, the octagonal. There are only eight surviving octagonal barns in the province. The style originated in the northeastern United States and spread northward in the closing years of the nineteenth century. To resume your trip, return to the main road and continue down the slope for 1 km, then turn right at another side road.

Here you will pass rolling apple orchards—some of the trees old and gnarled, others young and spindly, but all in neat rows. After 2 km, turn left at the crossroads. This road will take you through more shady orchards to a stop sign at County Road 13, the Beaver Valley Road (which runs the length of the valley). Turn left down County Road 13 and travel 2 km to the village of Heathcote. Just after you cross the concrete bridge over the Beaver River, turn left onto the main street of Heathcote.

This quiet residential community was once an important stopping place on the Mail Road, with three hotels and several businesses. You can still find reminders of those busy days—an old church, an Orange Lodge, several simple frame houses, and, on the main street, a carriage shop which is now an antique store. You will also find, if you need them, a gas station and a grocery store.

From the main street, recross the bridge, drive half a kilometre and turn left. This is the Mail Road, along which, during the 1840s, settlers trekked from Barrie to the newly opened lands of the valley and to the townships farther west. However, once the concession roads were opened, the Mail Road fell into disuse, and the short section from Heathcote to Griersville is the only portion to survive.

From the turn, the road rises for 1 km to the crest of the valley's western wall. Stop here at a small lookout point, where a historical plaque commemorates the road, and where a wide view extends over the fields of the lower valley. Then continue west a few metres and fork right. Here the old Mail Road is narrow and rutted, a condition which the early travellers would find familiar. For 7 km the narrow trail twists past cornfields, woodlots, and past the farmsteads of early settlers, until it stops at Grey County Road 7 and the village of Griersville. Turn left at Griersville and drive 8 km to the Epping Lookout.

This lookout is one of the valley's most publicized. Managed

Epping Heights Farm overlooks the Beaver Valley.

by the North Grey Conservation Authority, the park covers several hectares and has parking for a hundred cars. There are toilet and picnic facilities, and the view is panoramic. You can look north to the wide valley mouth, or south to the narrowing rocky gorge. At your feet is a popular subject of artists and photographers, the Epping Heights Farm.

From the park, turn left onto County Road 7 and continue down the slope. Only a few metres away, at the first crossroads, is the abandoned Mount Hope Methodist Church, which has stood here since 1887 and marks the site of the vanished hamlet of Epping. The road then descends steadily in a straight line down the valley wall, until after 7 km it reaches the floor and the tumbling Beaver River. A popular canoe route, the Beaver River is also the scene of the zany River Rat Race. Each spring a flotilla of nondescript craft (anything *but* boats are allowed) bounce their way downstream, their navigators outlandishly attired.

The valley narrows here and its walls steepen to form a gorge and to provide some of Ontario's more popular ski slopes. In the valley bottom, County Road 7 stops at County Road 13. Here is the one-time mill village of Kimberley, which still has many of its original buildings and now caters to skiers. Even the old board-and-batten mill has become an antique shop.

As you drive south from Kimberley on County Road 13, a high, rocky cliff, known locally as Mount Baldy, looms over your left shoulder. After 1 km fork left. As the road climbs back up the east wall, the valley narrows until it is only 1 km wide, its walls almost sheer. After 2 km a small viewpoint on the right offers you a last view down the valley.

After another 2 km (you will be back up on the plateau now, above the valley), the road crosses two large wooden flumes. These carry water to drive the turbines of the Eugenia Falls power plant. This was originally a small wooden plant built by William Hogg to serve the local area, but it was purchased in 1915 by Ontario Hydro and expanded considerably. If you wish to see it, drive 1 km beyond the flumes, turn right, and drive a further 1 km down the valley to an intersection; turn right again and drive 1 km to the plant. If you do not wish to make this side trip, drive south from the flumes 2 km into the village of Eugenia.

Eugenia Falls

Yellow and brown signs in the village will direct you to the Eugenia Falls Conservation Area. Here again the North Grey Conservation Authority has been at work. One of their prime goals is to preserve the unique features of the escarpment, and at Eugenia they have created one of their most attractive parks. Covering 23 ha, this wooded park offers picnicking, hiking, and a view of the 30-metre-high Eugenia Falls.

This is a fitting place to end your tour of the escarpment—a location where one of the ridge's features has been so sensitively preserved for the public. It gives cause for hope that this unique and attractive limestone ridge may yet be saved from insensitive development.

To return home, continue south from Eugenia village for 4 km to the junction with Highway 4. Turn right and drive 2 km to the town of Flesherton, where you will link up with Highway 10.

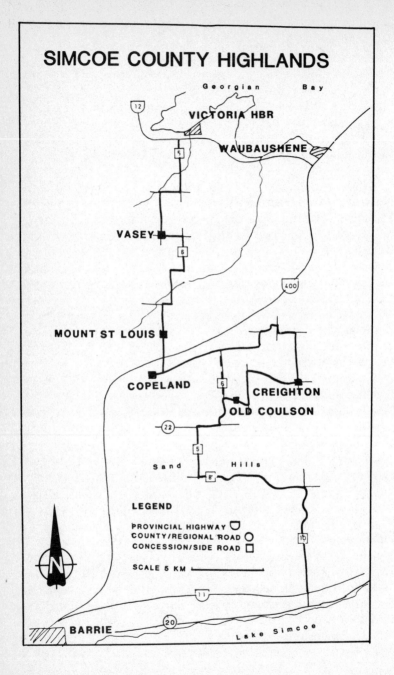

SIMCOE COUNTY HIGHLANDS

6 Simcoe County Highlands

Next time you venture north to Muskoka's cottage country, try and spend some time exploring the forgotten and often spectacular hill country of Simcoe County. This trip starts in the historic waterside mill town of Waubaushene, on Highway 12, and zig-zags southwards over 70 km of gravel concession roads through Ontario's forgotten hill country. Many of the views along this route are just as spectacular as those of the more famous Ottawa Valley or Niagara Escarpment.

What you can do depends on the season. Summer offers bass and trout fishing in Georgian Bay at the north end of the route and in Lake Simcoe at the south end. The fall season brings out some of Ontario's best colours in the maple forests that shelter the winding roads. For the photographer and country architect, there are some lovely farmhouses of stone, brick, and wood. And for those who prefer more strenuous activity, the forests and closed concession roads offer ideal hiking and skiing trails.

Although there are gas stations in a couple of the rural hamlets, there are no snack bars or restaurants along this route. But as the trip can be done in half a day, it could be fitted in between two meals if you don't want to pack a picnic lunch.

A Bit of History

Simcoe County's first roads were military. During the War of 1812, two supply roads were built to move troops and equipment to the forts that guarded northern Lake Huron. The first was the Six-Mile Portage, a wagon road that ran from what is now Barrie to Willow Creek, a tributary flowing to Georgian Bay. The second was the Penetanguishene Road which barged straight northwards from Barrie to where the town of Penetang now stands on

Georgian Bay. Today, the Penetanguishene Road has become Highway 93; the Six-Mile Portage has vanished.

After the war, the Penetanguishene Road was surveyed into farm lots, which were offered free to half-pay veterans of the war. After 1830 settlers began to take up land in the back townships. A mixed group, they included Germans, Irish, Scots, and some escaped American slaves, whose simple frame church still stands. Then, during the 1850s and 1860s, railways pierced the area and brought a new wave of growth, especially to the little ports that ringed the bay. A half-dozen of the ports quickly boomed into busy sawmill towns. But when the roar of the mills and the puffing of the trains faded, so did most of the towns. Meanwhile, on the hillsides, many farmers found the steep, stony lands awkward and unproductive, and they moved away. In recent years, both areas have revived through tourism—the milltowns because of the popularity of Georgian Bay's waters and shores, and the hills because of their potential for downhill skiing.

Waubaushene to Victoria Harbour

Beside the turnoff from Highway 400 onto Highway 12 sits what in 1860 was the largest of the mill towns, Waubaushene. Its industries and businesses, and many of its workers' cabins, have now vanished, and several new homes can be seen on the network of streets that overlook Georgian Bay. But a few reminders of the mill days still linger on.

If you wish to have a look around Waubaushene, turn right at the directional arrow on Highway 12 and follow Pine Street up the hill. At the crest is a ghostly sight. Here, the one-time commercial core has deteriorated into a handful of closed shops, dominated by a brick hotel. As you continue along Pine Street, the red brick Roman Catholic church comes into view. Continue down the hill to Hazel Street and turn right. On your left are Georgian Bay's waters and the combined Anglican–United Church with its slender white steeple. The road bends to the right to follow the shoreline, taking you past the Waubaushene Inn, an old hotel where, at the Captain's Table restaurant, you can have lunch before starting on your afternoon's trip. To begin the trip and get back onto Pine Street and Highway 12, stay on the shore road.

Follow Highway 12 for 8 km west of Waubaushene and look for the green arrow directing you into the village of Victoria

Although Waubaushene is in the tourist region of Georgian Bay, its main street resembles that of a ghost town.

Harbour. Drive down the hill, past the intersection that marks the main part of town, and continue straight on to the water. Here, beside a government dock, is a small park, so poorly kept that it is scarcely recognizable. But it is adequate for a quick picnic or a few casts for perch or bass from the dock, and it offers a view of the coastline of Hog Bay, an indentation on Georgian Bay. The large weedy fields beside the wharf were the site of the busy King and Fowlie mills during the last half of the nineteenth century.

Although Victoria Harbour is much smaller than it was, it has retained many of its early features. Several of the commercial buildings at the main intersection date from the milling days. (Look particularly at the weathered, wooden store, now closed, on the southwest corner.) Extending west on the main street for more than 2 km are the mill workers' simple cabins. Some have been renovated, their plank sides covered with insulbrick or aluminum. Others remain much as they were built, their wooden walls picturesquely weathered.

Victoria Harbour to Vasey

At the end of the long string of houses, the village road rejoins Highway 12. Follow it west for about 1 km and turn left onto Tay Concession Road 5. After 1.5 km you will see a blue and orange historical marker pointing left down a side road to the site of St. Louis. Near this spot, in 1649, the invading Iroquois tortured to death two Jesuits, Jean de Brébeuf and Gabriel Lalemant. The Iroquois went on to sweep the Hurons and the Jesuits from Simcoe County and to become kings of the fur trade. This site, open only during the summer, is a memorial to the Jesuits and their bloody demise.

Continue south on Concession Road 5, and be sure to keep your camera handy, for here the route enters picturesque ridge and valley country. After 4 km the road climbs out of the valley of Hog Creek and onto a high ridge. As you reach the summit, turn right onto an unmarked road. After 1 km this road takes you back to the crest, and suddenly a vista of pastoral serenity unfolds at your feet, revealing in the flat valley a quiltwork of traditional farms.

Considering the size of the valley, the creek that meanders across its floor is surprisingly small. Most geologists are of the opinion that this little stream did not carve the valley, but rather that it flows through the wide glacial meltwater valley that was already there. Because the valley runs at a 45° angle to the grid pattern of the roads, you must make one more "zig" into the valley before you "zag" back out of it. As you descend the hill, note the foundations of the barn on the right. You may at first think that these are rocks, but look closer; they are the ends of logs used in a rarely found construction method known as "stacklog."

Turn left at a crossroads as soon as you reach the bottom, and grind up another steep grade for more than 1 km. At the crest, you will emerge onto a wide, level, agricultural plateau, the summit of one of the north Simcoe mesas, and a further 2 km will bring you to the hamlet of Vasey.

Once a busy farmers' town, Vasey contained all the services that the nineteenth-century farmer could want—a church, a school, a store, a blacksmith's shop, and an Orange Lodge. Later, with road improvements and the advent of fast cars, residents began to venture farther afield to shop, and Vasey became a quiet residential hamlet. While the store sits abandoned and the black-smith's shop has disappeared, the red brick church and the Orange Lodge still see occasional use.

Vasey to Copeland Forest

Drive east from Vasey for 3 km and turn right onto Medonte Concession Road 6. After 2 km you will suddenly find yourself peering into the yawning valley of the Sturgeon River, which is even deeper and wider than the valley of the Hog. Its walls rise steeply 100 m from a flat valley floor that is nearly 2 km across.

The road you should follow turns right. Do not take the abandoned Concession Road 6 that leads straight ahead. In laying out their roads, the early British army surveyors ignored the topography, and settlers often found themselves with roads that ran into lakes or halted abruptly at cliffs. Although a road did once follow the survey line straight down the near cliff of the valley wall, it soon proved useless and was abandoned. You should therefore turn west and follow the side road for 1.5 km to the next usable road, Concession Road 5. Turn left here, driving down a far gentler slope into the valley. The valley floor is wider here, and once more the river is a mere creek.

About 1 km from the creek, you will begin to leave the valley. The south wall may loom higher than the north, but its grade is gentler. As you reach the summit, you will be rewarded with wide

Rugged pastureland on the slopes of the Coldwater Valley.

views across the valley below. Turn right at the first intersection and descend the valley again until you reach still another cross-roads, where you turn left and leave the valley for the last time and climb the next ridge. Once more extensive views appear on the right. After 1 km the road mounts the crest of the plateau and traverses a gentle landscape of pastures and farms with traditional houses and barns.

A little more than 2 km from the crest, the road enters the quiet, historic hamlet of Mount St. Louis. Although it never had more than a school, a church, a hotel, and a tavern, Mount St. Louis was a busy spot in pioneer times. The school, church, and hotel still stand, though they no longer enjoy their original uses. A few newer homes line the road to the left.

The village marks the intersection of two crossroads, but it was once noted for a more famous road that bisected the village. This was the Gloucester Road, which bustled with traffic for a few years, then was abandoned. In the 1830s, before the concession roads and the side roads were opened, the Gloucester Road guided pioneers from the Penetanguishene Road over the hills and through dark forests to Coldwater, 20 km east. Then, when the concession roads were opened, the old Gloucester Road was

The valley itself contains fertile farmlands.

forgotten and left to the weeds and trees. If you look behind the homes on the northeast corner of the intersection, you will see a double line of maples marching at an angle across a field. These once shaded the Gloucester Road and they are the only physical indication that the road ever existed.

South of Mount St. Louis you will begin to descend into the next valley, that of the Coldwater River. It is a two-step descent. From the lip of the first slope, you will garner your first glimpse of the Sand Hills. Steep and forested, they form a dark, wavering line on the horizon and mark the south wall of the valley. At the foot of the first step the terrain flattens out. About 1 km from Mount St. Louis, look on the right for a huge stone farmhouse. This massive building was constructed with stones gathered from the nearby fields and laboriously pieced together. It is one of the few such buildings in Simcoe County.

Carrying on along the road, you now begin to descend the second and last slope into the Coldwater River Valley. Before you lies the vast lowland of spruce and maple that was once the private forest from which Charles Copeland fed his mills. In 1907 Jasper Martin had built a mill beside the newly constructed CPR line and, to accommodate his 80 workers, he added the company town of

81

Martinville. Charles Copeland bought the operation in 1922, and his family continued operations until 1975, when fire destroyed the mill. So ended what was southern Ontario's last company mill town. Ontario's Ministry of Natural Resources bought the extensive tract and turned it into a forest management area that is open to the public.

As the road eases down the slope, it crosses a bridge over the busy four lanes of Highway 400 and stops at the Ingram Road. Copeland Forest, the park administered by the Ministry of Natural Resources, lies 1.5 km to the right. It has picnic tables and toilets, and is open to hunters, hikers, and skiers. The park office is located in the old Copeland store. With its attractive wood shingle siding, it and the family house nearby are the only survivors of Copeland's mill and the company town.

Copeland Forest to the Sand Hills

From Copeland Forest, your route follows the Ingram Road east through the dark woods and then emerges into the daylight among farm fields. After 4 km a stop sign marks the intersection with Medonte Concession Road 6. Here you can make a circular tour of a farming community that has retained the houses, barns, and traditions of the generations that preceded it.

Circle Tour

Continue through the intersection and cross a small bridge over the Coldwater River, which again is only a trickle and could never have carved the wide valley through which it wanders. Nestled beside the river is a small farming community with rolling fields, white homes, and red barns. Continue for 3 km to a T-intersection and turn left, then follow the road for about 1.5 km to a crossroads and turn right. Here the road winds past more rolling fields and farms. After 2 km turn right at a T-intersection, drive another half kilometre and follow a side road to the left. At the next crossroads, 1.5 km farther on, turn right again.

The road now climbs steeply from the valley of the Coldwater River, offering views on the right which span the breadth of the valley, views of farms and forests with the north valley wall looming up behind them. For 3 km the road traverses the plateau above the valley. The fences of cedar logs and the mighty boulders around the fields show that the wily pioneers used the materials they had to hand. These boulders were the bane of the early ploughmen; some of those that are now used as fences are as tall as the men who struggled to move them.

The road descends from the mesa into a little gully, and here you will find the tiny hamlet of Creighton. This hamlet once had a store, a post office, a blacksmith's shop, and a couple of mills, but today only two buildings remain—both of them made of brick and both standing at the crossroads. They have been altered little and are attractive survivors of agriculture's heyday in the closing years of the last century.

Turn right at the crossroads and follow the gulch as it opens into the wide Coldwater River Valley. The views once more are grand. Back on the valley floor, your route takes you straight ahead through the next intersection and across an area of flat bottomlands that are now luxuriant fields. Look on the right for the stone Carley School, with its bell tower still intact. Dating from the turn of the century, the school is still used as a community centre. At the next crossroads you will see the former Carley store and an old home. Continue straight on until, after 1 km, you come to a railway crossing and a handful of old houses. This used to be a busy village named Carley Station.

Travel on to the next intersection and turn left. After 2 km look for an unmarked dirt road and turn right. This road lurches into another of those little gulches that cross the valley floor. This one, however, had enough water power to spawn a little mill village named Coulson. It is still a pretty spot, and a few of the old village residences have been converted to modern homes. The road winds on through pasture lands, ending at Medonte Concession Road 6, where steep wooded slopes begin to loom on the left. These are the foothills of the great Sand Hills. Turn left and continue until you come to County Road 22.

(If you choose to bypass the circular tour, turn right from the Ingram Road onto the Medonte Concession Road 6. This takes you 5 km across the flat bottomlands of the Coldwater River Valley to the Sand Hills and to the junction with County Road 22.)

The Sand Hills

The Sand Hills were formed during the last ice age when the retreating ice sheets halted and the raging meltwaters hurtled sand, stones, and boulders into great mounds. On this rugged

An abandoned pasture in the Sand Hills.

ridge, early settlers purchased farm lots, sight-unseen. It was a decision most regretted, for the hills proved too steep and the sands too dry and bouldery for even the crudest farming. Most settlers left in disgust, and the Sand Hills today have reverted to forest.

Concession Road 6 ends at County Road 22. Turn right here and follow this paved road for 1 km to Oro Concession Road 5 and then turn left. This rugged, unmaintained dirt road (which should be avoided during winter and early spring) lurches without warning into the heart of the Sand Hills. Periodically, the forests open up to reveal abandoned fields and overgrown foundations— reminders of the heart-breaking attempts to wrest farms from this unyielding area.

After 3 km the road intersects with the Oro Eighth Line, or the Bass Lake Road. Turn left. This road is maintained by Oro township and is passable year round. It also marks the most rugged section of the trip. As it winds through a forest of pine and maple, it occasionally passes one-time pastures, long abandoned and overgrown. After 3 km follow Oro Concession Road 8 to the right for a few metres and then turn left to resume the Bass Lake Road. For the next 2.5 km the Sand Hills loom to the right, while below you on the left the fringe of productive farmland encroaches. Beyond lie the distant blue waters of Bass Lake. Although the lake is small and is becoming polluted, it remains popular with campers and cottagers.

At the next crossroads, that with Oro Concession Road 10, turn right. This road takes you directly across the Sand Hills at one of their highest points. Here, the road climbs a steep, wooded gully and passes a couple of farms that have struggled to survive on one of the few pockets of better soil. Although the ridge is 20 km long, it varies between only 1 km to 2 km in width. By the time you reach the next intersection, the Rugby Road, you will be on the south slope of the ridge. Stretching before you and on to Lake Simcoe, 5 km to the south, the terrain is flat and the farms productive.

Your trip ends 4 km from the Rugby Road, where Concession Road 10 links with Highway 11. This busy four-lane highway offers an endless line of gas stations and fast-food restaurants. If, however, you still have some time in hand, you can continue across Highway 11 and follow the concession road for another 2 km to County Road 20 and turn right. This road is called the Ridge Road, the ridge being an old shore bluff that parallels Lake Simcoe. A one-time pioneer trail lined with old farms and new country homes, it is an attractive way to enjoy the 15-km drive to Barrie, where Highway 400 waits to take you home.

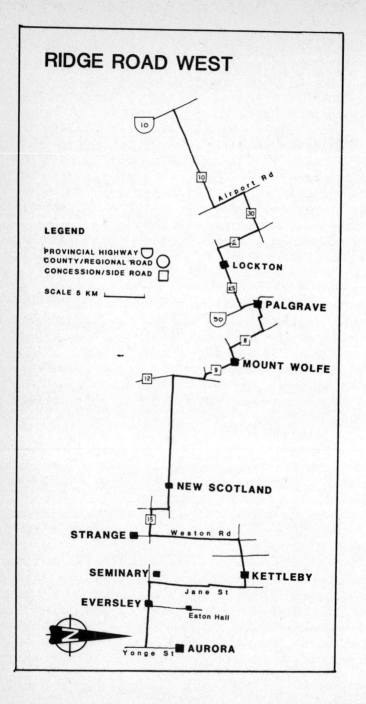

RIDGE ROAD WEST

7 Ridge Road West

Within the shadow of Toronto's skyscrapers there is a series of gravel roads that wind along a ridge of tossing fields, through hardwood forests, and past stone houses and churches that date back more than a century and a half. Here is a country landscape that has defied the sprawl of look-alike houses and fast-food drive-ins which mark Toronto's urban fringe.

The route starts at the intersection of Yonge Street and Bloomington Road, 2 km south of Aurora and about 30 km north of downtown Toronto. It zigzags westward along a series of concession roads and side roads for about 50 km and ends at Highway 10, just 19 km south of Orangeville.

Most of the land is private and the opportunities to hike or picnic are few. Snack bars, grocery stores, and gas stations are located along such main cross streets as Yonge Street, Airport Road, and Highway 10.

A Bit of History

Next to the Niagara Escarpment, central Ontario's most prominent landscape feature is the great Oak Ridge. About 50,000 years ago the waters from melting glaciers carried sand, gravel, boulders, and even great chunks of the glacier itself into a long fissure in the ice, leaving this ridge of rugged hills which stretches from Orangeville to Trenton.

Between the ridge and the lake lies a level clay plain that has provided some of the best farmland in Canada. Here, early settlers cleared their farms, gradually extending northward from Lake Ontario until they struck the great Oak Ridge. Its steep hills defied road building and only a few winding trails penetrated low saddles of the hills. Not until the 1830s did the pioneers penetrate the ridge. At first the tall pines gave rise to a prosperous sawmill industry. But because the high country cradled the headwaters of the rivers that flow into Lake Ontario, the streams were small and mill sites few. As a result, the villages were scattered and they served only the immediate needs of the pioneers. Moreover, farming was poor. Boulders and stones plagued the steep hillsides, and the sandy subsoils retained little water. Many of the farmers, weary and defeated, left.

During the 1930s, under a system of county forests managed by the Ontario government, the worst lands were replanted in pine. Later, during the 1960s and 1970s, much of the remaining land was sold out to developers or to wealthy commuters. Nevertheless, the area retains a landscape of spacious grasslands, dark forests, and spectacular views.

Aurora to Eversley

Follow Yonge Street north from Toronto, or take Bloomington Road west from Highway 404 to the intersection with Yonge Street. Continue west from Yonge Street. As you do so, you will leave the urban sprawl behind. At the corner of Bathurst Street, 2 km to the west, stands the Stone Haven Farm. A large fieldstone farmhouse, it hugs the roadside and dates back to the earliest days of settlement. Thoughtful owners have preserved it in its original condition.

Continue west for a further 2 km and you will come to Eversley and its old stone church. Begun in 1834 as a crossroads hamlet, Eversley takes its name from a village in Hampshire, England. On the northeast corner of the intersection is the one-time general store, now a private residence. The blacksmith's shop, which stood on the southeast corner, has long vanished. However, just 1 km south stands one of the most remarkable buildings on this route, the Eversley church.

Nearly a century and a half ago, area pioneers yearned for a place to worship. Assiduously, they gathered up the stones from their fields and laid them together to build the Eversley Presbyterian Church. The year was 1838. Services were held there until 1958, when the stone church was closed. Concern over whether this remarkable structure would long survive was relieved in 1960, when Lady Eaton purchased the building so that it could be preserved. It stands today, amidst its pioneer headstones, with a plaque in front to recount its story.

Eaton Hall, north of Eversley, is now King Campus of Seneca College.

Eversley to Kettleby

Near Eversley, two kettle lakes have given rise to two large estates, both of which are open to the public. The first is Eaton Hall. From the Eversley church, drive north 2 km, turn left into the grounds of Seneca College, King Campus, and follow the lane to the right which leads to Eaton Hall. Built in 1919 by Sir John Eaton of department-store fame, this estate was a popular summer retreat for the Eaton family. The last to use it was Lady Eaton, and upon her death in 1971 it became the property of Seneca College. The estate spreads over several hundred rolling hectares, covered by an attractive forest of pine and hardwood. In its midst is the turreted stone building of Eaton Hall, which overlooks the lake and is used by the college to host conventions.

The second estate in this area is the Marie Lake Augustinian Seminary. From Eaton Hall, return to Eversley and turn right onto Side Road 15. At the next crossroads, you will come to an arching stone gate, but it is a gate that never closes, for the grounds are freely open to the public. Drive through the gates and follow the lane as it winds through a tunnel of spruces. Where the woods give way to pasture (for the Augustinians raise Herefords) you will see a massive, red brick barn. Then the road forks, the right branch leading to the stone religious retreat houses, the left to the modern seminary and church. Here again the Eaton touch is felt, for the large organ in the church once rested in Eaton Hall. Beyond the buildings is the placid pond called Marie Lake. Remember that although the grounds are open, this is not a park. You may stroll and photograph, but you should not picnic.

Most of the side roads that lead west from the seminary have been blocked by Highway 400. The most attractive place to cross the highway is at the old village of Kettleby, which you can reach by driving 7 km north from the seminary gates. Unlike many of the other north-leading roads, this one is lightly travelled. Soon the road begins to rollercoast as it enters the steep hills that typify the ridge. Although there are a number of new country homes in this area, watch for large stone and frame farmhouses. Many of them date back to the 1840s and 1850s. Kettleby lies 1 km beyond the intersection with the 16th Side Road.

Kettleby has changed little since its early days, and many of its original buildings line the treed main street, though several have found new uses. The Methodist church, for instance, which was built in 1873, has become an antique store. However, the stone Anglican church (erected in 1891) still opens for worship each Sunday. The general store has added a pine gift shop and a small flea market to its more traditional functions. Look for two handsome early houses across the street from the store, Brunswick Hall and the Curtis House.

The road winds down the hill, through the village, and into the little valley that once hummed with grist mills and a distillery. It is now a grassy meadow. Then, as you begin to ascend the opposite valley wall, a curious sign points to the Herb Homestead, a store that specializes in spices and herbs of nearly every description. Ask to smell the curry plant.

Kettleby to Palgrave

Continue west, cross Highway 400, and then turn left onto Weston Road. This is a busy artery, but it leads you quickly to the next portion of the ridge backroad. When you have gone 7 km on Weston Road, watch for the 15th Side Road and turn right. Because the ridge has held the roads at bay, you will be doing a detour around its southern face, traversing a gentle land of prosperous farms. Then, at the 7th line, you will encounter a southerly thrust of the mountain, which causes the landscape to become one of rugged, grassy hills. Turn right, back towards the hill, where once more its steep slopes deflect the road sharply westward.

Just after the bend, you will pass a once-active pioneer community named New Scotland. Settled in the 1830s by Archibald Kelly and a colony of Scottish emigrés, this community contained a sawmill, a blacksmith's shop, an Orange Lodge, and a school. Today, these have been replaced by spacious country estates and the only relic of the early Scottish community is in the name of the small kettle lake at the foot of the peak, Kelly's Lake.

For the next 10 km the road lurches over scenic sand hills and through little gullies, until the side road halts abruptly at King Concession Road 12. Turn right here and travel 2 km to the next intersection, that with Side Road 17. Turn left and follow it for less than a kilometre to Concession Road 9 and turn right.

For 3 km your road grinds up a steep hillside and then enters the heart of the ridge, the Albion Hills. Here, the summit of Mount Wolfe overlooks a quiltwork of farms and country homes, and on the distant horizon the hazy towers of Toronto. Although

This rugged topography is typical of the Mount Wolfe region.

Snake-rail fences are part of the pioneer landscape to the west of Palgrave.

the slopes of the mountain are steep, the summit is level and is home to a community of farmers. On the northwest corner of the first intersection stands a well-preserved complex of traditional red barns. Turn left and drive 1.5 km across the plateau and down the side of the mountain to Concession Road 8, where you turn right and remount the hill. This is the west end of Mount Wolfe, and the views extend both south and west. It was on this peak that the Mount Wolfe post office and church once stood. However, all that remain are the headstones preserved in a common foundation.

Continue north and descend the mountain for the last time through a hardwood forest dotted with country estates. Turn left onto Side Road 2 and drive through rolling farmland to a T-intersection. Turn right and then, after 1 km, left onto a paved road which leads into Palgrave, the Albion Hills' only village.

Palgrave

Although they are surrounded by estate subdivisions, Palgrave's historic buildings survive. The village was originally known as Buckstown and was first gathered around Robert Campbell's grist mill. It remained small until the Hamilton and Northwest Railway was built through town. Then it boomed. In its heyday it contained several hotels and stores and a number of small industries. Today the industries are gone, though Campbell's millpond remains. On the main street, one old store sits abandoned; another now houses the *Advertiser Chronicle* newspaper. A number of old houses and churches still line the few narrow backstreets. Palgrave's most outstanding building is its former hotel; with its three peaks, white clapboard, and blue trim, its exterior has remained much as it was. If you wish to refill your gas tank or your picnic basket, Palgrave contains a gas station and a newer general store, Gladys'.

Palgrave to Highway 10

Today, Highway 50 follows Palgrave's main street, and you should follow this highway across the now-abandoned railway bed to Side Road 25, where you turn right. Once free of the jungle of estate subdivisions, the ridge becomes a range of smaller, wooded hills. Near the first crossroad, you cross the two branches of the Humber River; 3 km farther on, at the third intersection, sits the one-time village of Lockton, which now retains only a store and a log house. Continue west for 2 km to the next intersection. The road here winds around wooded hillsides and through dark gullies to the open farmland at the corner of Concession Road 2. Turn right, drive 3.5 km to Side Road 30 and turn left. Here the road resumes its winding way through a landscape of hills, forests, fields, and new country homes. After 3 km it stops once more, this time at the busy Airport Road.

Busy even in pioneer days, when it was known as the 6th Line, this is the same Airport Road that 40 km south carries six lanes of traffic past Pearson International Airport. Here it carries country commuters. Turn left and drive south 2 km to Side Road 10 and turn right. This is the last leg of the Ridge Road. It surges over the peaks of the rugged Caledon Hills. To the south, the views extend across pastures and woodlots, and culminate in the distant Toronto skyline. For 9 km you wind past fields—some overgrown, some replanted in pine, a few still grazed by slow-moving cattle. Finally, the great glacial ridge ends abruptly at the Niagara Escarpment. So high is the ridge that at this point it has buried even that great rocky cuesta.

It is here at Highway 10 that the Ridge Road drive, the only country drive left in the shadow of Toronto, ends. To the left lies Brampton and then, less than an hour away, the metropolis itself.

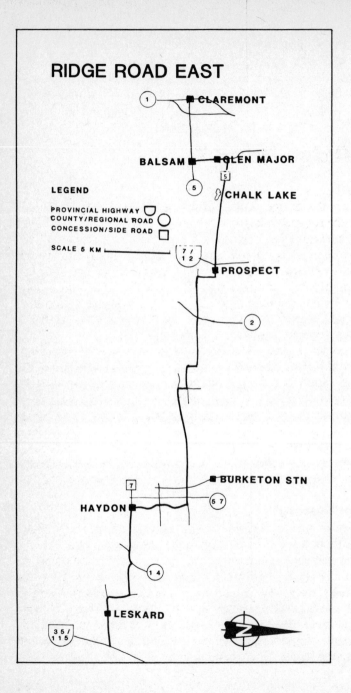

RIDGE ROAD EAST

8 Ridge Road East

Mirroring the Ridge Road West, this scenic route wanders through the rugged Oak Ridge hill country east of Toronto. To get to your starting point, drive east from Toronto on Highway 401, exit north onto Brock Road, and follow it 15 km to Claremont. The route follows a series of gravel concession roads and side roads easterly for about 50 km to Highway 35/115 at a point 3 km north of Kirby (the hamlet where Backroads Route 9, the Rice Lake Road, begins). While this route contains no restaurants, it does have a couple of snack bars and gas stations.

In contrast to the Ridge Road West, there are fewer estate homes on this trip and more of the simple settlers' farmsteads and churches. And while the views are less spectacular, the hills are more rugged, the gulches deeper and darker. So hostile is some of the terrain that early roads were abandoned or forced to detour entirely.

Again, this is a route for the recreational driver who wants a country getaway close at hand. The photogenic landscape, the old barns, cabins, and churches, and the historic hamlets are a bonus.

A Bit of History
The story of this area closely parallels that of the Ridge Road West. Although the lakeshore area was bustling with farms by 1810, the steep hills discouraged the movement of pioneers inland until after 1830. By then the government had constructed a few crude roads over low spots in the hills. But, again, being a headwater area, the region had few mill sites, and many of those that did attract mills dried up shortly after the forest was cleared. As a result, the landscape is one of abandoned farms, rough pastures, and small villages and hamlets that have long lost their

functions and have largely disappeared (though in recent years some have become dormitory communities for commuters to such cities as Oshawa and Whitby, and even Toronto).

Claremont

There are two Claremonts: Old Claremont, the original cross-roads village; and Claremont Siding, which came into existence after 1884 when the Ontario and Quebec Railway, now the CPR, pushed a branch line through the area.

As Brock Road approaches Claremont, it leaves its original route and bypasses the village. Continue past Durham Road 5 to the north end of the bypass and turn left to Claremont Siding. At the crossing sit two old feed mills. The one on the right is still in use, while the one on the left, a weathering, wooden structure, lies abandoned and is now used for storage. Across the track, forlorn yet solid, a brick carriage factory hugs the roadside. Along the side streets and the road to Old Claremont are the large frame homes of the early railway days. As part of the Canadian Pacific Railway's policy of eliminating all its redundant stations, the red railway station that was once the heart of the village has been demolished.

The village of Old Claremont lies 1 km from the crossing and

A side road near Balsam dips under this embellished railway bridge.

96

contains this route's most interesting building. Here, where the Brock Road intersected an important side road, an early settler named Noble built a general store. Known at first as Noble's Corners, the community had little more than a couple of stores and a hotel. But when the railway arrived to the north, the back streets of Old Claremont filled with houses, and more businesses moved to the village. Many still stand on these narrow roads and today mix with newer homes.

As Claremont gradually became a dormitory town to Oshawa, its residents paid less attention to their own stores. Now most are shuttered. Three of the four corners of the Old Claremont crossroads have been stripped of their original buildings, but the fourth boasts the most ambitious country general store in central Ontario. Built in the 1850s by John Mitchell, this large two-storey building with its elaborate brick façade greets today's visitors unchanged, and it is still a general store.

Claremont to Glen Major

Near the general store you can find a gas station, a craft shop, and a small restaurant. Drive east through Claremont to Durham Road 1. Here, several old village homes line the street. Two blocks along is the 1865 brick Baptist Church and near it two unusual board-and-batten cabins.

From the intersection of Durham Road 5 and Durham Road 1, continue east on Durham Road 5 and drive across the south face of the ridge for 6 km towards a historical crossroads hamlet called Balsam.

Halfway to Balsam two bridges cross the tumbling headwaters of Duffin Creek, which was once the power source for countless mills. The creek is now the focus for a string of conservation areas. Conceived originally as flood-control measures, these conservation areas fill a growing need for public recreation areas that neither the province nor the municipalities are prepared to fill. The 500-ha Claremont Conservation Area lies just 2 km south of Durham Road 5 on Sideline 10, and the 1,000-ha Greenwood Conservation Area is just 3 km beyond that. Both offer hiking trails, picnic tables, and playing fields, and both have gate fees.

To reach Balsam, stay on Durham Road 5. This village had its origins in 1869, when J. Palmer opened a crossroads general store to serve the needs of area settlers and to operate a post office.

Soon the intersection added a second store, a temperance hall, and a blacksmith's shop. But it failed to grow beyond that. Palmer's store closed after a few decades, though it still stands on the northeast corner of the crossroads. Graham's yellow brick store, which opened in the 1890s, is on the southeast corner, and it is still open for business. Here you can relax with a cone or replenish your supply of Warkworth cheese.

At Balsam, turn north onto the side road and follow it to one of the more scenic portions of this trip. For about 1 km you stay on the flatlands below the hills. But after you cross the railway tracks, the scenery changes dramatically. As you enter the valley of Duffin Creek, the wooded hills steepen and close in upon the road, forcing it onto the contours of the valley wall. About 3 km from Balsam, a string of simple homes cling to the steep slope, peering into the gulch. This is the picturesque valley village of Glen Major.

Glen Major

Although Duffin Creek at this point is little more than a brook, its source a mere 1 km upstream, it became the focus for a busy nineteenth-century mill town. Because of the steepness of the hills, this area was not settled until 1840, long after the plains below. Among the first to settle here were the Sharrards, who dammed the waters of Duffin Creek to power a sawmill and a grist mill. The bustling settlement became known as Sharrards Mills. By the 1870s, E. Major had acquired Sharrard's properties, and he ran no fewer than three sawmills and a grist mill. The name was then changed to Glen Major, and the community added a church and school. But when the forests vanished, so did the mills. The ponds, however, have survived and are now maintained by a private fishing club. Although they lie close to the road, you have no access to them. Beyond them is the village's feature attraction. Built in 1873, the white board-and-batten Methodist Church sits at the north end of the village, its simple pioneer architecture framed by a hillside of maples.

Glen Major to Burketon Station

North of Glen Major, the road winds out of the narrow, steepening gully onto a plateau. Watch for a rusting road sign that announces Side Road 5, and turn right. For 2 km the road winds through

A well-preserved farmhouse on the plateau above Glen Major.

pastures and fields long abandoned; then it plunges into the valley of Lynde Creek.

From the stop sign at Durham Road 23, continue straight on. Through the trees on the right, you will see the sparkling waters of Chalk Lake. Ringed by steep hills, Chalk Lake's waters fill a pothole that was left by a stray piece of melting glacier 50,000 years ago. For several years it has remained an enclave of large summer homes and country estates, shielded from prying eyes by the thick, hardwood forest that cloaks the hillside.

East of Chalk Lake, the road returns to the crest of the ridge. Continue for 7 km to the intersection of Highway 7/12. Over this section of road, the rugged knolls gradually diminish, and at the intersection they have levelled off to become prosperous farmland. Highway 7/12 was an early settlement road laid out by the government in 1825 and called the Centre Road. In 1852 a private company acquired the route and planked it from Whitby to Orillia. But in 1876 the company went bankrupt and the road was absorbed into the county system. The intersection was once the site of a little hamlet called Prospect, but all you will see of it today is the abandoned white church.

Drive east through Prospect on Side Road 5 and immediately turn right onto an unmarked gravel road. After 1 km the road

The waters of Chalk Lake sparkle through the trees.

plunges off the plain and into a gully. As you rise onto the next crest, you return to the heart of the ridge—and to a view that extends south to Lake Ontario. After 2 km, turn left at a T-intersection. Here the road follows the crest of the ridge, over its peaks, through its gullies, and past its simple farm homes. Of the latter, the most striking lies less than 1 km from the turn; it is the first one you see on the left. Built in that rare style known as board and batten, it yet retains its small window panels, its gable fretwork, and its graceful door. It is one of the photographic and architectural highlights of the trip.

A stop sign 2 km from the house marks busy Durham Road 2 (Simcoe Road North). Although a yellow sign announces that there is no exit on the 10th Concession, you can continue along it, for the road is in fact open to traffic, though it is very rough in patches. On the southeast corner, the Purple Woods Conservation Area is disappointingly no more than a roadside picnic park.

Continue driving east. Now you are on the north side of the ridge's crest and the views in that direction extend to the swampy bays of Lake Scugog. After nearly 2 km, at Wilson Road, the maintained road ends. For the next 5 km the road is safely passable only in the summer and fall, but it is not to be bypassed for it leads you into another of this route's more scenic segments.

After 2 km turn right at a T-intersection. Here, the hummocky hills are lined with neat rows of pine. Once cleared by hopeful pioneers, this rugged ridge proved too sandy and barren, and drove the farmers off to seek better lands. So infertile were these sands that they failed to regenerate even grassland and by the 1930s had become a dusty desert. Then, under the guidance of a provincial civil servant and leading conservationist, A. H. Richardson, and in conjunction with this (and other) counties, the province began to replant the blowing sands with pine. Today, this system provides not only recreation but a source of pulpwood.

Stay on the road as it bends left and then, at the next intersection, turn right to bypass another section of abandoned roads. Cross a set of railway tracks and continue to a T-intersection, where you turn left. Follow this road eastward for 8 km to the stop sign at the Scugog Road. Here, although the hills are lower, the terrain remains rugged, the soils sandy. Fewer than a half-dozen farms survive along this once-busy concession road.

Burketon Station to Haydon

About 1 km north of the intersection with the Scugog Road is a little railway village named Burketon Station, which is now a quiet residential community. Although a few freight trains rush through on the Canadian Pacific line, they no longer stop at Burketon. Like many early railway towns, its homes are modest and many retain their insulbrick covering, typical of railway homes of the last century.

Continue east from the Old Scugog Road for 1 km to the New Scugog Road, Durham Road 57. Proceed through the intersection for almost 2 km and watch for an unmarked dirt road leading to the right. For 3 km this quiet road winds through a gully that erosion has carved into the ridge. Beside the road a tiny creek bubbles beneath hillsides which are forested and steep, here and there widening into pasture. A century ago, when the ridge was coated in pine, this little valley buzzed with a string of sawmills. Even today a sawmill still operates, using timber from second- and third-generation forests. About 3 km from the turn is a stop sign. Continue straight on until the road emerges from the valley onto a plain of farmlands, ending at the village of Haydon.

Haydon to Leskard

Haydon was the only mill site on the upper creek to develop into a village, and it quickly acquired the usual stores, shops, and institutions. The old wooden church has now become an auction barn, and the school is a private home, but among the buildings that line the village's two streets you will yet find a few original frame cabins.

At the stop sign in Haydon turn left onto Concession Road 7. Here, on the south face of the ridge, you traverse an undulating land of pasture, valley, and quaint old farm homes. About 2 km from Haydon, as the road ascends from a gully, look on the left for a white-frame farmhouse. This building is unusual in that it yet retains the frame and fretwork of its early façade. Another stands on your left near the stop sign at Durham Road 14. The extended style of this red brick house sets it apart from the more common styles.

At the stop sign turn left onto Durham Road 14 and drive 1 km. Then, as Durham Road 14 bends left, take the fork that branches right. This keeps you on your easterly course across the ridge's southern slope. As you branch right, look on top of the

The road rollercoasts over the south face of the ridge near Leskard.

knoll to your left. There you will see a well-preserved sample of a country school, now a private home.

After 3 km the road bends sharply south. Off to your left, you will see an abandoned side road disappearing over a crest of land—part of the network of roads that used to lead to the now-vanished hill farms. Although this road is impassable by cars, it offers a pleasant walk; and from its first crest, you can view rolling farmlands that extend to Lake Ontario, 20 km away.

Continue south for 2 km to a stop sign and turn left. The next 2 km maintain the sweeping southerly view before leading you into a deep, wooded valley and to the old village of Leskard. Now a commuter town, and once a partial ghost town, Leskard began with promise. In 1842, Ichabod Richmond started it all with a sawmill and a grist mill. In 1854, James Bauks laid out a town plan and Leskard quickly became a bustling regional centre. But like many a ridge mill town, it quickly lost its industries and for years several of its buildings stood vacant. However, the recent rush on country real estate has turned it into a dormitory village for such cities as Oshawa and Whitby. The general store on the southeast corner of the junction, the red brick Methodist church (c. 1885), and the school are all now private houses.

Highway 35/115 lies 3.5 km east of Leskard, and here you may end your trip by turning right. Alternatively, you can add a final scenic loop. For another 6 km the road rollercoasts eastward over the ridgetop, past fields and picturesque, weathered barns. Then it bends south to stop at Durham Road 9. Highway 35/115 lies 4 km to the right. To return home, follow that highway south for 20 km to Highway 401.

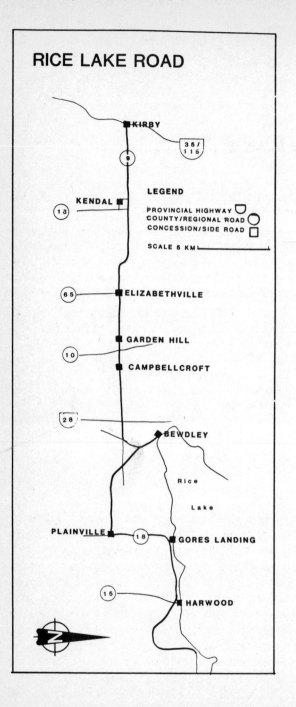

RICE LAKE ROAD

KIRBY

35/115

9

LEGEND

PROVINCIAL HIGHWAY
COUNTY/REGIONAL ROAD
CONCESSION/SIDE ROAD

SCALE 5 KM

KENDAL

13

65 **ELIZABETHVILLE**

GARDEN HILL

10

CAMPBELLCROFT

28

BEWDLEY

Rice

Lake

PLAINVILLE

18 **GORES LANDING**

15

HARWOOD

9 Rice Lake Road

Beginning in the tiny hamlet of Kirby, 75 km east of Toronto, this gentle rural route follows paved country roads through the counties of Durham and Northumberland, running eastward 50 km to Rice Lake. Along the way, there are ample picnic sites, general stores, gas stations, and even a few fast-food outlets. Items to bring: your camera, for there are some lovely views of lakes and old buildings; your sketch pad; and your love of Ontario's rural traditions.

Although this route is close to Toronto and runs through part of prosperous central Ontario, it lies inland from the lakeshore and has escaped the urban fingers that have stabbed out from the metropolis to turn the lakeshore into an urban sprawl. Here are gently rolling hills, where several rivers have carved quiet valleys as they rush south to the lake; and here are the wooded shores of Rice Lake.

To reach your starting point, follow Highway 401 to Highway 35/115 and then follow this shared highway 10 km north to Durham Road 9 and the crossroads hamlet of Kirby.

A Bit of History
Although settlers carved their farms on Lake Ontario's shore as early as the 1790s, four decades would pass before the frontier moved inland. By the 1830s, many of the interior lands had been opened and settlements had sprung up at key crossroads and at water-power sites on the numerous streams. As long as there were forests, the sawmills prospered. Then, as the woods disappeared, the wheat years took over. But American tariffs ruined the grain trade and by 1900 Ontario farmers had turned to dairy and beef farming. Today, this inland area remains one of family farms, quiet country villages, and rural traditions.

Kirby to Kendal

Kirby began during the 1850s after the opening of the Kendal Road, and it soon became a busy crossroads hamlet. Unfortunately, recent highway-widenings have left little of Kirby. Only a few interesting early buildings have survived. On the west side of the road is a 100-year-old brick Methodist church and beside it a house built in 1858. On the northeast corner are a few other old homes and a school that has been converted to a museum, which is open on weekends. Unusual in that it is so well preserved is a turn-of-the-century dairy barn with its wooden silo and its red preservative paint. Few barns have survived unaltered as this one has.

From the stoplights at Kirby drive east along Durham Road 9, which was once known as the Kendal Road. It developed as a municipal toll road and was opened around 1850. The first 6 km roll over gentle hills and past lush fields and a few new country homes. Then the road descends into the valley of the Ganaraska River and to the village of Kendal.

Although Kendal contains a number of newer homes, several early houses and shops still line its shady streets, preserving the appearance it must have had in its palmy days. Kendal was laid out not on the main road, but slightly to the south of it, for it was here that in 1848 Theron Dicky built his sawmill and later added a grist mill. Only twenty years later the village contained two sawmills, four shingle mills, two hotels, two churches, and four stores.

Enter the village on the first road to the right, soon after crossing the bridge over the Ganaraska. This is Church Street, and it contains the white-frame United Church, built in 1870, and the one-time Loyal Orange Lodge. At the intersection with Mill Street stands one of the old hotels, now weathered and unpainted, its original windows and doors still in place. The mills used to stand on the road to the right. Turn left and drive past attractive homes, their white-frame exteriors little changed, and a tiny general store with unusual, arching wrought-iron window frames. This store no longer operates, but if you need to buy anything, there is a new store at the east end of the village.

Kendal to Garden Hill

Kendal's main street ends at Durham Road 18. Turn left here and drive back to the Durham Road 9. Turn right. Along this stretch of the route you will see the evidence of another collapsed farm

The church and Orange Lodge still stand in the village of Kendal.

industry, tobacco. The kilns, sometimes up to six or eight in a neat row, stand abandoned, surrounded by fields of hay or oats.

After 5 km you will come to the hamlet of Elizabethville, which was first settled in the 1830s and became a small stopover village at the intersection of the Kendal Road with the Decker Hollow Road. Today, the Decker Hollow Road is closed and the village of Decker Hollow has vanished, as have many of Elizabethville's original buildings.

Drive east from Elizabethville and after 3 km watch for the sign to the Richardson Lookout. This lookout was named after the father of Ontario's conservation movement, Arthur H. Richardson. It was he who devised the notion that municipalities sharing river watersheds should pool their resources with the province to prevent flooding, to encourage improved farming techniques, and to replant forests on infertile soils. A beneficial byproduct has been the development of conservation areas, and small recreation parks have been established beside reservoirs and at flood-control dams and old mill dams. In parks where an old mill still stands, the conservation areas have sometimes mushroomed into "pioneer villages," with nearby buildings of historical interest being moved to the park to create a living museum.

107

The general store at Garden Hill used to be the centre of a far larger and busier village.

From the Richardson Lookout, look north. There, the irregular peaks of the great Oak Ridge indent the horizon. This 150-km mound of sand and gravel was laid down during the last ice age, 50,000 years ago, by the swirling meltwaters from two huge glaciers. The Ganaraska River pours off the ridge into the plain below you, where it has carved its gentle valleys. Here lies a landscape of green fields, red barns, and white houses.

Return to the road and continue east. For 3 km your road descends the hill into the valley of the Ganaraska River. Beside the bridge over the river is a millpond and the village of Garden Hill, which was one of the busiest villages on the Kendal Road. It began in the 1830s when one Kirkpatrick arrived and built a mill on the river. By 1880 Garden Hill had five sawmills, two grist mills, and the largest woollen mill on the river. Its population stood at 450.

Although the mills are now gone, there remain a few interesting vestiges of Garden Hill's former days. The general store dates back to the turn of the century and unlike most of its contemporaries still retains its wooden porch. Then there is the old brick church and several white-frame houses. Take a short spin around the single residential block. Little wider than a laneway and lined with trees and simple homes, the street appears much as it did during the town's heyday. Beside the pond, the conservation authority has developed one of its picnic and swimming parks.

Garden Hill to Bewdley

Continue east from Garden Hill. This swampy lowland is the flood plain of the Ganaraska Valley, where several little tributaries seem to meander without purpose. If you had been travelling this road a century ago, you would have been stopped 1 km east of Garden Hill and asked for a toll. The tollgate was at the intersection with one of the earliest roads to penetrate the interior from the lake, the Port Hope–Millbrook Road. Here, too, was an early mill settlement called Waterford; but, like the tollgate, Waterford has disappeared.

After 2 km, look on the right for a rambling and weathered building—originally a general store and post office. This was the centre of Campbellcroft, a village that began with Thomas Campbell's mill but did not take off until the late 1850s, when the first steam engine of the newly opened Midland Railway puffed across the road. By the 1870s, Campbellcroft had been renamed Garden Hill Station and was an important shipping centre. Lumber and grain were loaded onto freight cars for the 15-km journey down to Port Hope and thence for export to the United States or England. Apart from the old store, few buildings remain from these busy times, and the village has reverted to its original name.

The next 5 km continue through the lowland, past a string of farms and country homes. From a stop sign on Highway 28, continue straight on, travel another 1 km and turn left at the next intersection. This is the old Highway 28, which was originally known as the Port Hope–Peterborough Road. One of its stopover towns was Bewdley.

Bewdley

Bewdley sits at the west end of Rice Lake—one of Ontario's most beautiful lakes. Pastures and woodlands that are gentle and green roll down to the shore, and islands dot the placid waters. As the name implies, waving fields of wild rice once surrounded the lake's low shores. They sustained not only the Native population but the pioneers as well. But at the turn of the century, the builders of the Trent Canal dammed the lake and drowned the rice fields.

Long and narrow, Rice Lake stretches 30 km west to east yet is only 5 km across. It is fed by the Otonabee River from the north and drains east into the Trent River. Being near to Ontario's urban heartland, it has become a popular destination for cottagers and boaters—but not for campers and picnickers, for Ontario's park planners have fallen behind and have provided few sizable parks on this especially suitable lake.

Like the lake itself, Bewdley is a resort area, and there are few indications that it was once a busy port of call for the Rice Lake steamers. Today, the wharves have been replaced by an attractive lakeside park, while the pioneer Halfway House has become the Sportsman's Centre Hotel and Restaurant.

Bewdley to Gores Landing

Leave Bewdley south on the road on which you entered it, and 1.5 km after you pass the marina and swing inland, look for a road forking to the left. Here you encounter another of those early pioneer roads, the Bewdley–Plainville Road. Follow it for 2 km to the intersection with County Road 9. Cross County Road 9 and stay on the old pioneer road.

As in its early days, the road bends and twists around the hills and valleys. Now paved and widened, it passes handsome family farms with their farmhouses of brick or clapboard. Here the landscape changes as you enter the land of the "whalebacks." These hills, so named for their resemblance to the smooth, elongated back of a whale, were moulded when the great glaciers readvanced over their earlier deposits of sand and gravel. Geologists call them "drumlins."

About 5 km from County Road 9 you will encounter the Plainville United Church, which was built in 1903 as a Methodist church. Its tall steeple soars above its red brick frame in the midst of gentle farmland. About 1 km beyond it are the few houses and the feed mill of Plainville itself.

At the T-intersection in Plainville, turn left onto County Road 18 and drive 4 km back to the shores of Rice Lake. Here, with its century-old summer estate homes, is Gores Landing. This village began in the 1820s as a landing at the end of the Cobourg–Rice Lake Road. Stagecoaches from Cobourg and Port Hope turned passengers over to steamers like the *Forester*, which puffed across the lake and up the Otonabee River to the fledgling mill town of

Peterborough. Among its early travellers were Peter Robinson's Irish colonists fleeing the killer potato famines at home to seek the promise of Canada's wilds.

With the building of a railway to nearby Harwood, Gores Landing lost its importance and settled down into a resort community of summer homes—a role that was enforced during the 1950s when the great Toronto cottage boom gobbled up the Rice Lake shoreline.

As you enter the village, follow the left fork (the high road). From this road you can see the length of the lake. Dotted across its waters are small forested islands—the crests of partly submerged whalebacks. By the water, where the high road meets the low road, are the large summer mansions of an earlier wealthy class. Built of clapboard and painted white, many are two-storey or three-storey houses overlooking wide green lawns. From a small park where the two roads meet, a short side street leads left. Along this remnant of an abandoned shore road is St. George's Church, a small stone building that is one of the most photographed churches in the Rice Lake area.

Gores Landing to Harwood

Continue along the shore road, County Road 18. For the next 4 km, between Gores Landing and Harwood, the road hugs the scenic shore but never allows you access. Crammed into even the narrowest beaches are shacks, cottages, and mobile homes.

Harwood began as a railway town but did not remain one for long. In 1852, to rival the Midland Railway from Port Hope, a group of Cobourg merchants formed the Peterborough Railway Company. Across the shallow lake, they built a 5-km trestle, much of it only a few metres above the water, and on 29 December the first train rumbled across it. But after only six years, the spring ice movements on the lake had so weakened the trestle that it was no longer safe and had to be abandoned. Shortly afterwards it collapsed. Harwood's life as a railway town collapsed with it.

Like Gores Landing, Harwood is now a resort community, but a few vestiges have survived from the days of the Peterborough Railway Company: its main street, named Railway Street; an empty insulbrick store; and the dense street network atop the hill overlooking the lake. Then there are the remains of the causeway itself. A broken finger of fill extends several hundred metres into

Red brick church to the east of Harwood.

From the Alnwick Conservation Area, the views extend the length of Rice Lake.

the lake. Again, because of the sad lack of public access, although you can see the causeway, you cannot explore it.

Return along Railway Street, the alignment of the old railway, to County Road 18. At this corner is the A and B Country Store, which also dates from the railway days. It sells handicrafts and sandwiches, and even has a hitch where the local horsey set can tie their horses.

Continue east on County Road 18 and drive 5 km to the Alnwick Conservation Area. Here you can finish your trip with a picnic and a hilltop view of Rice Lake. Atop a small hill, the Conservation Authority has constructed a lookout tower. From it you can look west down the lake and view its islands, its wooded shore, and the Harwood railway causeway. Again, however, the authority has failed to acquire any shore land, and while you may look at the lake, you may not touch.

There are two ways to return home. If you are bound for Ottawa or points east, stay on County Road 18 east until you reach Highway 45. Turn left to Highway 7 and Ottawa. If you are returning to the Toronto area, turn right onto Highway 45, which takes you to Highway 401 in the vicinity of Cobourg.

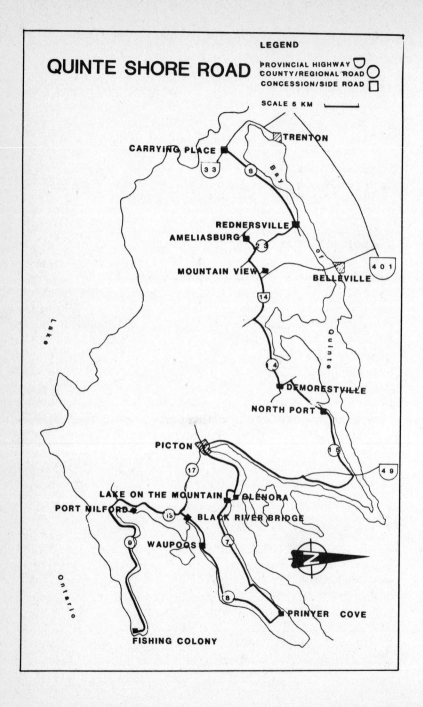

QUINTE SHORE ROAD

LEGEND
PROVINCIAL HIGHWAY
COUNTY/REGIONAL ROAD
CONCESSION/SIDE ROAD

SCALE 5 KM

TRENTON

CARRYING PLACE

33   8

Bay

REDNERSVILLE

AMELIASBURG

23

MOUNTAIN VIEW

BELLEVILLE

401

14

of

Quinte

4

DEMORESTVILLE

NORTH PORT

16

PICTON

49

17

LAKE ON THE MOUNTAIN   GLENORA

PORT MILFORD

13   BLACK RIVER BRIDGE

9   WAUPOOS   7

Lake

Ontario

8

PRINYER COVE

FISHING COLONY

10 Quinte Shore Road

The cliffs of Prince Edward soar above the Bay of Quinte, rising in places to heights of 100 m above its swirling waters. This route guides you on a shoreline drive along the crest of these cliffs. It starts 150 km east of Toronto, at the northwest corner of Prince Edward County, and follows 120 km of paved county roads to Point Traverse, the county's southeastern corner. Most villages on the route contain gas stations and general stores, and some have a snack bar. Midway, Picton offers opportunities for shopping and licensed dining. If you prefer a picnic lunch, there are frequent roadside and waterside parks, at some of which you can swim or fish.

Prince Edward is both a county and an island, for it is separated from the Ontario mainland by a narrow Z-shaped body of water called the Bay of Quinte. Its long limestone peninsulas jab amoebalike into Lake Ontario. A tilted limestone plateau, the island's north and east shores form grey rugged cliffs, while its west and south shores slope gently under the lapping waters of the lake.

The Quinte Shore Road offers something for almost everyone. If you are a photographer or artist, you will stop for the red cupola-roofed barns, reminiscent of New England, or the stone farmhouses; if a sailor, you will linger at a fishing cove or at one of the lighthouses that are among the oldest on the Great Lakes. If your penchant is nineteenth-century architecture, you can stroll past the century-old mansions and workers' homes of Picton. And if, like most, you are a pleasure driver, you will find on this route all the fields, orchards, and clifftop vistas that you could want.

A Bit of History

If you trace your roots to United Empire Loyalist stock, you may find them here, for Prince Edward is one of Ontario's oldest white settlements. In 1783, when American persecution of British supporters peaked, John Weese fled the hostility of New York State to the peaceful shores of Prince Edward County. Others followed him, and within a decade Prince Edward's shores and coves were well populated. During the peace that followed the War of 1812, the county farmers began to ship barley to American breweries across the lake. Barley ports popped up in every cove that could shelter a schooner. Later, as steamers replaced the schooners, and as the barley trade died, the little ports dwindled. Farmers turned to cheese making, and soon the county could claim 28 cheese factories. But this too declined, and now only one factory remains. However, the flat fields and moderate climate have ensured Prince Edward of agricultural prosperity, and today it leads Ontario in vegetable growing and canning.

Carrying Place

The trip begins at Carrying Place, in a small, treed park beside the Murray Canal. To reach it, exit from Highway 401 south onto Wooler Road about 150 km east of Toronto. At Highway 33, 3 km south, turn right and drive another 1 km to the park, which is on the left side of the road. Here you can watch sleek schooners or antennae-laden cruisers edging their way under the lift bridge. Here too you will realize that Prince Edward was not always an island. Until 1889, a swampy neck of land connected Prince Edward with the mainland. This is why the location was called Carrying Place, for it was a popular portage of the Indians. Then, in 1889, when Great Lakes shipping was at a peak, Thomas Murray eliminated the long, perilous outer voyage by chopping a canal through the portage.

Carrying Place is also the site of a long-lost fort. In 1668, responding to the pleas of local Cayuga Indians, the Sulpician priests Claude Trouvé and François de Fénelon built a mission fort. It prospered only briefly, and by 1680 the dispersal of the Indians and soaring costs forced the mission to close. Its exact location remains a mystery to this day.

Carrying Place to Rednersville

Drive south from the park, over the bridge, until after 1 km you come to County Road 3. Turn left and drive 10 km to Rednersville. This is now popular estate country for Belleville and Trenton commuters, and modern homes mingle with the nineteenth-century farmsteads and large apple orchards. Although manicured estate lawns generally separate the road from the shore, you can view beyond them the waters of Quinte and the spires of Trenton and Belleville on the far mainland shore.

Clustered about the intersection with County Road 23 are the homes and shops of Rednersville. The village was founded by the Loyalist Henry Redner, and it prospered as a barley port during the mid-1850s. There are two interesting buildings that predate the barley era. One, Henry Redner's home, is a solid stone house set back from the road on the south side, just west of County Road 23. The other is his store at the southeast corner of the intersection. This store has been in operation since 1803; it is Ontario's oldest general store and one of the oldest in the country. The brick façade was added following a fire in 1860.

The store at Rednersville is the oldest country store in Ontario.

Rednersville to Ameliasburg

Turn right at the store and follow County Road 23 for 4 km to County Road 19; turn right and continue another 1 km into Ameliasburg, where a string of white-frame buildings line the road. This was once a busy farm village, but its shops are now silent. The tall, stone United Church has been converted into a museum and houses pioneer farm and household utensils, as well as a large collection of old area maps and photographs. On the grounds, the curators have reconstructed a log cabin and also a blacksmith's shop, where you can watch blacksmithing as it was done a hundred years ago. The museum is open daily during the summer and on weekends through the spring and fall.

West of the museum on the south side of the road, you will find an unusual eight-sided house. This style flourished briefly during the mid-nineteenth century, but fewer than a dozen samples survive in Ontario, four of them in Prince Edward County.

Ameliasburg to Demorestville

Leave the village east on County Road 19, then left on County Road 2 and travel 3 km towards Mountain View. Here, although the road begins to follow the brink of one of the county's limestone escarpments, the view from it is often blocked by a forest of maples and cedars. Tucked under the cliff is the village of Mountain View. To take a short side trip to its twin-spired church and abandoned cannery, follow the directional arrow to the left.

At Mountain View turn right onto Highway 14 and drive 3 km to County Road 14 and turn left. Once again the road edges up to the brink of the cliff, but here the view is not impeded. On the left side are a couple of undeveloped lookouts, where you can park and gaze down at the waters of Muscote Bay, 50 m below. A swampy indentation on Prince Edward's north coast, this bay separates the northwestern peninsula from the northeastern.

After following the rim for about 3 km the road inches inland and 2 km farther along enters the village of Demorestville.

Demorestville

In Demorestville a handful of homes, old and new, mingle on a small grid of streets. This hamlet is a mere ghost of what it was a century and a half ago when it was the county's grandest village. It began in 1800 when William Demorest dammed the waters of Fish Creek and built a mill. By 1824 the busy new town contained four taverns, six stores, and had nearly 2,000 residents. However, the growth of the barley trade and the coming of the railway turned this inland town into a backwater, and it soon declined. Although many of the empty lots now sprout new homes, you can still spot the old streets—weedy dirt tracks that vanish into the fields.

At Demorest's old dam, the Prince Edward Conservation Authority has established a small park. Here you can picnic and follow a short nature trail, but the weedy pond is unsuitable for swimming.

Demorestville to Picton

From Demorestville, follow County Road 15 north as it plunges down the cliff and bends east to follow the low Quinte shore. After 10 km the Highway 49 bridge looms into view. Stay left on County Road 15 and drive under the bridge. Here, at Prince Edward's northeastern shoulder, the road bends south and for 3.5 km follows a 100-metre cliff top to Highway 49. Turn left here and follow the provincial highway south towards Picton.

After 7 km on Highway 49, just after crossing a railway track, watch for a historical marker to the White Chapel. This two-storey clapboard church was built by William Moore in 1809 and has been fully preserved. It holds an annual service each June and is Ontario's oldest Methodist meeting house that is still in use.

About 2 km past the White Chapel, Highway 49 joins Highway 33, which is Main Street West in downtown Picton. The town has provided parking spaces behind the stores on Main Street West, so you can park here and enjoy Picton's attractions on foot. The intersection of Highways 33 and 49 marks the head of Picton Harbour, though there is no public access to this historic bay.

A Walking Tour of Picton

This short tour of Picton's historic core encompasses twelve city blocks. With a stop in a museum and hidden fish market, it will take about an hour.

From the intersection with Highway 33, walk north on Highway 49 (Main Street East). These two tree-lined blocks contain Picton's most prized mansions and some of the finest in the

The White Chapel in Picton is Ontario's oldest Methodist meeting house that is still in use.

province. On the west side, between Paul and Johnson streets, stands the slender Italianate form of the McMullen mansion (1850) and the Georgian mass of the Striker mansion (1868).

Return to the intersection and walk south on Union Street four blocks to the corner of Church Street, where the tall spire of a stone church stabs the sky. Built by the Rev. William MacCauley in 1823, this church now houses the county museum. On the first floor is a display of nineteenth-century furniture and telephone equipment, and on the second floor is a rare collection of nineteenth-century children's books.

As you return north on Union and Bridge streets, walk left on Mary Street just before the main intersection. It parallels Main Street and contains vintage workers' homes. Despite the narrow lots, no two houses are alike. Farther west are some attractive terrace houses which have been designated by the town as heritage features. After three blocks turn right onto a short street named Bowery. On the west side is a plain white building with no exterior identification. This is the Jarvis fish market, and here you will find a choice of trout, perch, and salmon, all caught fresh each day by Prince Edward's fishermen.

Bowery Street leads quickly back to Main Street West and the heart of downtown Picton. Shops and restaurants line these three blocks. Businessmen have cleaned away unsightly overhead signs and wires, and have decorated the sidewalks with plants and benches. In the central block, on the north side, a three-storey stone building rises above a Rexall Drug Store. This was originally the Striker Pharmacy, and it has been in operation since 1829; it is Ontario's oldest drug store.

Should you wish to eat before you leave Picton, you will find the fast-food "strip" on Main Street West, west of Bowery. Or, if you prefer to dine in a historical atmosphere, you can go to the Waring House (built in 1833) 1 km west on Main Street; or to the Castle Villeneuve, which lies 0.5 km east on Highway 33.

Picton to Lake on the Mountain

Leave Picton on Provincial Highway 33 east, and after driving 3 km look north across the bay. There you will see the sprawling bulk of the Canada Cement Company, with its limestone crushers, its quarries and conveyors.

After driving 7 km from Picton, turn right onto County Road 7 and follow the signs to Lake on the Mountain Provincial Park. Designed for picnickers and viewers, this park includes the county's highest lookout point and one of the province's most mysterious lakes. The lake sits on a lip of cliff 100 m above Lake Ontario, and for many years it puzzled geologists. Only recently did divers at last determine its depth at over 50 m and its source as underwater springs. The lake's origins remain a mystery, though its surface level fluctuates with that of Lake Erie over 200 km to the west.

Beside the park are the remains of a village. In 1796, Loyalist Peter Van Alstine built a mill on the cliff and spawned a village named Mountain Mills. In 1813 he built a second mill below the cliff and created the village of Glenora. Van Alstine's store, long closed, still stands adjacent to the picnic grounds. A newer store across the street is also now closed.

Van Alstine's first mill was demolished in the last century, but his second mill, a three-storey stone building, still stands. To see it, return to Highway 33 and turn right to Glenora (which today is the terminal for the free government ferry to the mainland). The large stone building beside the dock is a Ministry of Natural

The Waupoos tomato cannery—one of the many in Prince Edward County.

Resources fish hatchery, and it provides tours during working hours. Beyond it is Van Alstine's mill, now a private residence. West of the mill sits a white-frame house. It is the one-time Glenora Hotel, where a young lawyer named John A. Macdonald passed many evenings.

Lake on the Mountain to Waupoos

Follow County Road 7 east from Lake on the Mountain along the north coast of Cressy Point. For the first 3 km the road opens onto unimpeded views across Adolphus Reach to the Lennox and Addington shore. There the yellow bulk of Ontario Hydro's Lennox and Addington thermal generating plant, with its twin chimneys, soars far above a coastline that is otherwise pastoral and green.

Over the next 3 km the cliffs subside, reaching water level at Prinyer Cove. In 1784 this cove witnessed the landing of one of Ontario's first parties of Loyalist refugees, led by Colonel Archibald MacDonald. A busy shipping and fishing centre during the barley days, the cove is now a retirement and cottage community. A few fishermen still sail from Prinyer Cove; their modern silvery tugs have replaced the wooden skiffs of the last century.

Prinyer Cove signals the end of the Bay of Quinte. Here, its waters swirl into the vastness of Lake Ontario. The long, thin, fingerlike peninsula, which is called Cressy Point, is the county's most easterly point of land.

County Road 7 cuts sharply south near the head of the peninsula to the south shore and to County Road 8. Turn right here and follow the low shore. For 3 km waves lap on your left, while on your right are the farms and orchards that were started by the Loyalists. After 5.5 km, look on the right for a red board-and-batten house. This, the Marysburg Museum, contains rooms decorated and furnished in the style of 150 years ago, when the house was built.

Continue west and descend the mesa, past more orchards and white wooden farmhouses. Then, 3 km from the museum, look for a sign to the Waupoos Cannery, and follow the short side road left to the shore. Like most coves, Waupoos grew into a fishing and barley port. Today it is home to cottages and also to one of the county's canneries. During the tomato season, dump trucks plunge their shining red loads into a large bin, from which the tomatoes bounce along a conveyor, splash into a swirling wash tank, and then disappear into the factory.

Waupoos to South Bay

Continue west from the cannery 2.5 km and turn left onto County Road 13. For 3 km the route teases the lip of the cliff and offers views over the waters of South Bay. It then descends, through a dark forest of maples and oaks, into the Black River Valley. The village of Black River Bridge was another of the island's once-busy ports. It has the last of Prince Edward's 28 cheese factories. Located at the east end of the bridge, the factory is open most weekends and offers a wide range of cheeses.

Stay on County Road 13 for 3.5 km. If the squat stone lighthouse on the left side seems far from the water, it is. The second oldest Canadian lighthouse on the Great Lakes, it guided ships around the distant Duck Islands from 1838 to 1965. It was then moved, stone by stone, to this the South Bay Mariners'

Museum. A modest frame building beside the lighthouse houses relics of the Great Lakes. Anchors, bells, oars, and lamps date from the days of sail and steam, some salvaged from wrecks that occurred in the shoaly waters off Prince Edward's coast. Take time to leaf through the scrapbooks containing photos of the many vessels that sailed over (and some that sank into) the turbulent waters of the lakes.

South Bay to Point Traverse

This is the last segment of the Quinte Shore Road and it follows the shore of Long Point to the county's southeast tip. From the museum, County Road 13 continues south as County Road 9. It then bends around the head of South Bay to follow the Long Point shore easterly, passing through a scattered string village, also called South Bay. After 4 km follow the signs to the Little Bluff Conservation Area. The view from this clifftop picnic ground extends from the tip of Long Point in the east to the far shore of South Bay. Be careful, for there are no safety fences, and 20 m straight down the waters crash against the limestone cliff.

Leave the park and continue east. For 10 km the road hugs the shore, although the cliffs subside to just a few metres. Then, at the entrance to the Long Point Migratory Bird Sanctuary, the pavement ends. The tip of Long Point was acquired in 1979 by the

The little harbour at Point Traverse is the home of Lake Ontario's last colony of fishermen.

Canadian Wildlife Service. Although hunting is of course forbidden, the sanctuary is open to the public and attracts large crowds when duck and geese migrations are at their height during spring and fall.

Stay on the gravel road as it follows the windswept headland of Point Traverse. Below the 10-m cliffs, a beach of boulders washed smooth by the clear lake waters offers swimming that is secluded but cool. The road ends at Prince Edward Point, where the still waters of a tiny unexpected bay reflect the round, white forms of a dozen fishing boats. Around the shore are the weathered ice houses, the spidery net racks, and—brightly painted in oranges, whites, and blues—the small cabins of Lake Ontario's last colony of fishermen. From a public wharf on the north side of the inlet, you can watch sleek American yachts glide in from the open lake; or you can fish. Although the rest of the shoreline is private, you may follow the narrow dirt track around the head of the bay to the ancient wooden lighthouse and stroll over the boulders on the beach. Here, in a setting that is silent and idyllic, your trip along the Quinte Shore Road ends.

To return home, retrace your steps to Black River Bridge. Turn left and follow County Road 17 north to Picton, where three provincial highways (49, 14, and 33) all lead to Highway 401.

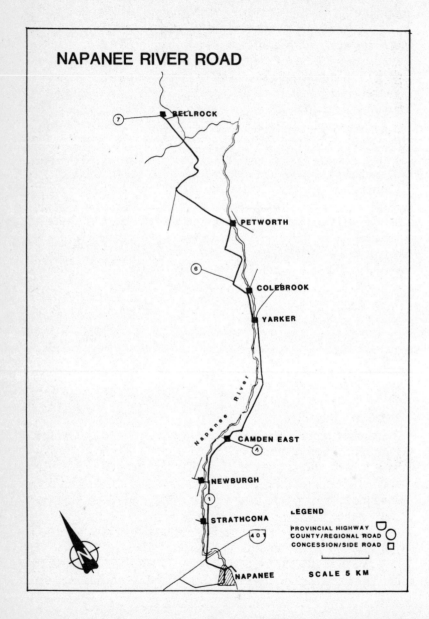

NAPANEE RIVER ROAD

BELLROCK

⑦

PETWORTH

⑥

COLEBROOK

YARKER

Napanee River

CAMDEN EAST

Ⓐ

NEWBURGH

①

STRATHCONA

④0①

NAPANEE

LEGEND

PROVINCIAL HIGHWAY
COUNTY/REGIONAL ROAD
CONCESSION/SIDE ROAD

SCALE 5 KM

N

11 Napanee River Road

Much of Ontario's early settlement was determined by its rivers. This route probes the fertile valley of the Napanee River, which, with its string of unusual old mill villages, marks one of the thrusts of pioneering into what was then a dark and mysterious back country.

The trip begins at the town of Napanee on Lake Ontario, 200 km east of Toronto, and follows the river valley 45 km northeastward. To arrive at your starting point, exit off Highway 401 at interchange 96 and follow Highway 41 south into Napanee. While most of the villages you will visit contain gas stations and general stores, only Napanee has a selection of restaurants. So either snack beforehand or pack a lunch to enjoy in one of the several riverside parks.

This route contains much for you to see and do. For the photographer, stone houses, country stores, and old mills provide ample subject material, while the angler can pause to cast for bass or perch in the rushing river or in one of the tranquil millponds.

A Bit of History

The gentle slopes of Lake Ontario's backshore are cut by many rivers. In a day when roads were seldom negotiable, if they existed at all, the rivers were the highways, giving early settlers their first opportunities to move inland from the communities along the lakeshore. The rivers also provided much-needed power sites for the vital sawmills and grist mills.

Yet settlement along the Napanee progressed slowly. In fact, five decades passed before the pioneers finally overcame the obstacles of rapids and windfalls, and completed the settlement of the valley. While the many rapids and falls provided power sites

127

for the early sawmills, not until the river road opened did the first settlers trudge up the fertile valley. Soon, busy farms lined the concessions, and the mill sites boomed into farm-service towns.

Gradually the era of the mill passed and the towns declined. Today, although most of the old mills are gone, the early townscapes and farmscapes have survived with little alteration.

Napanee

The outskirts of Napanee now sprawl outward to meet Highway 401. But 200 years ago there were no highways and Napanee was little more than a sawmill settlement. Robert Clarke was Napanee's founder. At the falls on the river, he built a sawmill, a store, and a handful of houses. Mill manager James Clarke gave the settlement its first name, Clarkeville. In 1787 he added what was the first grist mill between Toronto and Kingston. But Clarkeville remained small until 1812 when Allan MacPherson took over the mills and built a large store and later a school. By then the surrounding area was bustling with pioneer farms, and the village began to grow. Then, in 1831, Sam Benson surveyed a townsite, and Napanee began to take the form it has today.

Drive to the stoplights at Highway 2 in the heart of Napanee and turn left. This, Dundas Street, is Napanee's business district, with its century-old commercial buildings. In downtown Napanee the sidewalks have been widened and trees planted. Its nineteenth-century commercial buildings have been spared from fires and from the needless demolition and insensitive alterations that have decimated so many Ontario towns of Napanee's size. One block north of the main street is the market square, with its pillared town hall. Built in 1856, the town hall has recently been restored and painted; it is one of the oldest in eastern Ontario.

Across the street, and half a block north, looms a massive red sandstone building, the Napanee post office, which was built in 1888. If you drive north on John Street and then right on Thomas Street, you will come to a large limestone building. This is the Lennox and Addington county courthouse, which was built in 1864 when Napanee was proclaimed the county seat. Its domed cupola and arched pillars dominate what is otherwise a shady residential street. Behind the courthouse, and predating it by several years, is the old jail, now a museum, where you can still see the cells.

Napanee's market square is dominated by the town hall.

By following Dundas Street eastward from the downtown area and passing under the railway bridge, you will come to Clarke's old mill site, set in an appealing little riverside park. Here, at the falls on the river where Napanee began, you can enjoy a picnic before setting out on your backroads drive.

From the park, retrace your steps along Highway 2 to the bridge. Watch for Camden Road and turn right. Turn right again onto Elizabeth Street and park by the historical plaque in front of a large white house. This is the mansion once owned by Napanee's co-founder, Allan MacPherson, and built around 1825. Having stayed in the MacPherson family until 1896, the house has recently been refurbished by the Napanee Historical Society and it provides you with a glimpse into upper-class life in early nineteenth-century Ontario.

Napanee to Newburgh

Leave Napanee north on Camden Road, which swings right 2 km from the MacPherson house and becomes County Road 1. After crossing Highway 401 and the Napanee River, it follows the pioneer road up the Napanee River Valley, leading through gentle farmscapes to a string of historic mill villages. The first of these is Strathcona, 6 km from Napanee.

Strathcona owes its existence to John Thompson, who—in Windsor in 1864—perfected the modern pulp-making process. Moving to the Napanee Valley in the 1870s, he established paper mills near Camden and Newburgh, and also at Strathcona, which was at the time a tiny sawmill village that had been known for most of its life as Napanee Mills. Not only is the mill at Strathcona one of the only two among the valley's mill towns to survive, but it is the only one that grew. Today, its 250 employees produce daily 130 tonnes of heavy paper for boxes.

Strathcona's buildings line a pair of parallel streets that strike westward from County Road 1 and continue up the opposite side of the river. Turn left, and as you cross the bridge you will see the sprawling bulk of the Strathcona mill on your right, the original section now so engulfed by additions that it is barely distinguishable. After crossing the bridge, fork right onto an old village street. In addition to the workers' houses, there are two outstanding stone structures—the old Methodist church, built in 1875, and the handsome two-storey public library. They face each other across the road about half a kilometre from the bridge. At the north end of the village street, turn left onto the bypass; return to County Road 1 and turn left.

The Newburgh Academy, which was one of Ontario's leading teaching colleges, has been preserved by a group of local citizens and former students.

As you continue up the valley, you will pass stone farmhouses with their wide pastures that drop gently towards the valley floor; and after 3 km you will come to Newburgh. At the green directional arrow, turn left and drive down the valley wall into this unusual village.

Newburgh

In contrast to Napanee and even to Strathcona, Newburgh exudes an air of quiet, a memory of days past. The streets are deserted, one-time stores empty. The few shops that do remain now serve only the village's small population. But it wasn't always that way.

In 1824, when David Perry built a sawmill on a waterfall in the woods, he probably didn't foresee a bustling mill town that would challenge Napanee for the county seat. By 1832 settlers were coming in growing numbers, and soon there were factories, mills, stores, and hotels in this thriving community that was known throughout the area, somewhat ingloriously, as Rogues Hollow. Then, in the 1870s, came John Thompson and his paper mills, and the town entered its glory days. But its booming growth was shattered when in 1887 a raging fire razed 84 buildings. By then Napanee was the county seat and the area's leading town. So most of Newburgh's destroyed industries either relocated in Napanee or else were not rebuilt at all. More fires in 1902 and 1908 reduced the town still further to a mere shell of its former self.

As you descend the hill to the first bridge, you will find a clutch of fine stone buildings, the only part of the main street spared by the many infernos. Here, a one-time hotel and some stores and handsome old homes are a "must" for the photographer and historian alike. Cross the bridge and turn right to the conservation area which has been developed upon Thompson's mill site. Here you can enjoy a lunch break or take a stroll beside the gurgling river.

To see Newburgh's most celebrated building, continue north on the main street to the hardware store and turn left onto County Road 11. Drive half a kilometre to the top of the hill and park. Rising above a field of wild flowers is a massive stone building topped by a domed cupola. This, the Newburgh Academy, is the oldest such institution in Ontario to survive in its original form. Started in 1839 by three local residents, it grew to become one of the province's leading teachers' colleges. The present building replaced the original in 1856 and, despite a fire in 1887, retains its original appearance. Thanks to a fund raised by local residents and former students, the college has been restored and preserved.

Newburgh to Camden East

Retrace your trail to the main street and then to County Road 1. Turn left and continue up the valley. On this stretch of road, the valley walls retreat and the pastures roll gently towards the river. At 2 km from Newburgh, where the road swings sharply to the right, there is a small group of old buildings on the left. Marked on some maps as Thompson's Mills, they are just that, the original site of another of Thompson's mills. But the mills are long gone and the site is now a quiet residential area. After another 1 km, you will come to the village of Camden East.

To describe Camden East as a "picture postcard" village is not an exaggeration, for that is what it was—a subject of artist Manly MacDonald for the Coutts Hallmark Christmas cards.

Camden East got off to an early start, considering the difficult transportation problems that the settlers faced. By 1850 the village could claim mills, factories, stores, hotels, and even a distillery. When the railway arrived in 1871, Camden East's prosperity seemed assured. But rather than enhancing the town's trading position, the railway weakened it, for the line was extended to Napanee, and Camden East faltered in its shadow. Today, there are so few shops that it is hard to imagine that this small village was ever a thriving industrial centre.

Camden East to Yarker

Continue east on County Road 1. Beyond Camden East the views across the river to the left encompass a pastoral landscape of fields and barns. Then, after 6 km, the road bends steeply to the left and descends into the village of Yarker.

Yarker is a relative newcomer to the Napanee Valley. It began in 1840, when David Vader built a sawmill, and it received a boost nine years later when George Miller established a grist mill. The falls at one time dropped 10 m straight down, but so consistently did the log drives wear away the soft limestone riverbed that the lip of the falls now lies 15 m back of the base.

As Yarker grew, it attracted an array of mills and businesses, and in 1871 the railway. Although the village has slipped from its population peak of 600 to just around 200, it has retained its narrow winding streets and many of its older buildings. The best grouping is at the corner of Water and Bridge streets where the old hotel, now home to the Free Methodists, faces the attractive W. M. Wright store that was built in 1902.

Cross the bridge and turn right onto Vanluven Street, County Road 1.

Yarker to Petworth

As County Road 1 leaves the village and proceeds towards Colebrook, the wooded valley wall closes in from the left, while the river laps the roadside on the right.

Attracted by the riverine landscape, new country homes have lined the 2 km between Yarker and Colebrook, and the two villages are now nearly one. However, you will find the heart of Colebrook beside the bridge over the river. Like Yarker and its sister river towns, Colebrook began as a sawmill village. But when the railway bypassed Colebrook in 1871 the village stagnated, becoming no more than a roadside string village; what little it had was destroyed in 1877 by a fire that gutted two sawmills, three stores, two hotels, and five homes. Few were rebuilt. The gaps are still there.

A small conservation area beside the millpond has replaced

The millpond at Colebrook is the site of a small park.

the mills and provides a picnic park. Below the dam you can still see the foundations of the grist mill, the victim of a more recent fire in 1961. (The original mill, spared by the 1877 fire, had burned in 1939.) Across the road from the park is the only remaining general store, Ducharme's. However, the stone church, a few metres north of the store, escaped the conflagration and is now a private residence. It was built in 1874 to serve the Methodist congregation. The village's grandest home, and one of its oldest, sits south of the bridge facing the river. Built of stone, it was occupied by the Wolfe family for several years.

Leave Colebrook north from the store on County Road 6 and drive 1 km. Then look for the Petworth Road sign on the right and turn onto this gravel road. Here the landscape changes. Rock outcrops and boulders scar the surface. For 3 km the narrow road winds through rugged pastures and past scattered farms.

When you arrive at a fork in the road, keep right. This will take you into a village that is strangely silent and along a street that is lined by vacant buildings, staring windowless; for Petworth is a semi-ghost town.

Petworth started with a sawmill and then grew with the settlement of the area's farmlands. A stone grist mill was added in 1845, and at its peak Petworth possessed two hotels, several stores, an Orange Hall, a cheese factory, a blacksmith's shop, and a carding mill. Most of what wasn't destroyed by fire now lies empty. The school, the blacksmith's, and the stone walls of the grist mill all brood silently along the single street in picturesque ruin—a delightful photo subject.

Petworth to Bellrock

Return to the fork in the road and turn right, or north, towards Bellrock—the second village on this trip with an active mill. After almost 3 km, turn right at a T-intersection. Once again the route is narrow, and the barns and homes beside it have an appearance that is a century old. Then suddenly the road plunges down a short but steep hill into Portland Swamp. The swamp is dark and forbidding. Dense woods rise high overhead as the Napanee River divides into a myriad of small tributaries, which wind aimlessly through the bush. Although the swamp is over 10 km long, your crossing is less than 2 km. Just as you are getting accustomed to the stillness, the road rises steeply out of the swamp to the intersection with County Road 7 and to the mill village of Bellrock.

Although most of the old village buildings have long vanished, Bellrock contains a vestige of old Ontario—a waterpowered sawmill, one of the few in the province. At the intersection turn left, drive across a bridge and then almost immediately turn right. This takes you through Bellrock's old streets to a conservation area that contains the mill.

Bellrock rose on the fortunes of the Rathbun Lumber Company. One of the logging giants of the 1800s, Rathbun logged the area and drove the logs down the Napanee River to their mills at Deseronto. Bellrock not only grew into a supply centre for the Rathbun Company but also into a milling centre in its own right. In addition to hotels, stores, a blacksmith's, and a cheese factory, the village also had two sawmills, one grist mill, and a carding mill, all powered by the rushing falls on the Napanee River.

The sawmill in the conservation area was built in the 1920s, but it carries on an activity that goes back more than a century. The Napanee Region Conservation Authority purchased the property in 1976, and rather than turn the mill into another museum, continued to cut wood for the area's farmers. Under the same roof are a shingle mill and a grist mill, which the authority also operates. To tour the mill, check in at the information booth, and a guide will conduct you. There are toilets and picnic tables on the grounds. The falls on the river not covered by the mill pass through private lands and are unfortunately out of bounds to the public.

This finale to the trip is appropriate, for it was mills such as these that created the towns on the Napanee River and brought prosperity to the valley.

To return to Kingston or points east, travel 6 km east from Bellrock on County Road 7 and then take Highway 38 south for 30 km to Kingston and Highway 401. If you are returning to the Ottawa area, turn left, or north, at Highway 38 and follow it 45 km to Highway 7, which leads east to the nation's capital. For returning Torontonians, travel west on County Road 7 (which becomes County Road 14 upon entering Lennox and Addington County). After 20 km, you will come to Highway 41. Follow it south for 15 km to Napanee and Highway 401.

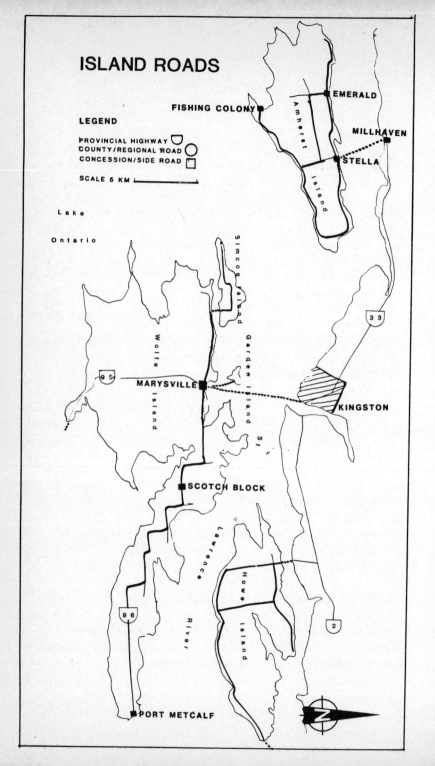

ISLAND ROADS

LEGEND

PROVINCIAL HIGHWAY
COUNTY/REGIONAL ROAD
CONCESSION/SIDE ROAD

SCALE 5 KM

Lake

Ontario

FISHING COLONY

EMERALD

MILLHAVEN

Amherst

Island

STELLA

Simcoe Island

Garden Island

33

Wolfe

Island

95

MARYSVILLE

KINGSTON

St.

SCOTCH BLOCK

Lawrence

River

Howe

Island

96

2

PORT METCALF

N

12 Island Roads

Few routes could have a better claim to being backroads than those which you cannot drive to. You need to take a ferry to get to the backroads of Lake Ontario's largest island communities—Wolfe, Amherst, and Howe islands. Side trips to the smaller Simcoe and Garden islands also await you on this route.

These low, limestone outcroppings crowding the outlet of Lake Ontario and the beginning of the St. Lawrence River are linked to the mainland near Kingston by frequent ferries. While Wolfe Island provides a full range of services for any traveller, Howe and Amherst have only small stores and few gas pumps. Garden and Simcoe have none.

Allow about half a day to visit each island. You can base yourself in Kingston, which has a wide choice of accommodation and the best collection of early nineteenth-century stone buildings west of Montreal.

This is a trip for the traveller who likes tranquility. On these islands you may stop in the middle of the road to take in a view, without fear of an impatient horn behind you. Just as there is little traffic, there has been little pressure to demolish old farmhouses and stores. So if you love the simple architecture of the nineteenth century, you can find it here, usually little changed. On these island backroads you can take in history and scenery, all at your own pace.

A Bit of History

Wolfe, Howe, and Amherst islands were originally within the Seigneury of Cataraqui, which was once held by the Sieur de La Salle. After the British conquest of Canada in 1760, the islands passed to the British, though settlement did not begin until half a century later.

As the nineteenth century progressed, all three islands developed rapidly. The once-brooding forests were stripped clean and replaced by busy farms. Any cove that could shelter a schooner soon sprouted a wharf to ship wheat, timber, and farm produce. Wolfe Island's population peaked at 3,600 in 1860, while those of Amherst and Howe peaked at 850 and 400 respectively. Each was incorporated as a separate municipality.

With the turn of the century, urbanization reduced farm populations everywhere, and the populations of Lake Ontario's island communities plummeted to less than half. Today, the pace of island life remains leisurely. Traffic is light and the islanders have time to chat, even with a backroader from the mainland.

Howe Island

Howe Island is a flat limestone plateau about 9 km long and 4 km wide. Its roads follow the shore, offering views of the historic farmsteads and the sparkling waters of the St. Lawrence River.

To get to the island, leave Kingston on Highway 2 and travel east 15 km to County Road 16. Turn right and drive 1.5 km to the ferry dock. Here the nine-car cable ferry *County of Frontenac* shuttles back and forth, non-stop during busy periods and on request when traffic is light. It takes only 10 minutes to complete the crossing.

Howe Island has only four roads, two that hug the north and south shores, and two that connect them. At the dock you will find a small general store that has a snack bar and picnic benches. From the store, travel south on the gravel road and turn left at the first crossroad. This road was built to link the waterfront farms, and it winds through gently rolling pastures and past the once-busy farmsteads and barns. After a little more than 1 km, look on the right for St. Patrick's School, which was built in 1894 and is now owned by the volunteer fire department. It is the only survivor of the island's three public schools. Although it has lost its bell tower, it appears today as its pupils would remember it.

Shortly after passing the school, you will come to a fork in the road. Keep left and pass more handsome century-old farms. As you skirt and then descend the steep limestone cliff which forms the north shore of the island, you will be treated to a pleasant view of the mainland. Here the island's northern coast is interrupted by an inlet called variously Johnson Bay and Big Bay, and the farm road ends. Return all the way to the ferry road and turn left.

After 2 km you will come to the south shore road. Here, at a T-intersection, turn left. As the road winds in and out of the little coves, you can look across the sparkling St. Lawrence to the American shore. Beside the water is a sprinkling of new cottages and country homes. Most of the old farm homes line the road on the left. Many of them are now occupied by Kingston commuters and cottagers. A few lie neglected and weathered.

After 1 km look for a pair of renovated log cabins—one on the left beside the road and the other on the right close to the water. These are the original settlers' cabins and they are the oldest homes on the island. Over the next 2 km you will pass, almost imperceptibly, more than a dozen farm lots. Although they are not very wide, they are nearly 1 km deep, and they represent an old waterfront survey pattern which, in the days before roads, ensured that every settler had access to water. Of these dozen farms, only one is in operation today; and of the 40 original island farms, there are now a mere 8.

Halfway along the south shore drive, you will encounter the island's most imposing building, St. Philomena's Roman Catholic Church. Built in 1858, it is the only island structure that was built with local limestone. Continue driving east, and after 2 km you will come to the island's oldest store. Though it is no longer in business, it still has its old-style gas pump. The store was operated by the Goodfriend family for over a century, though it never occupied more than three rooms in what was otherwise a private house.

The final 2 km brings you to the end of the Howe Island drive and to Pickett's Ferry, which is run by the township. The ferry has a capacity for only two cars; along with the Simcoe Island ferry, it ranks as the smallest in the province.

Wolfe Island

Shaped like a long-handled dipper, Wolfe Island is the largest of the island townships, the closest to Kingston, the richest agriculturally, and the most populous. It is connected by ferry not only to Kingston but also to Cape Vincent in New York State. Although Wolfe Island is busier than Amherst or Howe, it contains quiet coves and unhurried farm lanes. Among its more interesting features are its photogenic stone halls, houses, and hotels, many of which predate Confederation. Two side trips—to Simcoe Island and to Garden Island—can be taken from Wolfe.

Although much of Wolfe Island contains prosperous farmland, some of the island farms were less successful.

The ferry for Wolfe Island leaves Kingston from the dock located at the corner of Ontario and Barrack streets. Here a large ramp accommodates the 50 cars and trucks that can be boarded onto the *Wolfe Islander III*. This ferry makes 16 crossings a day, but you should expect to wait your turn on a holiday weekend. Even on a regular summer weekend, it is wise to arrive early. The crossing takes 20 minutes.

As the ferry glides towards Wolfe Island's wooded shore, the buildings of Marysville, the island's only town, can be seen peering through the trees. On arrival, follow the ramp to the stop sign at Marysville's Main Street. Here, most of the ferry traffic turns right to follow Highway 95 to the Cape Vincent ferry. You should turn left, heading for the panhandle.

Drive out of Marysville east on Highway 96. After 1 km you will see the Kraft Cheese Factory on your left. This new building has replaced the long-standing Rattray family operation, and it represents Kraft's efforts to buy and close down eastern Ontario's family cheese factories.

A little further on, the road crosses what appears to be a weedy ditch. Incredibly, this was once a canal. In 1857, in an attempt to

A small limestone bluff on Wolfe Island's north shore.

attract barge and schooner traffic, the Wolfe Island Railway and Canal Company sliced a 2-km canal through the island's narrow midriff, eliminating the longer passage around the tip of the panhandle. But steamers had already begun to replace barges and schooners, and the company abandoned the narrow canal in 1870. It never built a railway.

Continue east on Highway 96. Although the pavement soon ends, Highway 96 remains the main road as it zigzags through the maze of concession roads that criss-cross the panhandle. After 3 km, follow the sharp bend to the right and then, after another 2 km, another sharp bend to the left. At the next crossroads sits a solitary boarded-up school. Built in 1890, this school was the focus of the panhandle's Scotch Block settlement—a band of hopeful Scottish immigrants who moved to the island during the last century.

About 1 km east of the school the road once more bends right, taking you into a portion of the Scotch Block that has long been abandoned. The homesteads stand desolate; despite the island's generally fertile land, the soil here proved too shallow for successful farming. Five more sharp bends (three left and two right)

141

over the next 4 km lead to the Scotch Block's Christ Church. Built in 1862 with local limestone, the church has seen steady worship ever since. From the church, continue east for 7 km to Port Metcalf. Here the panhandle narrows to a width of only one or two farm lots. You can still see many of the original shoreline farms that were built when the water was the only highway. Port Metcalf is the end of the road. You will need to retrace your route to return to Marysville.

Marysville

At some point during your visit to Wolfe Island, it is worth taking a walk round Marysville. The town started as a landing in 1802, though very few settlers arrived before the 1820s. The original wharf stood three blocks to the east of the present ferry dock, approximately where the Wolfe Island marina now sits. On the south side of the street, across from the old wharf, is the General Wolfe Hotel. Built during the 1880s, it has served Marysville for a century.

Walk west along Main Street, and at the southeast corner of Main and Division you will see a small limestone building. This is Wolfe Island's original town hall, built in 1859, just nine years after the island was incorporated as a separate municipality. It is one of Ontario's oldest and most attractive township halls. At the street corner is a red brick store. Built in 1878 by Edward Baker, it is still in the same family. One block past Baker's store, turn right to the village's oldest building, one of the oldest on the island. In 1832, Archibald Hitchcock built a wharf and a stone hotel, which he called the Hitchcock House. Two and a half storeys high, it was constructed of local stone; the frame addition on the back came later.

Simcoe Island

If you want to leave the traffic behind altogether and enjoy a quiet picnic beside a historic lighthouse, then tiny Simcoe Island is ideal, for it has only 3 km of road. From the ferry dock in Marysville, turn right onto Highway 96, following it west along the shore for 4 km until you see the directional arrow to the Simcoe Island ferry. Don't be surprised if the landing appears deserted, for Simcoe Island has little traffic.

This two-car ferry crosses from Wolfe Island to Simcoe Island once an hour.

The two-car ferry has a schedule which coincides with that of the *Wolfe Islander*. In other words, it runs about once an hour. On arrival at Simcoe Island, follow the only road west. Although it is a narrow gravel road, it is in good condition. Halfway along the road sits the island's only schoolhouse, which is now privately owned. The lighthouse is at the end of the road. Constructed of local limestone nearly a century ago, it no longer guides vessels through the shoal-stream waters. But it is a pleasant picnic spot, offering views westward to Amherst Island and northward to the mainland.

Garden Island

Garden Island is unique. For three-quarters of a century, this tiny island housed a busy shipbuilding community and was home to nearly 700 people.

The shipyards were begun in 1835 by an American named Dileno Dexter Calvin, and they continued to be run by the Calvins until 1916. During these years, the family launched 25 ships, ranging from barges to ocean liners. The wharves and factories were clustered at the eastern end of the island, while the workers'

143

simple frame homes lined a road that ran down the middle. At the western end was the company farm.

By 1866 the population had grown large enough to warrant independence, and for half a century Garden Island was an incorporated municipality with its own school, church, and post office. But when the shipyards closed, the population dwindled. Nevertheless, some of the residents remained, and they proudly preserved the company homes and shops, as their children and grandchildren do to this day.

There is no Garden Island ferry service available to non-residents, but you can charter a small boat for the short journey to this remarkable island. (Inquire at the Wolfe Island marina.) Garden Island is clearly visible 2 km northwest of Wolfe Island's marina dock, and there are no hidden shoals or sand bars in between. The Garden Island wharf is on the south side of the east point and is the only place to tie up. Most of the island's old buildings are within a few metres of the wharf.

From the wharf you walk between two buildings into the one-time shipyard area. Surrounding this now-grassy yard is a treasury of early buildings, among them the sail loft, the three-storey office building with its blue cupola, several workshops and houses, and the former post office. The latter still operates during the summer and it houses artifacts from the company days.

Walk west down the old tree-lined road. On the right is the sprawling White House, which was the residence of H. A. Calvin, who was the company president and the son of the founder. It was built in 1850, originally for one of the company partners, Ira Breck. Next is the Green House. Modest in comparison to the White House, it was built in the 1840s for founder Calvin himself. On the opposite side of the path are some of the original workers' cabins. They are maintained as they were built, even down to the doors and windows.

Garden Island is a museum piece. It is the only example of a nineteenth-century shipbuilding community to survive in such good condition. Although no authority assumes responsibility for its maintenance, its future seems in secure hands. One only hopes it will remain available for visitors.

Amherst Island

The ferry for Amherst Island leaves from Millhaven, 18 km west of Kingston on Highway 33. You will be unlikely to find a line-up here, for Amherst is the most tranquil of the three main islands and has the fewest cottages and commuters. Most residents continue to farm or fish, much as their forefathers did.

The 30-year-old *Amherst Islander* glides away from the dock every hour on the half hour and has a capacity for 18 cars. Half an hour later, the engines rumble into reverse and the gangway clangs onto the dock of the island's main village, Stella.

The roads of Amherst Island wind along wind-swept coastlines and cross lush farmlands. Happily, the lack of development pressure has left a legacy of old stores, farmsteads, and churches. So light is the traffic that even driving for its own sake becomes a pleasure. Whether you explore the village of Stella before or after your tour, be sure to set aside a few moments for that purpose. Although its buildings are few, they are a pleasure to photograph or sketch.

From the ferry dock drive a few metres to the intersection and

This tree-lined road bisects Amherst Island.

turn left. On the corner is the Glen store and post office. Shaded by its porch and covered in clapboard, it has occupied this site for over a hundred years. So have the frame buildings next to it; these include the public library in the former Methodist church, and the Orange Hall. Across the road is the village blacksmith's shop (now known as Brown's, but originally called Robinson's) which has stood here for more than a century.

Continue east as the road leaves the village to follow the shore. On your left you will see a small Royal Bank building. This was originally the Miller General Store and it was the site of Stella's lower landing. After 1.5 km you will come to Preston Cove. Here, tucked beside the shore, are two early estate homes, one of wood, the other of stone. They are among the oldest homes on the island.

The road now mounts a low mesa, offering views over the North Channel to the treed mainland. After 2 km the road bends right, leading you 1.5 km to the south shore. Here the road edges so close to the low limestone shore that, during a southerly blow, waves spray across the roadway. On the landward side you will pass a string of old family farms, most of them retaining their style of a century ago.

After 5 km the main road turns right towards Stella. But do not take this road yet. Instead, continue straight ahead on the narrower lane which leads to Emeric Point. Nestled in a small cove, where nets dry on racks and shacks lean into the water, Emeric Point is the island's last fishing village. Here the road ends in what appears to be a backyard; so, after photographing any of the several subjects, you will need to return to the intersection and then turn left towards Stella.

After about 1.5 km, you will come to a handsome Gothic church set against a backdrop of maples. This is St. Paul's Anglican Church, which was built in 1884, its grey limestone blocks having been wrenched from a quarry at Kingston Penitentiary by sweating convicts. Continue past the church for less than 1 km and then turn left down a side road. This narrow lane is one of only two interior farm roads on the island. Here the fields have long been stripped of their forest cover and the farmers carry on in much the same way as those in earlier generations.

Beyond the farmsteads, drive 3 km to a crossroads and turn right. A further 1.5 km will bring you into the tiny port of

Emerald. This was once a busy shipping village, but Emerald lost its purpose when the grain trade died. The store and the last of the port buildings sit empty and forlorn. If you wish to visit the homestead of the painter William Fowler, turn left in Emerald and drive 1.5 km to Fowler's home. Born in England, Fowler emigrated to Canada in 1843 and settled on this farm. Within this yellow house, he created the still lifes and bird paintings which earned him membership in the Royal Canadian Academy. Fowler died in 1894 and a historical plaque was erected here in his honour.

Return to Emerald and continue straight ahead along the shore road. Here, if the day is clear, you can see across the North Channel to the low shoreline of Bath, now dominated by the looming chimneys of the moth-balled Lennox and Addington generating station. This same road takes you back to Stella.

Like the other islands, Amherst has no public shoreline where you can enjoy a picnic lunch, nor does it have a snack bar where you can buy one. However, you won't miss them, for you can pull over to the side of almost any of the usually silent lanes and spread your blanket. Don't be surprised if a friendly islander stops to chat and to fill you in on island lore.

Once you have returned to the mainland and joined the rush of traffic home, you will soon realize why the Howe Islanders, the Wolfe Islanders, and the Amherst Islanders are in no hurry to trade the "disadvantages" of isolation for the conveniences of the mainland.

from 1848 to 1954 and were slated for preservation. But a raging fire destroyed them, and Parks Canada was left with only a few limestone walls to stabilize. Cross the second bridge and walk up the road to William Merrick's grand mansion. Set among stately maples, it was built with local limestone and has stood as the town's finest home since 1821.

Return across the two bridges to the town's commercial core. At the southeast corner of St. Lawrence and Main is another of Merrickville's outstanding buildings, the Jakes Block, which was built by Eleazer Whitmarsh sometime in the late 1860s. Its stone walls are three storeys high, its corner a graceful curve. What makes it particularly appealing is the fact that its façade has never been altered and still displays the arching doors and windows of Whitmarsh's early design.

Inevitably, Merrickville has been discovered. After lingering near death in recent years, the business district has revived with boutiques and cafés, especially in and near the Jakes Block. Amid the boutiques you will find a small, attractive restaurant called the Village Kettle. It offers light lunches at attractive pine tables. If you want licensed dining, there is Corky's Tavern a few doors away or, round the corner on Main Street, the Merrickville Hotel.

If you are returning to Ottawa, take Highway 43 east to Highway 16 and then follow this highway north for 50 km. If your route home is via Highway 401, follow St. Lawrence Street south out of Merrickville and drive 45 km to Maitland, 60 km east of Kingston, where you can pick up Highway 401.

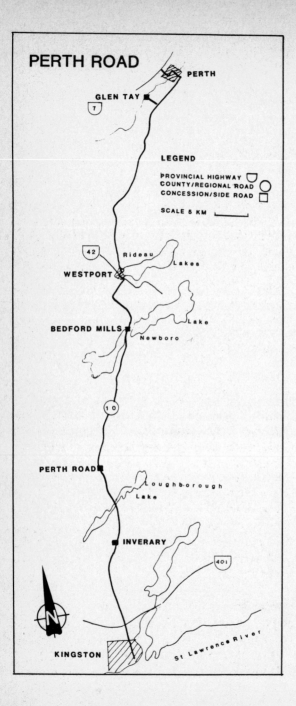

PERTH ROAD

PERTH

GLEN TAY

7

LEGEND

PROVINCIAL HIGHWAY

COUNTY/REGIONAL ROAD

CONCESSION/SIDE ROAD

SCALE 5 KM

42

Rideau

Lakes

WESTPORT

BEDFORD MILLS

Lake

Newboro

10

PERTH ROAD

Loughborough

Lake

INVERARY

401

N

KINGSTON

St Lawrence River

13   Perth Road

Ontario's two best-preserved stone towns, Kingston and Perth, are linked by one of the province's most scenic and historical backwoods roads. This 80-km-long paved road grinds over granite ridges and swoops into villages nestled in valleys. It passes through three counties—Frontenac, Leeds, and Lanark—in each of which it is marked as County Road 10. Good restaurants can be found in Kingston, Westport, and Perth, and picnic sites dot the route. Along the way are many barns, churches, and old general stores to photograph; a ghost town to explore; and holes to fish in. So pack well for this trip, taking fishing rod, camera, and a picnic lunch.

A Bit of History
The Perth Road began as a colonization road. Although both Kingston and Perth were growing towns by 1820, and in full bloom by 1850, the land between them lay empty and neglected. The opening of the Rideau Canal in 1832 brought settlers to the shores of the Rideau Lakes, and there Westport grew. The government then hired the Kingston and Perth Road Company to survey and cut a road northward from Kingston to Perth, thus opening up the interior. By 1854 the road had, however, progressed only 20 km, and in 1860 a series of lawsuits forced the company to relinquish its contract. So the government came to the rescue and completed the road.

Kingston to Perth Road Village
Before leaving Kingston, allow yourself time to visit its numerous historic sites and to sample its small but growing contingent of fine restaurants. From the massive, domed City Hall, leave Kingston north on Division Street. Or, if you are exiting directly

149

from Highway 401, do so at interchange 102 and turn right at the stop lights at the bottom of the ramp. Here, orange and blue "Perth Road" signs will show that you are on the right route.

The first portion of the route passes through a flat limestone plain, where early stone farmhouses mingle with the rural sprawl that emanates from Kingston. Soon after starting your trip, you will see on your left (1.7 km north of Highway 401) the Little Cataraqui Creek Conservation Area. This 400-ha park is a nature reserve with nearly 20 km of hiking trails. Continue north for 8 km. Here you will pass the large old farmhouses and the fertile countryside that gave birth to a prosperous farming community and the village of Inverary.

About 3 km north of Inverary a striking transition occurs. As the road descends a steep cliff, it suddenly leaves behind the flat limestone plain and enters the rugged granite rockland that is the Canadian Shield. Pink, rocky knobs jut from the earth as forests replace the level pastures and cornfields. The line of demarcation is the linear Loughborough Lake (pronounced locally "Lober"). This lake is so narrow where you cross it that you may easily mistake it for a river. Beside the bridge, a public boat ramp provides you with a place to cast for a few bass or perch. From the bridge continue north, where you will pass the last pocket of good farmland, and after 5 km you will come to the village of Perth Road.

If this had not been the site of the Perth Road's first toll gate, there would probably not have been a village here at all. County Road 10 now bypasses the quiet little place, and to reach it you will need to turn off at the directional arrow. With its old houses, stores, and churches, Perth Road village has altered little over the years. At the village intersection is the Perth Road General Store (now closed), a red brick building that 100 years ago was the Jabez Stoness Hotel. If you want a soft drink or an ice cream, Barrett's Store across the road carries on the country-store tradition.

Perth Road Village to Bedford Mills

Continue on your way along County Road 10. As you drive the next 25-km section of the route, with its bare rocks and dank swamps, you will understand why settlers shunned the area. The few who tried have left a legacy of overgrown clearings and sagging barns. However, the maze of lakes has attracted summer cottagers and restored some prosperity. Aside from a few cause-ways over swampy bays, there are no public access points to the lakes.

Bedford Mills

After 15 km, watch for an orange and blue directional arrow pointing to Bedford Mills, and follow it left. This narrow dirt track was the original Perth Road alignment up to Bedford Mills. From a high granite ridge, Buttermilk Falls cascades into a back bay of Loon Lake. Here, in the 1830s, Benjamin Tett built a sawmill. Not only was there water power to drive the mill, but Loon Lake led directly onto the Rideau Canal. When the long-awaited Perth Road finally arrived and settlers moved in, Tett added a store and a grist mill to serve the new community. Bedford Mills boomed and at its peak could claim a powerhouse, a church, numerous private dwellings, and a cheese factory. But after the turn of the century most of these shut down and the residents moved away. The place is now a ghost town.

You will probably want to spend some time exploring the site. The mill is a private residence, but its location beside both the road and the pond makes it an ideal photo subject. Near the mill stands the vacant powerhouse, its flume yet visible in the falls. St. Stephen's Anglican Church still stands, though services are held only in the summer. Beside the church is a plaque which summa-rizes the history of the little mill village.

Bedford Mills to Westport

Continue on the gravel road until it returns to the paved road and then turn left. After 3 km the road glides down from the rocky highlands into the flatlands that surround the Rideau Lakes. In this basin a pocket of silty and fertile soils has sustained a prosperous farming community. For 4 km the road passes neat fields and pastures, leading towards the historic town of Westport, its slender steeples and white-frame houses set against a picturesque background of field, forest, and lake. Stop at the T-intersection with Highway 42 and turn left. After less than 1 km, County Road 10 bends right and into Westport.

Westport

Westport's location at the head of Upper Rideau Lake ensured its prosperity as long as the canal, and later a railway line, operated.

These boomtown stores in Westport have long been closed.

But when commercial traffic stopped, the town slid from boom to bust. The upsurge of cottaging and boating in the last three decades has injected new life into the old town and made it a popular recreational spot. Despite its new prosperity, Westport has retained its historical buildings and old streetscapes.

Most of the town's early buildings are on Rideau Street, on County Road 10, and on Church and Main streets, which form the core of the small business district. Look particularly for a block of three wooden false-front stores on Rideau Street, and for the nearby post office, a bulky edifice built by local stonemasons, who used limestone quarried from a nearby farm. On Main Street, Murphy's barber shop, another boomtown shop, is not only the most colourful building in Westport but probably the busiest. Besides cutting hair, Murphy's dispenses hunting licences, fishing licences, motor vehicle licences, and also cold drinks. The town has several restaurants if you wish to stop here for lunch, or you may prefer to picnic in the conservation area just north of Westport.

Leave town travelling north on County Road 10. This road grinds up the steep side of Westport Mountain, a granite cliff which soars 100 m above the lake and the town. The lofty

A picnic-site view of Westport and the Rideau Lakes.

escarpment extends along the lake for 20 km. The view over the town is spectacular—church spires poking through the trees, and lake and fields stretching into the distant haze. But don't stop here. Continue to the summit and to the 240-ha Foley Mountain Conservation Area (no gate fee), where you can enjoy both the view and your picnic lunch. To help you work up an appetite, the area has 13 km of hiking trails.

Westport to Perth

Leave the conservation area and continue north on County Road 10. For 15 km the route twists around rugged granite hills where pioneer bush farms are tucked into rock-walled vales. Defying the stony soils, many of these farms are still in operation, though the owners supplement their income with off-farm jobs. Suddenly the road emerges onto a lush, flat plain. Here the soil is deep and fertile, the farms large and prosperous. About 7 km farther on, look for the side road to Glen Tay, where you will find one of the area's most photogenic stone mills. Built in the 1860s, it looms above the rushing Tay River against a backdrop of rocky river bank and cedar woods.

Backtrack to the Perth Road (here called the Scotch Line to

The mill at Glen Tay sits silently on the river bank.

commemorate the settlement of the area by Highland Scots) and drive into the town of Perth. Turn left onto Gore Street and after eight blocks park by the town hall.

Perth

Allow yourself plenty of time to stroll this town of old stone buildings. Perth has been spared the highrise intrusions and senseless demolitions that have scarred Kingston, that other stone city of eastern Ontario. Much of the credit is due to Perth's concerned citizens and far-sighted planners. They have designated much of the downtown as a "heritage district," an area to be spared demolition or incompatible new development. All this has made Perth one of the most photogenic of Ontario's small towns.

Perth is also one of Ontario's oldest towns. Along with Richmond, 40 km to the east, Perth was surveyed in 1816. Its town lots were to be a reward to the officers and men of the Glengarry regiments who had served in the Peninsular War and the War of 1812. Mills were built on the swift Tay River and stores appeared on the main street. In 1834, when the Tay Canal provided a link with the Rideau, Perth experienced a boom in growth; and in 1859, when the railway rumbled into town, new factories and mills propelled Perth's population towards 3,000.

154

But its unrivalled stone heritage must be credited to the builders of the Rideau Canal. To construct the stone locks and lock buildings, the canal mastermind, Colonel John By, lured a bevy of Scottish stonemasons to Canada. When the canal was completed, many of these men settled in local towns, and there they applied the trade they knew best. During the boom years, these skilled builders erected, particularly in Kingston and Perth, Ontario's finest stone structures.

Perth must be enjoyed on foot. The short tour which follows covers only Perth's core. Detailed walking-tour brochures are available in the town hall, and that is the best place to start your tour.

The town hall, with its domed clock tower, was built in 1863 of cut stone, and it combines the Georgian and federal styles of architecture that were popular in the early 1800s. From the town hall, walk north up Gore Street through the commercial core, where many blocks date back 130 years. All are of stone, peak-roofed, and some with a front gable. A few paces north, cross a bridge over the Little Tay, a branch of the larger river. Here you will find a clutch of Perth's oldest stone stores, many built in the 1840s, and a riverside restaurant.

Continue north another block and a half to the mansion built in 1840 for Roderick Matheson. This house was saved from demolition in 1966 by a concerned citizens' group, and with the help of an Ontario Heritage Foundation grant it was turned into a museum. For a nominal entrance fee, you can tour the grand rooms which have been furnished in the style of the period of its construction.

Carry on along Gore Street another half block to Foster Street. On the southeast corner stands the beautiful stone block housing Shaws, one of Ontario's oldest family stores—in business since 1859. Across the road is Maximillian's Restaurant, which was built as the Perth Hotel in 1838 and is Perth's second oldest hotel. Turn right onto Foster Street and walk half a block to the Heritage Silversmiths. Located in a renovated stone building, one of Perth's earliest, this is an outlet for a wide variety of silver- and gold-plated cutlery, and it draws customers from throughout southern Ontario and upper New York State.

Continue on to Drummond Street and turn right. Before you lies one of the town's oldest residential streets, a street of stone houses large and small, most of them predating 1850 and all nicely preserved. On the northeast corner, now owned by St. Andrews Presbyterian Church, stands the former Merchant's Bank of Canada building, which was constructed in 1850. A block south, on the southeast corner of Herriott, is one of Perth's first stone houses. It dates from 1835. Walk south another block to the turning basin of the Tay Canal. Here a small waterside park provides a watery foreground for a photograph of the town hall and the other early buildings on the opposite side of the canal.

From the park, cross the bridge and walk up the hill to the corner of Harvey Street, the site of two of Perth's more interesting buildings. On the southeast corner is St. James Anglican Church, built in a high-steepled Gothic style in 1861. Beside it sits the courthouse, erected in 1842. On the courthouse lawn are two 200-year-old cannons which have seen action in three wars. On the northeast corner is another of Perth's most celebrated homes, Summit House. Built in 1823 for James Boulton, Perth's first lawyer, this house combines the two architectural styles known as Adamesque and American federal. It was modelled after Toronto's famous Grange, which was the home of James Boulton's

Inge-Va has been described as the most beautiful house in eastern Ontario.

156

uncle, D'Arcy Boulton. When Summit House was built, it was eastern Ontario's only brick house. It has now been declared a historic site.

Turn right onto Harvey Street and walk west a block to Gore to another of Perth's famous homes, the MacMartin House. Dating from 1839, it too reflects the federal style. Although much of its original woodwork has been removed, its three cupolas set it apart.

From Harvey Street, walk south one block to Craig. On the northeast corner is Perth's oldest building, which was built of logs in 1816 and was originally a busy inn. In 1819 a famous guest, the Duke of Richmond, suggested remodelling with red clapboard and the inn became known as the Red House. Even though the siding is now white, the name has stuck.

One block west on Craig Street sits Inge-Va (Celtic for "come here"). Set back from the road on a gracious, curved lane, and shaded beneath a canopy of willows and maples, Inge-Va has been described as the most beautiful house in eastern Ontario. It also has an unusual chapter in its history. Ten years after its construction in 1823, it played a role in Canada's last fatal duel, the duellists being two young law students named John Wilson and Robert Lyon. When the gun smoke cleared, Lyon lay wounded and he was carried to Inge-Va, where he died. In its 150 years, Inge-Va has known only three private owners—its builder the Reverend Michael Harris, the Radenhursts, and the Inderwicks. In 1966 Mrs. C. Inderwick, who still resides there, donated the house to the Ontario Heritage Foundation. It is open for tours by appointment only.

Perth contains much more to see—more mansions, century-old factories and stores. This tour has touched only the highlights of the core area. If you are ready to rest your feet, you can do so in the attractively landscaped Stewart Park behind the town hall. And if you want to have a meal, Perth has a variety of licensed and unlicensed restaurants, both in the downtown area and on the northern outskirts along Highway 7.

Highway 7 is the route to lead you home. Ottawa lies 65 km to the east, Toronto 300 km to the west. If the prospect of the long drive is too much, there are a number of motels in and around Perth and a pair of provincial campgrounds about half an hour's journey westward on Highway 7.

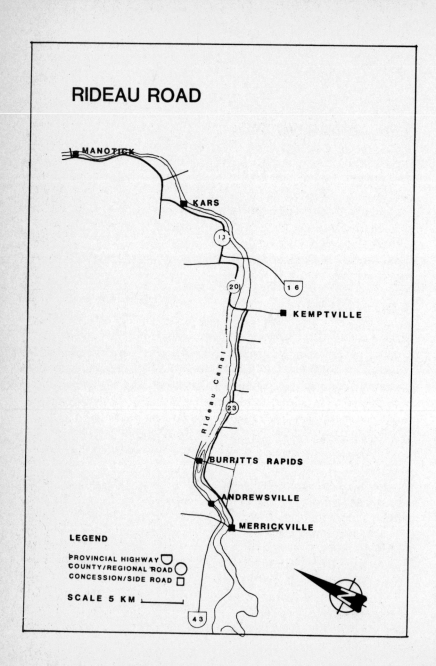

RIDEAU ROAD

MANOTICK

KARS

13

20

16

KEMPTVILLE

Rideau Canal

23

BURRITTS RAPIDS

ANDREWSVILLE

MERRICKVILLE

LEGEND

PROVINCIAL HIGHWAY
COUNTY/REGIONAL ROAD
CONCESSION/SIDE ROAD

SCALE 5 KM

43

14　Rideau Road

This is a short route, just 45 km long, following the Rideau Canal between two early mill towns, Manotick and Merrickville. Most of the villages en route have restaurants, gas stations, and parks, so keep preparations simple. But be prepared to do some walking, for the towns on this trip are exceptionally rich in historic buildings. They need to be enjoyed in a leisurely manner, and that means on foot.

A Bit of History

In the 1820s, when there was a constant threat of war with the United States, the British army engineer Colonel John By built the Rideau Canal between Ottawa and Kingston. Its purpose was military—to provide a transportation route for troops and supplies at a safe distance from the American border. The canal was a remarkable engineering achievement. Rapids had to be dammed and bedrock blasted. Great stone blocks had to be hauled through roadless backwoods and fitted exactly into locks and lock buildings. The canal was completed in 1832, and it remains a marvel to this day.

Even before the canal was completed, the many waterfalls and rapids had spawned mill villages. Then, when the Rideau became a busy commercial highway, the little villages grew into towns. They thrived until the 1870s and 1880s when the railways heralded another transportation era. Then the canal traffic dwindled and the towns stagnated. Ironically, this is one reason for the wealth of early, unaltered buildings.

The canal left another even more enduring legacy. The Scottish stonemasons who hewed the canal's great limestone blocks settled in the Rideau Valley, where they applied their trade to the construction boom. They built many of the limestone houses, mills, and stores that are found in such numbers between Kingston and Ottawa, and are among the most photographed and praised of Ontario's nineteenth-century buildings.

In 1975, Parks Canada recognized the unique heritage role of the Rideau Canal and its buildings, and declared the entire system a historical park. Locks, lockmasters' homes, and the protective blockhouses have been thoughtfully preserved, as have the century-old techniques of operating the locks and swing bridges by hand.

Manotick

The starting point of your trip, Manotick lies 15 km south of Ottawa. Follow Highway 16 south to Regional Road 13 and take this road west across the Rideau River bridge into Manotick. A left turn down the first side street will bring you into Dickinson Square, the historic heart of Manotick. Here you can park by the stone mill. There is much to see in Manotick before setting out on the Rideau Road.

Dickinson Square is bounded by three historic buildings—the F. E. Ayers building, Dickinson House, and the Watson mill. The Ayers building, a handsome, flat-top, brick structure, was built in 1902 and originally housed the Union Bank. Its arching doors and windows still retain the façade that greeted its early customers. Today, the building is the headquarters of the Girl Guides of Canada and is also a reception area for the Rideau Valley Conservation Authority.

The second building, the yellow-frame Dickinson House, was constructed in 1867. It has been a store, a post office, and the home of Moss Kent Dickinson, who was a mayor of Ottawa and one of the Watson mill's first owners. The Conservation Authority bought the house in 1972 and restored it right down to the pioneer herb garden.

The star attraction of Dickinson Square is the Watson (or Long Island) mill. Built by Scottish stonemasons between 1857 and 1860, this five-storey stone mill was the centre of an industrial complex that included a sawmill, a carding mill, and a bung mill. It has been described as one of Canada's best remaining examples of a nineteenth-century grist mill. It is now a living museum, and flour is ground there three times a week.

The Watson mill in Manotick is now a living museum, and flour is ground here three times a week.

From Dickinson Square, stroll west along shady Mill Street. Beside Dickinson House stands Waddel House, a turn-of-the-century sister to the Ayers building. It housed the town tailor. Halfway along Mill Street, look for the Millers Oven teashop. Built in 1870, this mansard-roofed frame shop was originally a village store and a popular gathering spot. Across the street from the tearoom is an example of the simple residences of the mill workers.

There are many other interesting buildings which have also been carefully restored by the Rideau Valley Conservation Authority. If you wish to know more about Manotick's buildings, you can help yourself to the booklets available at the Conservation Authority's reception area in the Ayers building.

Manotick to Kars
Drive along Mill Street to Regional Road 13 and turn left. Here are Manotick's more modern amenities, including restaurants and

gas stations. For the next 2 km the green, sloping banks of the Rideau have attracted commuters, who have converted a small cottage community into an expensive Ottawa suburb. But soon the road leaves the backsplits behind, following the river as it churns past old barns and farmhouses, many of which have been well preserved. Then, 5 km from Manotick, County Road 13 bends right to follow Regional Road 9 to an intersection. Turn left and continue on County Road 13. Almost immediately, you will enter the 150-year-old village of Kars.

Kars

With its parklike river bank, its narrow streets, and nineteenth-century homes and shops, Kars beckons you to amble and photograph, and perhaps to picnic or cast a line from the wharf. Drive through the village to Walter Murphy's store and turn left onto Wellington Street. A little farther on is the river, where you can park beside the government wharf.

Kars traces its origins back to 1829, the year James Lindsay arrived and built a wharf to ship lumber a little to the south of the present dock. Three years later the Rideau Canal brought a commercial boom, and Lindsay's wharf became a busy spot. North of the wharf, a six-street town plot was laid out and named Wellington. It became the focus for the homes, shops, and churches that collected at the site. But in 1854, when the railway shunned Kars, the community's growth faltered and to this day the village has changed little.

From the wharf, walk back along Wellington Street two blocks to Nelson Street. These waterside blocks retain their narrow streets and their canopy of trees. At the northeast corner of Wellington and Nelson is Adam Eastman's old home. Built in 1854 by one of the settlement's first mill owners, this white-frame house still has its original windows with their irregular panes. Walk north on Nelson two blocks to Anne and turn left to Rideau River Drive, the main street. Just north of the corner is St. John's Anglican Church, a white clapboard building that was constructed by John Eastman in 1850. It is Kars's oldest church.

Continue your walk south on Rideau back to the corner of Wellington. The house on the southeast corner is the former Zena Ault Hotel, a boisterous spot during the boom days. Return along Wellington to your car.

Kars to Burritts Rapids

Continue south on County Road 13. Half a kilometre from Kars, look for a stone farmhouse. This is James Lindsay's original home, built in 1829. Today, more than 150 years later, it still remains in the Lindsay family. South of Kars the shoreline is flat. Even so, it has attracted cottagers and commuters, whose homes mingle with old farmhouses and barns. At 7 km from Kars you will come to Baxter Conservation Area, where you can fish or picnic and even swim if the algae growth is low.

From the park, continue to the stop sign at Highway 16. Turn right, drive 1.5 km and then turn left onto Regional Road 20. This is the former Highway 16, and it takes you to Rideau River Provincial Park, which offers camping as well as other amenities. At the west end of the park, the road soars over the river. The high-level bridge allows tall-masted cruisers to glide beneath and it gives you a glimpse of a river that here is wide, sluggish, and often swampy.

After crossing the bridge, turn right onto River Road, unless forestry or hiking interest you. If they do, ignore the River Road for the moment and drive straight ahead for 1 km to the entrance to the G. Howard Ferguson Forest Station. Named for a former Ontario premier, who was born in nearby Kemptville, this 1,000-ha tree garden offers hiking and gives tours during most of the year (though it is closed in January, February, and July). It provides you with an opportunity to see just how they really do cultivate those young trees.

From the bridge, drive west on River Road 6 km to County Road 23 and turn right. This quiet gravel road winds along the Rideau's swampy shores past century-old riverside farms, many of them built by the Scottish stonemasons who laboured beside John By to build the Rideau Canal. Follow County Road 23 for 6 km to one of the highlights of the trip, the village of Burritts Rapids.

Burritts Rapids

Beside the road is the Burritts Rapids lock; the village is across the canal. Park in the small parking lot beside the lock station and explore this museum-piece village on foot. As part of Parks Canada's preservation efforts, the locks on the swing bridge are operated by hand as they have been for 150 years. But the village predates even the canal.

In 1793 two Loyalist brothers, Stephen and Daniel Burritt, fled from Arlington, Vermont, and made their way up the Rideau River to a set of rapids which they felt could power their mills. By the time the Rideau Canal opened nearly 40 years later, Burritts Rapids was a flourishing mill village. But the railways bypassed the village. Businesses fled, and for years many buildings stood empty. Today, most are residences maintained by owners who care for the past.

Cross the bridge and walk north up Grenville Street. Here the tight rows of wooden nineteenth-century homes and former businesses present a century-old streetscape. At the first cross street you will find a craft shop in an old village home, as well as the old hotel, which has half a second-storey porch and is painted a light blue. Venture down the dirt side streets and you will find a row of simple frame cabins, a large white-frame house with an elaborately fretted wraparound porch that architects call Gothic revival, and a 130-year-old Methodist church that is now a private home. Then continue north to the next bridge. In a small park beside the river is a plaque commemorating the founding of the village. Beside it is a former store, which now functions as a community centre. Beneath the bridge tumble the rapids where the Burritts located their mills, and beside them is a disused blacksmith's shop that has been painted a brilliant red.

At the head of Grenville Street, set back from the road in a large churchyard, is Christ Church, one of eastern Ontario's most photographed churches. It was built in 1831. A square, crenellated tower soars above its white-frame body, and in its gable is an unusual circular window. The cemetery surrounding the church contains headstones that date back nearly a century and a half.

Burritts Rapids to Merrickville

From Burritts Rapids continue west on County Road 23. Here the river's banks are steeper, its flow swifter. Over the next 6 km the river plunges so steeply that the canal builders had to construct four separate sets of locks. This is a shoreline that displays several handsome stone houses, most built by canal stonemasons around the middle of the last century and each subtly different from the next. But one in particular is strikingly different. At 2 km from Burritts Rapids the road bends sharply left and then back to the right. At this second bend, watch for the house set back on the left.

Many of the locks on the Rideau Canal are still operated by hand.

While its storey-and-half style is typical, its alternating pattern of red and yellow bricks is found among only a few old houses and is unique to this area.

Just past the house is the entrance to the Poonamalie Locks and half a kilometre beyond that are the Nicholson Locks, with a bridge and side road to Andrewsville. Founded in the 1830s by pioneer Rufus Andrews, Andrewsville grew into a busy mill village with a store, a cheese factory, and a population of 150. Today, it is little more than a ghost town—its one-time grid pattern of streets now just trails into the bush. The mill is gone, and fewer than a half-dozen original houses remain, with a few new cottages between them.

Return across the bridge to County Road 23 and continue 1.5 km to Provincial Highway 43. Turn right, and after 1 km you will come to Merrickville, the finale of the trip.

Merrickville

On this particular trip the best comes last, for Merrickville's buildings, many of stone, have changed little in more than a century. Like Burritts Rapids, the town began with a Loyalist fleeing the oppression of post-revolutionary America. William Merrick arrived in 1793 and built a sawmill at the rapids. The

Merrickville's century-old main street.

steep drop in the river called for three sets of locks when the canal was built, so Colonel By chose the site for one of his four protective blockhouses. When the canal opened, Merrickville boomed. In 1848 Merrick's son Stephen built extensive woollen mills and a grist mill. Then, when the railway passed through town, Merrickville boomed again. Most of its buildings date from one of these two boom periods.

The stoplight marks the corner of Main and St. Lawrence, and is the centre of town. Either turn left and park by the stores on St. Lawrence or continue straight ahead, past the blockhouse, and park by the river.

Merrickville is another town that is best enjoyed on foot. Start with the blockhouse. Built in 1832, it is the largest of John By's four blockhouses. Like the others, it never saw military duty, and today it is a museum of military and pioneer paraphernalia. It is open daily during the summer months.

Walk north from the blockhouse across the bridge to an island in the river, the site of Merrick's woollen mills. On one side of the island are By's locks, on the other the tumbling rapids that powered Merrick's early mills. The mills operated uninterrupted

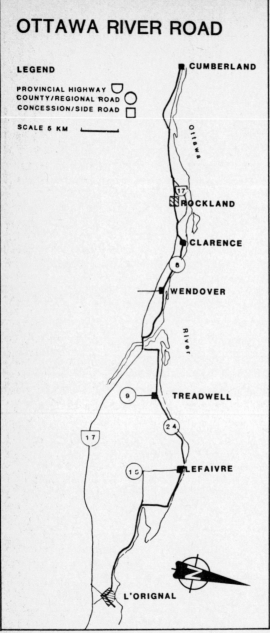

OTTAWA RIVER ROAD

LEGEND

PROVINCIAL HIGHWAY
COUNTY/REGIONAL ROAD
CONCESSION/SIDE ROAD

SCALE 5 KM

CUMBERLAND

Ottawa

17 ROCKLAND

CLARENCE

8

WENDOVER

River

9 TREADWELL

24

17

15 LEFAIVRE

L'ORIGNAL

15   Ottawa River Road

Although brightly painted barns and curved silvery roofs are common in rural Quebec, they are not often seen in Ontario. Yet many are to be found along the Ottawa River Road, which winds past numerous buildings whose styles proudly proclaim their French Canadian origins. Silver steeples of village churches dominate the landscape. French Canadian "ski jump" roofs crown village homes and farmhouses. Barns are brightly painted in orange or green, contrasting cheerfully with the drab brown of most Ontario barns.

This is above all a riverside drive. The road begins at Cumberland, east of Ottawa, and winds easterly along the Ottawa River, following paved county roads for most of its 70-km length. It ends at L'Orignal near the Quebec border.

This is a well-populated area, and the villages contain gas stations, grocery stores, and a wide selection of restaurants, so preparations for your trip can be minimal. The trip offers pleasant views to the mountains on the Quebec shore, as well as providing the opportunity for a picnic or stroll beside the Ottawa River.

A Bit of History

This route was originally known as the L'Orignal–Bytown Road. Completed around 1850, it was the first road to open up the south shore of the Ottawa River and to link the little steamer villages that huddled on the banks.

Settlement in the region began with an American called Abijah Dunning, who in 1801 purchased an extensive tract of land around Cumberland. Meanwhile, 70 km downstream, another American, Nathaniel Treadwell, was creating L'Orignal. At first there was little settlement between the two towns. The shore was swampy and thickly wooded, and was remote from Ontario's early roads. Most immigrants shunned the area in favour of the lighter, more accessible soils of the Lake Ontario shoreline. Then, in 1848, Pierre Lefaivre left the crowded confines of St. Benoit in Quebec and made his way up the Ottawa, where be bought a portion of land from the Treadwell family. His son Hercule encouraged others to move from St. Benoit, and settlement began in earnest. By 1867 half a dozen little wharf villages had sprung up along the shore.

Cumberland to Rockland

Cumberland lies on Highway 17 about 36 km east of Ottawa. As you enter Cumberland you will see a sign pointing left to the ferry. Turn right, taking the road across from the ferry, and drive two blocks to Cumberland's one-time main intersection. On the northeast corner sits one of the town's oldest buildings, a house and store started in 1844 by G. C. Dunning, the son of the town's founder.

Proceed east through Cumberland along the old L'Orignal Road. Here, shaded by mature maples, are houses dating from the times of dirt streets and horse-drawn wagons. One of the more striking is on the north side, four blocks from the Dunning store.

A team of horses pulls a wagon through the back lanes of Cumberland.

This three-storey stone house, completed in 1883, was the home of Dr. James Ferguson, the town's first doctor. Note its wraparound wooden two-storey porch, one of the few still existing in the area. A little farther along the road is the Cumberland Township Heritage Museum, where the curators have assembled a wide variety of nineteenth-century buildings, including log cabins, churches, and the railway station from the nearby town of Vars.

Your road continues east, and after 3 km it crosses Becketts Creek, the site of an early sawmill, and rejoins Highway 17. Stay on Highway 17 for 3 km and then watch for a directional sign to Rockland. Turn right into Rue Laurier and follow it into this historic town.

With a population of 4,000, Rockland is the largest town on this route. Yet it was no more than a small wharf village until 1889 when the merchants lured the Canada Atlantic Railway to their community. This brought a prosperity that is reflected in Rockland's main street buildings. Rue Laurier, Rockland's main street, is one of the most striking in eastern Ontario, for the buildings still have their traditional balconies and porches. Especially noteworthy is the string of stores between the Panorama Restaurant and the Beauchamp Deli.

Rockland offers the widest range of facilities of any town on this trip. You can get more film for your camera at the Laurier Pharmacy, snatch a fast snack at Rolly's Takeout, or linger over a licensed lunch at the Castle Restaurant. If you wish to picnic, follow Rue Edward north from Laurier to the site of the wharfs and the riverside park.

Rockland to South Nation River

East of Rockland, Rue Laurier rejoins Highway 17. Follow it for 1.5 km to Clarence and turn left there onto County Road 8. When the L'Orignal Road was opened in the 1850s, this string village replaced the original wharfside settlement 2 km away. Although several newer homes have been constructed, there is a small stone Presbyterian church dating from those early days. A little more than 1 km beyond the church, a road to the left leads to the wharf. Here, two ferries still link Clarence with the busy industrial town of Thurso on the Quebec side. Look carefully towards the middle of the river. There, a swampy island known as Clarence Island was carved in two in order to speed the ferry service.

Before there were any roads on the Ontario shore, the farmhouses were built close to the only transportation route—the river.

Return to the L'Orignal Road and continue east. For the next 12 km the road meanders along the river bank. Modern homes and summer cottages now mingle with the older French Canadian farmhouses and barns. About halfway along this stretch of road you will enter Wendover, which was originally a wharf settlement. Another of the French Canadian string villages, it stretches 3 km along the road, yet has no back streets. In the middle of Wendover, a short lane leads to the old wharf. Here the Ottawa River widens and flows sluggishly around long swampy islands and over shallow weed beds. There are several restaurants in Wendover if you wish to stop here for lunch.

From Wendover, your route continues east on what is now County Road 19. After 2 km the road bends inland to follow the bank of the South Nation River. From the stop sign for the Trans-Canada Highway, turn left and cross the high concrete bridge. Below you swirls Jessups Falls, the site of the large, turn-of-the-century Anderson Hager sawmill. On the opposite bank is a small park called South Nation Provincial Park. With its mantle of pines, it offers a shady picnic site.

South Nation River to Lefaivre

The next 15 km follow a peaceful shoreline that draws you deeper into this "little Quebec." From the South Nation Provincial Park, turn north past a motel onto an unmarked gravel road. After 2 km

172

turn right at a T-intersection and follow the south bank of the Ottawa. Below you in the river lie the twin islands of Grande Presqu'ile and Petite Presqu'ile, while on the horizon is the hazy ridge of the Gatineau Hills. The farm buildings on this road are close together, set on long, narrow lots which stretch about 2 km from the river. This was a common pattern of French settlement when the river was the only highway, for it ensured that the early settlers all had access to the vital water route.

Continue for 4 km to Treadwell, a cluster of buildings at a crossroads. Like the other villages, Treadwell originated as a wharf settlement and saw little activity until the road opened up the interior. The small frame church with its slender silver steeple was built in 1923. At the church, jog left and then follow County Road 24 east from Treadwell. Here the road winds along the river bank, descending through wooded gullies and past old farmhouses and barns, many of which date from the early days of settlement. On the opposite bank, the Gatineau Hills loom higher.

After 6 km the road climbs a wooded ridge and emerges to a panorama of farm, river, and mountain. A further 3 km brings you to a string of houses. This is the village of Lefaivre, the heart of Pierre Lefaivre's historic colony.

Lefaivre

During its early years Lefaivre grew slowly, for its low and swampy backshore discouraged settlers. The village remained little more than a shipping point until the 1850s, when Lefaivre's colonists began to stream in from the crowded parishes of rural Quebec, giving this area the appearance and culture it has retained to this day.

Lefaivre is unarguably the most "French" of the villages along the shore. Silver, ski-slope roofs and a tall church steeple dominate this string village. At the main intersection is the Hotel Present, the Lefaivre Boucherie, and Cadieux's Magasin-Général. If you are a photographer, you will find plenty of subject material here.

Beside the school, less than 1 km beyond the main intersection, is a driveway that leads down the bank to a quiet little riverside park. The wharf here has been out of use since 1923, but only half a kilometre away is a modern wharf, where a six-car ferry shuttles back and forth across the Ottawa.

Lefaivre to L'Orignal

Continue east from Lefaivre on County Road 24. It was along this section that, in the 1850s, Lefaivre's colonists carved out their farms. As the land was handed down from father to sons, the farms were severed lengthwise so that each lot had access to the river. Today, there are 25 of these strip farms on a section of road that is only 5 km long.

Leaving the river and the farms behind, the paved road turns sharply inland 5 km from Lefaivre. For 2 km it crosses a flat plain, pock-marked by small, swampy depressions, and then abruptly halts at a T-intersection. Turn left. Here, at a swampy arm of the Ottawa called Baie des Atocas, the route rejoins the river and continues along the bank 8 km to L'Orignal. As you approach this quiet and historic town, you will see its large steel foundry looming above the plain.

L'Orignal

Now a dormitory town of the larger Hawkesbury, L'Orignal contains two of the more interesting buildings in eastern Ontario, a cottage called Riverest and Ontario's oldest county courthouse. Drive across the bridge and turn left into King Street, where you can park if you wish to take a short walking tour.

It was on the banks of the creek by the bridge that in the early 1800s, Nathaniel Treadwell's sawmills belched steam and smoke into the sky while mountains of lumber awaited the next schooner. L'Orignal was one of the busiest ports on the river and a major reason for the construction of the L'Orignal–Bytown Road. Today it is a quiet residential village of 1,800 people, most of whom are French Canadian.

The intersection of King and Queen is the focus of L'Orignal's small downtown core, and here, in an attractive turn-of-the-century building, is the old Hôtel de Ville, or town hall. However, L'Orignal contains few examples of French architecture. Even the stout turreted houses on King Street smack more of Victorian England than of the French town that L'Orignal subsequently became.

Continue east on King Street to Wharf Street. At the foot of the street you will find, nestled under the shade of stately elms and pine, a cottage called Riverest. It was built in 1833 by John Marston, using local rubblestone. With its wraparound porch, it is

The L'Orignal county courthouse is the oldest in Ontario.

considered by architects to be the best remaining example of
Ontario's few Regency cottages. The house and grounds are
privately owned, but you can see the building clearly from the
road. The road ends at the large federal dock, where you can view
the mountains of Quebec across the wide river.

Return to the downtown area and walk south from the Hôtel de
Ville. Brooding over the village from the head of Queen Street, its
roof a glowing red, is the L'Orignal courthouse. Although several
sections were later added, the original portion was built in 1825,
making this building the oldest county courthouse in Ontario.
Beside the courthouse is St. Andrews Church, constructed in
1836 as a Church of Scotland. It is now a United Church and is
one of eastern Ontario's oldest churches still in use.

Leave L'Orignal by turning left past the church. After 1 km
you will meet the Trans-Canada Highway 17. Turn left for
Montreal or right for Ottawa. To reach Highway 401, turn left and
drive 5 km to Highway 34; then turn south and travel 60 km to the
expressway.

Ontario's countryside harbours many cultural groups. Few,
however, have left their distinctive imprint so indelibly on the
landscape as have the Franco-Ontarians of the lower Ottawa
River.

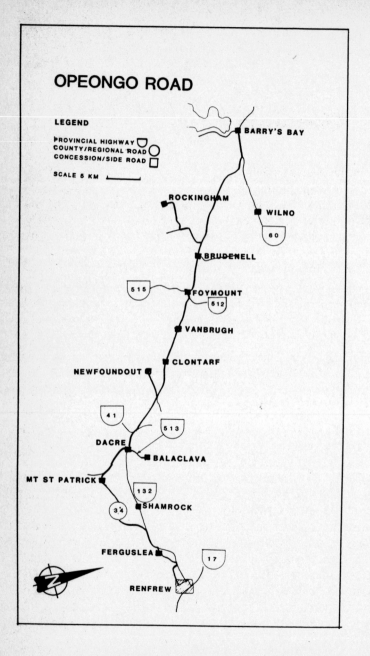

OPEONGO ROAD

LEGEND

PROVINCIAL HIGHWAY
COUNTY/REGIONAL ROAD
CONCESSION/SIDE ROAD

SCALE 5 KM

BARRY'S BAY

ROCKINGHAM

WILNO

60

BRUDENELL

515

FOYMOUNT

512

VANBRUGH

CLONTARF

NEWFOUNDOUT

41

513

DACRE

BALACLAVA

MT ST PATRICK

132

34

SHAMROCK

FERGUSLEA

17

RENFREW

16　Opeongo Road

Deep in the Black Donald Mountains of Renfrew County lies a pioneer landscape of log cabins and barns, of snake rail fences and simple churches. Through it winds the Opeongo Road. This route begins at the town of Renfrew, 320 km northeast of Toronto and 130 km west of Ottawa, and it follows paved county roads and a provincial highway for 110 km to Barry's Bay.

Fill your lunch bag and your gas tank in Renfrew for you will find few facilities along this route. To get to Renfrew from Toronto, follow Highway 401 east to Highway 41, then drive north to Highway 132 and east to Renfrew. From Ottawa, simply follow Highway 17 to Renfrew.

A Bit of History

It was in 1854 that Peter VanKoughnet, chief commissioner for Crown lands, announced that the unsettled wilds of central Ontario would be thrown open for settlement. A dozen settlement roads would breach the timbered highlands, and along them the land would be free.

The Opeongo Road, which was begun in 1855, was among the first of these settlement roads, though its condition was deplorable for many years. Nevertheless, in its first nine years, the road attracted 300 settlers. Mill villages sprang up at water-power sites and at stopping places and major road junctions. But the rush soon subsided. The harsh climate, the infertile soils, and rumours of starvation sent prospective settlers in search of friendlier regions.

Reflecting upon the road's collapse, a Renfrew journalist wrote in 1900: "Immigrants who came in considerable numbers were disappointed.... Those who had means mostly fled the country, ...those who were poorer had to stay and make the best of it." Those who did stay could scarcely afford major improvements, and so the agricultural landscape today retains the log cabins and barns and even the family traditions of the pioneers who settled it 125 years ago.

Renfrew

The homes, shops, and even the industries of Renfrew have changed little since the turn of the century, and they provide an appropriate atmosphere in which to commence this historical tour. Enter Renfrew on Highway 17B, follow it to Arthur Street and then turn east to the McDougall mill and museum. The mill was built of stone fired locally by one John McDougall in 1857. On the second floor are nineteenth-century clothing and furniture, while the basement houses an unusual collection of early farm tools and the main floor displays a miscellaneous collection of local artifacts. The museum is open daily during the summer and has picnic tables located beside the scenic gorge of the Bonnechere River.

From the mill, follow Raglan Street south through the main business district. Many of the commercial blocks were built around the turn of the century by wealthy lumbermen.

Renfrew to Dacre

From Raglan Street, turn right onto Opeongo Road, which follows the original alignment west for 3 km to its junction with Highway 132. Turn left along the highway, and after less than a kilometre turn left again onto a dirt road and drive 2 km to Ferguslea. Once a busy village of hotels providing rest for weary travellers, Ferguslea contains today only a handful of early homes, a couple of them log cabins.

Continue through Ferguslea, drive 1 km to rejoin Highway 132, and turn left. From this junction to its intersection with Highway 41, about 20 km west, Highway 132 has buried the winding old road beneath a layer of asphalt. But the landscape is little changed. The terrain is still rugged, the swamps frequent. The few farms along here were small, and today the log barns and weathered houses peer from fields that are overgrown and forgotten. Occasionally, a new house has been built upon one of the old farm lots.

About 8 km from Ferguslea a small collection of buildings marks the site of another former road village, this one with the very Irish name of Shamrock. Even before the road was built, a band of Irish settled here, chased out of Ireland by the killer potato famines of the 1840s.

At 3 km beyond Ferguslea, turn left onto County Road 34. Here you leave the Opeongo Road for a 22-km side trip through a landscape of mountains, forests, and bush farms. After 14 km of twisting road, you will come to Mount St. Patrick Roman Catholic Church, its slender steeple reflecting the sun. Mount St. Patrick was originally a mill village, and it served as the agency headquarters for the Opeongo Road. Here the prospective settlers could meet the road agent and then select their free lots.

Although the village is little more than a string of houses straddling the road, it contains an interesting variety of early building styles. Three of the houses display an unusual turn-of-the-century flat-top roof, while the church itself dates from 1869. As you continue through the village, you will pass the one-time general store, which is now a tearoom.

About 1 km beyond Mount St. Patrick, turn right at a T-intersection. Here, the broad flat lowland of the Ottawa Valley halts abruptly at the looming form of the Black Donald Mountains—a great granite ridge with peaks that soar more than 300 m above the lowlands. For 7 km the road winds past the foot of these peaks and through a valley of log barns and cabins, until it comes back to the Opeongo Road itself and to the village of Dacre.

Dacre

The first impression of Dacre is that of a ghost town. Nearly half of the buildings on the main street lie unused or weathered. Dacre was once a stopover village at two important crossroads, and the four corners of the intersection each housed hotels. Today only one remains, that on the southwest corner.

Side Trip to Balaclava

Near Dacre there lies the little sawmill village of Balaclava—a virtual museum piece with its picturesque mill and handful of old buildings. To visit Balaclava, turn north from Dacre onto Highway 513 and drive 2 km. Here, gathered about a weedy mill pond at the outlet from Constant Lake, stand a sawmill, a blacksmith's shop, a store, and a hotel, all of which have changed little since the pioneer days. The massive wooden mill was built by Duncan

Balaclava's picturesque buildings are reflected in the village millpond.

Ferguson in 1855, before the Opeongo Road was opened, and it continued to be driven by the waters of the creek right up to the late 1960s. Its flume, burner, and machinery all remain in place. Sadly, no agency has come forward to preserve this unique piece of early Ontario for future generations.

Dacre to Brudenell

Return to Dacre and continue west on Highway 132. After 1 km you will come to an intersection with Highway 41. Turn right onto Highway 41, drive 1.5 km, and then turn left onto a side road.

The Opeongo here follows a municipal road which, although it has been straightened and asphalted, still retains many of its pioneer curves and bumps. For 10 km it winds along the foot of the lofty Black Donald Mountains. Bordering the road are dense woodlots and rugged pastures; and, in the small clearings, pioneer farms with their string barns, a style unique to this region. At the first crossroads you will see an outstanding example of this barn style. Four attached log barns enclose the small barnyard near the original log cabin, which was built by the pioneering Davidsons. Their descendants now occupy a newer dwelling. There are other string barns along this road, but they are smaller, and few enclose the barnyard so completely. Fewer still remain in the family of the original pioneers.

High in the mountains lies a settlement which failed. As the lands along the Opeongo filled, branch roads were pushed into the high mountain gulches. There, the soils were at their worst, and many of these side settlements were abandoned. One was Newfoundout. If you wish to make a side trip to look at it, turn left at the Davidson farm onto a rugged dirt trail. After 5 km you will see the collapsing shells of half a dozen log cabins and barns lying amid the rugged terrain that defeated the settlement's pioneers. This side trip takes you up the steep mountainside, so it is best avoided in wet weather.

Continuing on your main route, the road wanders along the foot of the mountains and into a pocket of relatively productive soil. Here, a rural settlement known as Clontarf sprang up, and many of its buildings are still intact.

At McDonalds Mountain, the road begins its long climb to the summit. As you grind slowly up the hill, the roadside drops away. Below you shimmer the waters of Lake Clear. Beyond the lake the fields and forests of the Ottawa Valley roll into the distance until they reach the Gatineau Hills of Quebec, 70 km away. Geology books will tell you that the Ottawa Valley is a huge block of rock that cracked away from the adjacent rock and sank. The Gatineaus and the Black Donalds are the rocks that held firm. The land in between them is still sinking today. You may hear your Ottawa friends tell of their earthquakes. This is the reason.

For the next 10 km the road rollercoasts over the lofty peaks. Even here, pioneers tried to wrest their fortunes from the rocky ground. Again, many of their log buildings still stand. After about 6 km you will come to the former Vanbrugh school, now a private residence. It is one of the few log schoolhouses in Ontario that is still on its original site.

This section of road joins Highway 512 at a T-intersection. Turn left, and after 1 km you will come to a startlingly modern town, Foymount. Built after the Second World War, this was a federal radar town. Here modern homes, apartments, and even a recreation hall and library, line curving suburbanlike streets. Now that the base is closed, most of the houses are empty.

From Foymount continue west on Highway 512. Here the Opeongo Road swings back from the crest of the mountains to wind over the highland plateau. Although lofty rock outcroppings still peer down, the pockets of soil between them are wider and deeper; the fields are larger and the farms more numerous. Then, 10 km from Foymount, at the road's only junction with a sister colonization road, you will come to the partial ghost town of Brudenell.

Brudenell

The Peterson Colonization Road began several hundred kilometres to the west, on Lake Muskoka, and wound its way through forest and over rock to link with the Opeongo. The intersection quickly sprouted several hotels and stores, and Brudenell became one of the road's earliest villages. But as road traffic diminished and farm families moved away, Brudenell fell into a decline from which it never recovered.

At the southeast corner of the intersection sits an old store, a small portion of which is in use as a residence; across from it is an empty shop. Beside the store is Costello's Hotel. With its elaborate wraparound porch, it was the grandest hotel in town—and still is, for it has remained almost unaltered. The porch, the clapboard, and the shutters are still there, though the paint is worn and peeling.

At Brudenell, Highway 512 follows the Peterson Road north. But your route continues straight ahead. Beyond the intersection is the Brudenell church; and beyond the church on the left is a side road leading to Rockingham.

Side Trip to Rockingham

If you wish to make a side trip to this pioneer village, follow the side road for 4 km and then fork right. After a further 2 km, the road descends into the gully of Rockingham Creek.

Rockingham sits nestled in this wooded hollow, its rustic pioneer buildings little changed, its simple wooden church the oldest on this trip. Rockingham dates from 1859, when John Watson led a band of English colonists to a mill site on the Peterson Road. The village grew quickly and soon contained a

The pioneer village of Rockingham nestles in a mountain valley.

grist mill, a sawmill, several stores, taverns, and hotels, and St. Leonard's Church. Many of these buildings still remain, including the church, though it is no longer in use. It is one of the few churches in Ontario that was built in the board-and-batten style. Fortunately, the far-sighted residents of Rockingham still preserve it, and in doing so preserve the heritage of Ontario.

Brudenell to Barry's Bay

Continuing west from Brudenell along the Opeongo, the road enters its most truly pioneer state. For the next 10 km the terrain is rugged, the farms few. Most of the old farmsteads retain their early log barns, and some their log homes. Here too the road becomes narrower, the curves and hills steeper. But all too soon the road emerges from its pioneer past and stops at Highway 60. Only 3 km to the left lies Barry's Bay, a lakeside lumber town and the heart of Canada's first Polish colony.

Since Barry's Bay had more locational advantages than the other towns on the Opeongo Road, it grew larger and stayed that way. Its position on Kamaniskeg Lake meant that logs could be

The wooden water tower still stands at Barry's Bay.

floated in from much of the extensive Madawaska River watershed, an area particularly rich in pine. Barry's Bay became a busy sawmill town, greatly increasing in activity when lumber baron J. R. Booth built his railway from Ottawa to Georgian Bay, passing through Barry's Bay.

During this period the Poles began to arrive. Between 1864 and 1895 more than 300 Poles migrated to Canada to settle the Opeongo Road and nearby lands. But the harsh conditions caused many of them to give up farming, and they moved to Barry's Bay and to Wilno, a nearby village, where they engaged in lumbering. Wilno is named after a town in Poland and although smaller than Barry's Bay, it remains the cultural focus of the Polish community. More than a century later, the people here preserve the language and the folkways of their pioneer ancestors. The village, with its twin-spired cathedral, stands 8 km east on Highway 60.

Many buildings in Barry's Bay date from its lumber days. Look in particular for the Balmoral Hotel, an early lumbermen's hotel, and for the old red railway station, now a senior citizen's centre. This building is the oldest J. R. Booth station still standing, a rare find, with its wooden railway water tower.

After your long drive with neither refreshment stop nor picnic site, you will appreciate the town's other features. Set at the junction of two modern provincial highways, 60 and 62, Barry's Bay caters to the travelling public and has a selection of stores, restaurants, and picnic facilities. For your return journey to Renfrew, Highway 60 east is the quickest route.

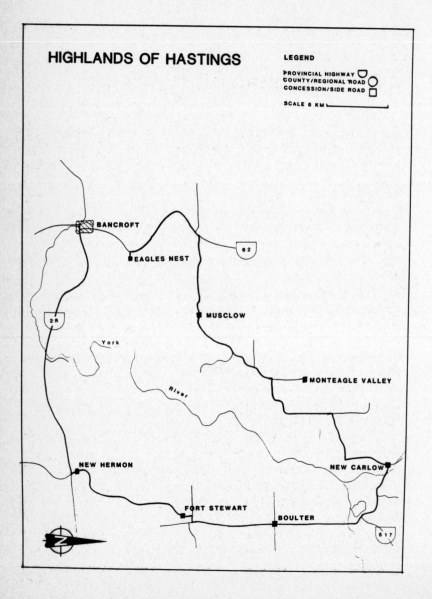

HIGHLANDS OF HASTINGS

LEGEND

PROVINCIAL HIGHWAY
COUNTY/REGIONAL ROAD
CONCESSION/SIDE ROAD

SCALE 5 KM

BANCROFT

EAGLES NEST

62

28

York

MUSCLOW

River

MONTEAGLE VALLEY

NEW HERMON

NEW CARLOW

FORT STEWART

BOULTER

517

17   Highlands of Hastings

Between Toronto and Ottawa, in the north part of a county called
Hastings, there is a remote community of mountain people and
glorious scenery that is matched only by America's Appalachia.
This backroads trip takes you through the region on a circular
route that begins in Bancroft, 220 km northeast of Toronto, and
follows a chain of gravelled mountain roads for about 80 km.
Although the route has no facilities other than general stores (and
even they are few), you will never be more than half an hour's
drive from Bancroft, where there are restaurants, motels, and a
full range of services.

This is a tour that will appeal to the rockhound in particular,
for the hills around Bancroft have become internationally known
for their gemstones. Each summer Bancroft hosts a rockhounds'
"gemboree." The beauty of the hills is a naturalist's delight, while
the many pioneer homes, barns, and general stores offer much for
photographer and historian alike.

If you are coming from the Toronto area, you can reach
Bancroft via Highways 401, 115, and 28. From Ottawa, follow
Highway 17b to 60 and 62.

Although two good provincial highways bisect the area, the
Highlands of Hastings remain remote. Bancroft has only 3,000
residents, and its nearest neighbour of comparable size, Madoc, is
more than 70 km away. The highlands themselves are a high,
rugged plateau deep in the Canadian Shield, surrounded by the
deep, spectacular canyons of the Madawaska, Mississippi, and
York rivers. Here you will find some of southern Ontario's finest
scenery and some of its hardiest people.

A Bit of History

Settlement came late to north Hastings, and with good reason. Although loggers had swept up the Madawaska Valley and decimated much of the area's forests during the early decades of the nineteenth century, settlers had been kept at bay by the poor soils, the swamps, and the forbidding rocky highlands. It was not until the 1850s and 1860s, when the government held out the twin carrots of roads and free land, that pioneer farmers finally began to cultivate the land.

The first of the colonization roads, the Hastings, barged straight up the centre of the county. It was begun in 1855 and finished by about 1860. Soon, other branch roads were opened, including the Mississippi Road to the old Perth settlements in the east, the Monck Road to the west, and, across the north, the Peterson Road.

The site that would be Bancroft had an advantage from the very beginning. Not only was it the junction of the Hastings and the Monck colonization roads, but it possessed excellent water power—a steep falls on the York River. As Bancroft boomed as a lumbering town, the hills began to fill with settlers. But when the trees disappeared, so did the lumbermen. However, the area had one more natural resource that would help retain its prosperity— minerals. In the rocks lay deposits of graphite, mica, and uranium, the latter a discovery that seemed certain to bring lingering prosperity to an otherwise depressed area. Today, however, the uranium mines are shut. The region is one of the most isolated in southern Ontario, though its beauty and its abundance of semiprecious gemstones have brought some tourism.

Bancroft

Bancroft began in 1879 when the Bronson Lumber Company moved its headquarters to the falls on the York River. Mills, churches, and hotels quickly sprang up by the falls and around the intersection of the two settlement roads. Then, in 1900, the Central Ontario Railway rumbled into town, followed in 1903 by the Irondale, Bancroft, and Ottawa Railway.

Although many of the original stores have been replaced or been covered with plastic and plate glass, Bancroft retains a frontier appearance. One of the town's most attractive and historic buildings is the Bancroft Hotel, built in 1899, which still provides

Bancroft's main street has a frontier boomtown appearance.

rooms and meals. On Railway Street, one block north, is the Bancroft Museum. Its centrepiece is a large log cabin built for the Bronson company in 1853 and moved to town as a centennial project in 1967. Close to it is the Central Ontario Railway station, which has been well preserved.

Bancroft to New Hermon

Leave Bancroft east on Highway 28, which follows the route of the Mississippi Colonization Road. After 3 km look for the Princess Sodalite Mine on the left. A rare decorative blue stone, sodalite is found in only a few locations throughout the world. This once-busy mine is now a commercial tourist operation. For a fee, you can prowl for samples in the quarry, or you can buy them in the store.

Continue east for another 4 km to the York River. If you want to do some more rockhounding, you can take a side trip, turning left down a rough dirt trail on the opposite side of the bridge. After 0.75 km, watch for a footpath leading to the water, where you will find a quantity of magnetite. About 0.5 km farther along the road, you can search amongst the talus of an old mine for fluorescent chondrodite, spinal, and wollastonite. And if you continue a further 1.5 km and then fork right and carry on for another 1 km, you will come to an abandoned mine where you can find cancrinite, fluorescent hackmanite, and possibly small quantities of sodalite.

Your main route continues east along Highway 28. As you emerge from the York River Valley, you will see the Hastings mountains looming ahead. A drive of 8 km brings you into their foothills and to the junction of the Hermon Road (originally known as the New Carlow Road), which was built to link the Peterson Colonization Road in the north with the Mississippi Road. At its junction with the old Mississippi Road (a little to the south of today's Highway 28) was the village of Hermon, which has long since vanished. But its successor, New Hermon, still exists only a couple of kilometres from the old village.

Drive north from Highway 28 and almost immediately you will come to New Hermon's simple frame homes, clustered at a disused crossroads. You may look twice at the red schoolhouse, for a hand-painted sign proclaims it to be a Mennonite meeting house. The latest wave of settlers, a small group of Mennonites, moved here from Kitchener when land prices there proved too high. Don't strain to look for horses and buggies, though, for this group is not Old Order.

New Hermon to Fort Stewart

Keep right at the fork and continue north from the schoolhouse. Here the Carlow Road twists its way into the hills, passing the scattered clearings of pioneer farms. After 5 km it arrives at the breezy summit of a high plateau and at the hamlet of Fort Stewart. This hamlet was an early stopping place on the road, and its hotels provided rest and nourishment for weary stagecoach travellers. The Stewart part of its name derives from an early hotel keeper, the Fort from the height of land the hamlet occupies. Although the hotels are gone, the village still contains early frame homes and a white-frame former store, which is striking in its simplicity.

Fort Stewart to New Carlow

Drive north for 1 km to a T-intersection. Turn right and after half a kilometre you will come to a view worth lingering over. Here the

Fort Stewart's general store.

plateau plunges 100 m into the valley of the Little Mississippi River, while beyond the valley another range of forested mountains rolls towards the horizon.

Turn left at the intersection and continue on your route, which follows the top of the plateau for 5 km. The northern peak of the plateau is crowned by the village of Boulter, which was named after an early county warden. Boulter began as a roadside stopping place for travellers and developed into a farm-service village. With its century-old Presbyterian church and still-active country store, the village continues to fulfil this role.

North of Boulter, the scenery shifts dramatically once more. As the York River Valley opens at your feet, the road glides down the slope of the plateau and into a swampy lowland. Here it crosses over the York River, which is meandering northeastward to the mighty Madawaska.

About 1.5 km north of the bridge, look for a narrow gravel road to the left. This short lane leads to one of the few lakes that are tucked into these highlands, and to the area's only municipal

The hamlet of New Carlow sits at the foot of the mountains.

beach and picnic ground. If you have packed a lunch, this is the place to have it, for there are no other lakeside parks on this route.

Continuing north from the park, the road bends westward to complete half of the circle trip. Rockhounds should look for a bush trail on the right 2.5 km from the park exit. It leads to the site of the once-busy mining town of Burgess, one of Canada's leading corundum producers during the early decades of this century. Although the trail is rugged, it is passable, and after 1.5 km it will bring you to the collapsing buildings of Burgess. On the hill behind them, in the old pits, you may find some crystals of corundum. But be sure to take a pick and hammer, for corundum is one of the world's hardest minerals.

Back on the road, you will come, after 3 km, to a T-intersection. Here is the picturesque hamlet of New Carlow, which was once a busy crossroads village. Its store, school, and shops are closed now, but the frame buildings still cluster about the intersection and dot the wooded hillside over Papineau Creek.

192

New Carlow to Musclow

Turn left and cross the bridge over Papineau Creek. The road now climbs out of the valley and onto another mountaintop plateau. Here, again, the level and relatively fertile soils have sustained a small farming community. At the first intersection look for an old log school, now boarded up. It is one of the few schools on the backroads of Ontario that has not been removed or in some way altered. It sits as it was left.

Beyond the school the road bends right and descends into a dark, swampy valley, then mounts yet another plateau, which has the curious name of Monteagle Valley (the Monteagle part being named after an English lord). Here you come to a T-intersection, where you should turn left. As you drive south from the intersection, look to the left for views across the valleys of Quirk Creek and York River to the plateaus and mountains which you have just travelled. Here the landscape changes once more as the road twists through the rugged foothills and descends through a chain of ravines to the flat sand plains that lie north of Bancroft.

At 6 km from your last turn, the road bends to the right and meets another T-intersection. Turn left and continue straight for 2 km to yet another T-intersection, where you turn right. Throughout this area, the mountainsides have been dissected by the rivers and creeks that are slowly eroding their way into the plateau. Tucked into the steep, narrow gulches are the small bush farms and the simple frame homes of the mountain folk who settled the Highlands.

Nestled in one of these peaceful gullies, 3 km from the last T-intersection, is the hamlet of Musclow, which took its name from a pioneer family. Musclow began life as a busy service village at a once-important road junction, but it ceased to serve this purpose when the road that led east to Fort Stewart was closed. The buildings, however, still guard the intersection—the grey wooden church built in the 1880s, the school that was later used as an Orange Lodge, the general store, and several homes. A solid pioneer log barn and several smaller log outbuildings dot a field opposite the village and provide prime subject material for the landscape photographer.

Turn right at the village corner and follow the Musclow–Greenview Road west for another 6 km. This road descends

View from Eagles Nest lookout.

through forested ravines and emerges onto a wide, sandy plain. Here, at the intersection with Highway 62, you have come almost full circle and are 7 km north of Bancroft. And here, if you want, you can end your day's outing by taking two side trips.

Rockhounds' Side Trip

To locate a deposit of amazonite, the attractive, green semi-precious stone, turn right onto Highway 62. Drive 2 km to the first road on the right, follow it for 2 km, and then fork right and park by the abandoned railway line. Walk south along the railbed for 600 paces and then climb the hill on the right. Here, in the talus heaps of mines that have been closed since the 1920s, you can find fist-sized chunks of amazonite.

This area harbours many other rock-collecting sites. The Treasure Shop in Bancroft sells a guidebook which gives their locations.

194

Clifftop Side Trip

This side trip leads to a high lookout. Turn left onto Highway 62, drive for 3.5 km, and then follow the signs to the Eagles Nest Park. From this vantage point, the wide valley of the York River opens at your feet. The cliff itself is an outlier of the plateau from which you have just descended. Looking north, you can easily discern the high plateau wall as it winds its way along the York Valley.

Bancroft lies just 3 km south of the park, and from there you can make your way homeward.

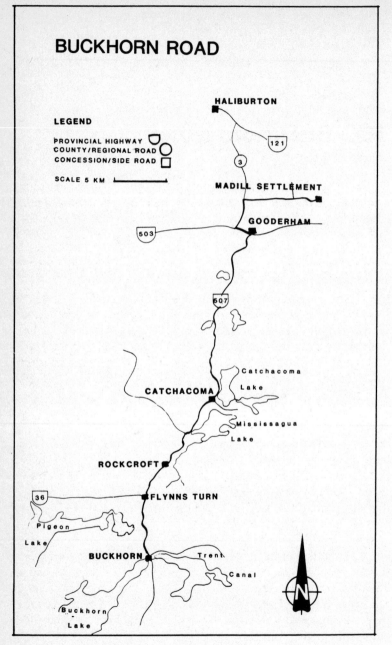

BUCKHORN ROAD

HALIBURTON

LEGEND

PROVINCIAL HIGHWAY
COUNTY/REGIONAL ROAD
CONCESSION/SIDE ROAD

SCALE 5 KM

121

3

MADILL SETTLEMENT

GOODERHAM

503

507

Catchacoma
Lake

CATCHACOMA

Mississagua
Lake

ROCKCROFT

36

FLYNNS TURN

Pigeon
Lake

BUCKHORN

Trent

Canal

Buckhorn
Lake

N

18 Buckhorn Road

Of the more than one hundred highways on Ontario's provincial road map, Highway 507 is the only route to give the warning: "Road very narrow and winding. Use caution." Not only does this highway follow the route of a century-old colonization road, but it retains nearly every curve and hill.

This 48-km trip, one of the shortest of the backroads, starts in Buckhorn village, 30 km north of Peterborough, winds north into the heart of Haliburton County, and ends at the village of Gooderham. Both Buckhorn and Gooderham contain minimal facilities (small take-out restaurants, general stores, and gas stations) so if you need more than you can obtain there, you should do your shopping in Peterborough. To reach your starting point, take Highway 28 north out of Peterborough, and after 10 km take Highway 507. Follow this highway 20 km to Buckhorn.

A Bit of History

To the south of the Trent Canal the terrain is level, the soils deep and fertile. As early as the 1820s colonizer Peter Robinson led 2,000 Irish immigrants into these lush lands. They were followed in the 1830s by English settlers, including authors Susanna Moodie and Catharine Parr Traill. Settlement spread quickly to the shores of a chain of lakes called the Kawarthas, but there it stopped, for the land beyond was bare and infertile.

"Along the northern boundary of the township I have scarcely seen a rougher country," lamented surveyor Theo Clementi in 1864. "Fires have destroyed all that the lumbermen have left." Surveyor William Drennan backed him up: "I regret that I cannot give a favourable report on the quality of the land, much of it being little better than bare rock."

197

The Trent Canal has continual traffic during the summer months.

Nevertheless, the government decided to push one of its colonization roads northward from the river. The hard, granite ridges and the countless swamps proved to be horrendous obstacles, and it was not until 1873 that the road was opened. Since there were only small and scattered pockets of soil, this remained one of the least used of the settlement roads, a characteristic that the road has retained through the years. Save for some crude paving, it is the least improved colonization road in Ontario.

Therein lies its appeal. Although the few bush farms have long vanished and holiday cottages now line the shores of the lakes, the road has changed little. As it twists around granite knobs, over ridges, and through swamps, the young forest closes in from the sides. In some parts, the log roadbed, known as corduroy, pierces the surface. The two or three hours that you require to complete this trip cannot compare to the three days which the pioneers needed, yet along this route you will experience a roadscape close to that which intimidated its early travellers.

Buckhorn

In 1863 John Hall built a small sawmill at the falls on the Trent River which drains Buckhorn Lake into Lower Buckhorn Lake.

He also built a bridge across the rushing river, and for many years the village was known as Hall's Bridge. In 1883 work began on a canal that would link Georgian Bay, northwest of Hall's Bridge, with the Bay of Quinte on Lake Ontario. This canal was not completed until 1920, and by then the timber had all been stripped from the area and the railways were carrying freight faster than steamers could. The canal saw little traffic until the cottage boom struck after the Second World War and yachters discovered the wooded waterway.

Before setting out on your drive, you can park beside the Trent Canal lock and enjoy the scene at Buckhorn's modernized lock station. From the grassy park (which has picnic facilities) you can watch bulky white cabin cruisers ease into the concrete enclosure of the lock and then slowly disappear below the ledge to the level of the lower lake. From here, you can also wander through the village. On the main street, a store, church, schoolhouse, and a few old houses have resisted the cottage wave. Dead-end lanes bear testimony of Hall's ambitious street plan, while atop a knoll of pink granite is the Cody Inn, which dates from the earliest days of tourism.

Buckhorn to Gooderham

From the lock station, drive north on Highway 507. For a little over 6 km this highway shares a roadbed with Highway 36 and is a high-speed route. At Flynns Turn, Highway 36 forks to the left. Your route continues right on Highway 507.

For the next 5 km you pass through an area known as Rockcroft. Here the soil, although stony, was deep and relatively fertile, and this led to the development of one of the Buckhorn Road's few farming communities. Much evidence of this early community has survived, including the Rockcroft church, which is situated 1.5 km north of the turn. This white-frame building, simple in its design as most pioneer churches were, was once the centre of the settlement. Along with the original log cabin that stands beside it, the church now sells antiques and handicrafts. About 2 km farther on, a handful of pioneer farms cluster about a crossroads. But as the road wanders northward, the old bush farms are more scattered, the clearings smaller. These farms have long since ceased to operate, and those which have not been totally abandoned now sprout retirement homes.

The Buckhorn Road leads many cottagers to their lakeside retreats.

At 5 km from the Rockcroft church, the road leaves the last of the farms behind and enters the country of rock and swamp that was so vividly described by the surveyors Clementi and Drennan. Then, 8 km from the Rockcroft church, there suddenly appears in an otherwise unbroken brush a small restaurant and tavern. Behind it lap the waters of Mississagua Lake. Until the late 1960s, this was the site of the Mississagua Landing sawmill—the wooden mill, a few workers' homes, and a post office were all perched on the rocky shore. These buildings have now been replaced by cottages, but some debris lingers yet amid the crevices and under the maple saplings.

Continue north from the tavern and after 2 km look for a small blue on white "boat launch" sign. Follow it to the right along a 2-km bush road, which is maintained by the Ministry of Natural Resources and is passable for all vehicles. At the end of the trail, the ministry has cleared a small park. Developed in conjunction with the boat launch, which is no more than a gravel ramp leading under the water, the little park sits on a quiet bay of Mississagua Lake and is a place to stretch your legs or enjoy your picnic lunch. (If you're not hungry yet, another lakeside park, quieter still, lies near the north end of the road.)

About 2 km from the launch, Highway 507 intersects a side road. Around the intersection is a clearing with a few old buildings. This is the site of the former stopover village known as Catchacoma. The few travellers who ventured along the colonization road found that a day's travel from Hall's Bridge took them no farther than here, where a small log hotel provided them with a straw bed and a hot meal. Today, the name is associated with a store and with a campground 1 km east along the side road on the shores of Catchacoma Lake.

About 1 km north of the abandoned hamlet, the warning on the highway map takes effect. Suddenly the road begins to twist to the right and then back to the left. Rocks and potholes grab at your tires. Craggy granite ridges peer from the woods; between them are small swamps, many with a beaver pond or lodge. After 5 km you will come to the only farm to survive on this stretch of road. Its picturesque log barns and wood-shingle cabin, now disused, overlook the waters of Greens Lake, where the sandy backshore contained enough stone-free soil to support this lonely bush farm. Today, while a couple of ponies graze in the overgrown pastures, campers use the shoreline.

North of the old farm the road resumes its serpentine path. Then, 6 km from Greens Lake, a small dirt road ventures left. This was a link road to the more settled Bobcaygeon Road, 20 km to the west. A few pioneer families settled along this road, but only their clearings (and, in a couple of places, their barns) survive in memory of their hardship.

Continue north and after 3 km watch for another "boat launch" sign. It leads left for a few metres to a lake so small that even the maps do not name it. From this little park, where irises and orchids grow wild in a swamp, you can look across to Greens Mountain, the highest in the area. The park contains a few picnic tables and some pit latrines.

About 2 km north of the park the road bends to the right and suddenly becomes a little straighter and a little wider. As it winds down off the rocklands into the valley of the Irondale River, you will see more rural homes. Here, a pocket of soil comparable to that at Rockcroft attracted a small community of farmers and a network of concession roads. However, most farming activity has long since ceased and the land is now used for country homes. It is in this little valley, at the junction of Highway 503, that Highway 507 ends. Most colonization road junctions gave rise to small villages, and here, where the Buckhorn and Monck roads met, Gooderham grew.

Gooderham

Cross Highway 503 and drive into the village. Although Gooderham was partly scarred by a fire in the 1930s, it has managed to survive much of the modernization and road widening that has defaced many a nineteenth-century village. Most of its early buildings huddle about the main intersection at the foot of the falls from Gooderham Lake.

Gooderham began around 1876 when John Hunter and Anthony Hall used the falls to power sawmills, shingle mills, and the only grist mill in Haliburton County. Later, S. S. Hadley opened a store and Andrew Young started a hotel. The hotel burned in the devastating fire of 1931, while Hunter's second sawmill, also water powered, survived until 1970. Other buildings were luckier; the general store is now Food Town, the Orange Hall still stands at the intersection in its white clapboard simplicity; and there are several frame homes dating from the 1880s. Although the Monck Road once barged through the centre of town, highway improvements have created the bypass that Highway 503 now follows.

On Highway 503 near the junction of Highway 507 there are a couple of fast-food outlets, and a small picnic park has been built along the river. Despite the noise of traffic on busy weekends, this is an attractive picnic site.

The Madill Settlement

Don't return home without visiting the Madill Settlement. The most pleasant way to get there is to drive west from Gooderham on Highway 503 for 1.5 km and turn right; then drive north for almost 3 km and turn right onto South Glamor Lake Road. This was originally called the Bear Lake Road, and it opened the area north of the Monck Road during the 1870s and 1880s.

Follow this road for 5 km to its end (look out for a jog to the

Deserted schoolhouse in the Madill Settlement.

left after 3 km) and here you will find the Madill Settlement. Named after an 1880s pioneer, the settlement consisted of a school and a few log cabins clustered about an intersection. In its abandonment, this is what remains. On one corner, a cabin sags in a field of wild flowers, and beyond it are the collapsed shells of barns; on the opposite corner, the school bell tower peers above a second growth of lilacs and poplars.

The conditions that confronted the Haliburton pioneers, and especially those on the rugged Buckhorn Road, were harsh. Most of their abandoned settlements have long since vanished, or have been replaced by rural homes, so the sight you see at the Madill Settlement is one that you will see in few other places.

If you are returning to Toronto, go back to Highway 503 and follow it west to Highway 35. For eastern Ontario, drive east to Bancroft and then take Highway 62 south. For Ottawa, follow Highway 28 past Bancroft.

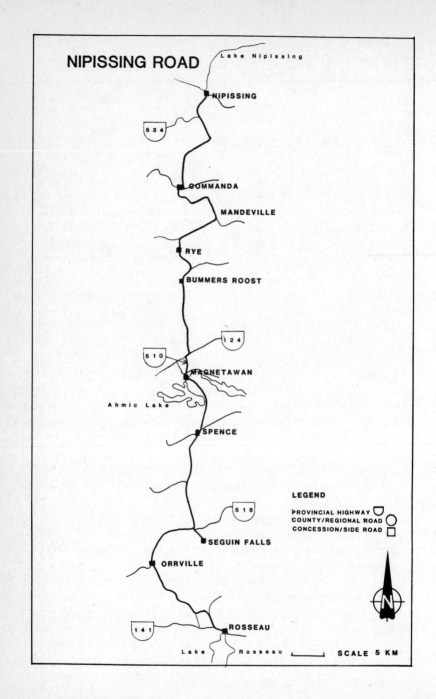

NIPISSING ROAD

Lake Nipissing

■ NIPISSING

534

■ COMMANDA

MANDEVILLE

■ RYE

■ BUMMERS ROOST

124

510

■ MAGNETAWAN

Ahmic Lake

■ SPENCE

518

LEGEND

PROVINCIAL HIGHWAY
COUNTY/REGIONAL ROAD
CONCESSION/SIDE ROAD

■ SEGUIN FALLS

■ ORRVILLE

141

■ ROSSEAU

Lake Rosseau

SCALE 5 KM

N

19 Nipissing Road

The Nipissing Road is Ontario's ghost town trail. Once home to a settlement of hopeful pioneers, it is guarded by their abandoned cabins and weathered barns. The road lies in the District of Parry Sound and winds along 120 km of gravel road from Rosseau on Highway 141 to Nipissing on Highway 534. As the road runs north, it roughly parallels Highway 11, which can be reached by any crossroad. Highway 11 abounds with motels and campgrounds, but if you intend to stay overnight it would be wise to check the Government of Ontario's accommodation booklet.

A ghost town trail has no facilities, so fill your lunch bag and gas tank in Rosseau, especially if you plan a leisurely drive. Magnetawan, halfway along the route, has gas stations, shops, and restaurants, but after that there is nothing until you reach Nipissing. Although the road is gravel, its condition varies. Some stretches are wide and well kept; others are little more than two ruts plunging into dark woods, much as the pioneers might remember it.

What does the Nipissing Road offer? If you are an artist or photographer, the empty cabins and log barns offer unusual and rugged images. If an explorer or collector, empty cellar holes and vanished village sites could replenish your supply of old bottles or square nails. But leave the metal detector at home, for most of what is abandoned is also heavily overgrown. You are unlikely to find old coins.

A Bit of History

Poorly conceived government schemes are not just a modern-day phenomenon. The Nipissing Road was one of a network of colonization roads devised by the government of the Province of Canada in 1850 to settle the virgin uplands between the Ottawa

River and Georgian Bay. Although these lands were touted as a Utopia for land-hungry immigrants, the roads were built mainly to help the great lumber companies gain access to their distant lands.

By 1877 the Nipissing Road was open between Lake Rosseau and Lake Nipissing, and the first of the thrice-weekly stages rattled into the new village of Nipissing. But with the forests laid waste and the fertile Canadian prairies ready for settlement, the Nipissing Road was doomed almost from the start. Settlers streamed away. Behind them they left overgrown bush farms and vacant villages. Only four settlements prospered, and today they are still regional centres: Rosseau and Nipissing, the centres of modest farm and cottage economies; Magnetawan, born of a long-forgotten canal; and Commanda, which has one of Ontario's most unusual general stores.

Rosseau

Clinging to the granite shores of Lake Rosseau, the white-frame houses and shops of Rosseau village deserve a look before you start on your drive. A century ago Rosseau harboured the fleet of steamers that plied the bays and channels of Lakes Muskoka, Rosseau, and Joseph. Settlers and businessmen disembarked here to follow the Parry Sound Road west or the Nipissing Road north. Tourists soon followed, and today Rosseau, with its population of 225, survives primarily as a summer cottage town. Of the houses, stores, and churches that line the little town's few streets, most were built by pioneer labour and they still display their clapboard construction. Best known is the white clapboard general store, built in 1875, which stands at the corner of River Road and the Parry Sound Road.

Before you leave Rosseau, you can have a morning coffee at one of two snack bars, G C's or the Rosseau Garage; the latter has a gas pump, and both are near the main intersection. Across the street, in the general store, you can stock up a lunch bag with cheese, fruit, bread, and canned drinks.

Rosseau to Orrville

Leave Rosseau along Highway 141 north. After 1 km or so, just past a small pioneer cemetery on the left, you will come to an intersection with an unnumbered gravel road. This is the starting point of the Nipissing Road and the site of a village called Ashdown. Named after a pioneer family, Ashdown could once claim a store, a school, an Orange Hall, a blacksmith's shop, and a hotel. Today, nothing remains except for vague cellar holes and rotting lumber.

Turn right onto the gravel road and drive north for 1 km to a fork. Take the left branch. (The original Nipissing Road followed the right branch, but it soon degenerates into a bush trail that is suitable only for hikers or winter snowmobilers.) Follow the left branch 10 km to Orrville, keeping right at the two intersections you encounter on the way. This takes you through the Turtle Valley, where fields of hay and oats bend in the breeze and beef cattle graze lazily in their pastures.

One of the first buildings you will see in Orrville is Campbell's blacksmith shop. Popular with local artists and photographers, this frame shop with its hand-painted sign dates from the turn of the century. Its doors, however, have been closed for several years. Apart from this, there is little to pause for in the village, for modern retirement homes are rapidly replacing Orrville's pioneer buildings.

Orrville to Seguin Falls

At the stop sign beside the general store, turn right and follow Highway 518 east. Here young forests flank the road, reclaiming the exhausted soils of the pioneer fields; surrounded now by shrunken clearings are many pioneer cabins (still lived in) which display the frame or shake construction of their pioneer builders.

After 11 km, Highway 518 meets a T-intersection, bringing you back onto the original Nipissing Road. Although your route lies north, to the left, a side trip right leads to the ghost town of Seguin Falls. To take this side trip, stay on Highway 518 for a few metres until it bends left, then follow the gravel road straight ahead for 1 km. As the road twists around rock outcrops, vacant cabins peer from their granite perches. And then you come into Seguin Falls: a red brick schoolhouse, long abandoned, which is now a private residence; and just beyond it, a white two-storey frame hotel and a cluster of weathered wooden houses, which mark the centre of the one-time village.

Seguin Falls owes its birth to lumber king J. R. Booth. In 1895 this Ottawa millionaire acquired extensive timber limits in Algonquin Park, 160 km to the east. To tap his new riches he extended his Booth Line Railway into the park and then to Georgian Bay. By providing the shortest link between the Upper Great Lakes and the Atlantic, he quickly captured the lucrative grain trade. For more than three decades, puffing steam engines strained under the load of grain, lumber, manufactured goods, and passengers. At the Nipissing Road crossing, the Spence Lumber Company erected a mill, and this marked the beginning of Seguin Falls. The settlement grew to have a population of 500, with a general store, a post office, shops, a church, a school, and the King George Hotel. The town prospered until 1933, when a trestle in Algonquin Park was washed out and the rail traffic dropped drastically. During the following years, as the timber vanished and the farms failed, the town's residents moved away. Finally, in 1954, the line was closed and the tracks lifted. When the hotel and its confectionery shut their doors forever, Seguin Falls became a ghost town.

As you photograph the many buildings in Seguin Falls, remember that most are privately owned and that some are used seasonally. Two "musts" include a glass gravity-feed gas pump in front of the hotel (a legacy of the early auto era) and the picturesque three-storey frame mansion which stands beside the hotel.

Seguin Falls to Spence

Turn around at Seguin Falls, return to Highway 518, cross it, and continue north. For the next 25 km the road is wide and well maintained, although still gravel. Here it passes farmsteads and villages—once bustling, now dead.

After 5 km you will see on the right the St. James pioneer cemetery. With its fading white limestone headstones, some dating from 1876, the cemetery marks the site of the one-time village of Dufferin Bridge. A few metres beyond lies the Dufferin Methodist Cemetery, which tells a sad story. On the weathered tombstones of James and Janet Morden are the names of six children, their ages between one and a half years and ten years, who died between January 14 and January 19, 1902. The Ashley stone nearby lists four more children who died in the same period.

About 2 km farther on, the Nipissing intersects the Inholmes Road. This was another branch colonization route, and it leads west over scenic hilltops for 15 km to the Broadbent church and the Hurdville mill, a photographer's side trip if you have the time.

This gravestone in Dufferin Bridge cemetery records the deaths of six children who all died during one week in 1902.

The Inholmes intersection also marks the site of the one-time village of North Seguin, again a site with no trace of its former activity.

Then follows a scene not unlike that which awed the Nipissing Road's first pioneer travellers. The road plunges into a dark, forbidding forest. Trees close in from both sides and meet overhead. Through this tunnel the trail twists one way and then back upon itself; it lurches over granite outcroppings and slogs through muddy swamps. And after 6 km it brings you to Spence.

Spence

After Seguin Falls, Spence is the Nipissing Road's most extensive ghost town, described as follows by an early traveller: "At the junction of the Ryerson Road and Nipissing Road is Spence post office, a good store, boarding house, and public school." The boarding house became Simpson's Hotel, and Spence acquired a church and a population of 150.

Abandoned pioneer cabins border the Nipissing Road near the ghost town of Spence.

Today, the shells and foundations of the buildings lie buried under weeds or peer from among young trees. Most cluster about the more southerly of the village's two intersections. It is the other intersection, 1 km north, that was the site of the store, church, and hotel. The hotel has been moved to Huntsville's pioneer village, and now only a part of a picket fence tells that anything at all stood at the crossroads. Nevertheless, Spence has revived slightly. The pressure for new country lots has brought four new homes to the old village lots.

Spence to Magnetawan

North of Spence the road suddenly widens and enters a pastoral farming area. On the left lie the waters of Ahmic Lake, a bulge in the Magnetawan River. For 10 km rolling green fields and solid barns mingle with forested hills and overgrown pastures as the road leads along the valley's flat floor to the homes and stores of Magnetawan.

Magnetawan

Unlike the ghosts of Spence and Seguin Falls, Magnetawan is very much alive, with a population of about 230. Solid frame homes line the village's half-dozen streets, while shops and restaurants cluster by the bridge over the Magnetawan River. In a park beside the bridge is a historical plaque commemorating the story of the Nipissing Road.

Magnetawan grew quickly during the nineteenth century, for it was situated at the junction of the Nipissing Road, the Ahmic Road, and the Magnetawan Canal. Settlers and loggers flowed in and turned the valley from forest to farm and mill. In 1925 the area's first hydro-electric plant whirred into life, powered by the falls on the river. Although commercial traffic on the canal ceased in the early 1930s, and the hydro plant fell silent soon after, Magnetawan continued to prosper because of the cottage and recreation trade.

The old hydro plant, with its original generators still in place, is now a museum. It stands a few paces east of the Nipissing Road on Highway 520. The town offers a selection of services. You can dine in the Schmeler Hotel north of the bridge or take a quick, unlicensed meal in a restaurant simply called June's, which stands beside the bridge. Magnetawan also has a general store, a hardware store, gas stations, and, beside the museum, a liquor store. If by this time you have filled your day and wish to spend the night in the area, two provincial highways, 520 and 124, lead east 22 km to motels on Highway 11, while Highway 124 also leads west 56 km to Highway 69.

Magnetawan to Commanda

Leave Magnetawan north on Highway 520 and turn right onto Highway 510 (which, at 4 km, is one of the shortest in the provincial network). Cross Highway 124 and after 1 km turn left beside a cemetery onto a gravel road, as usual, unnumbered. Here the road again is as the pioneer stage travellers might have known it. The forest is tall and dark, and the dirt ruts bend and twist around each obstacle. There are no clearings, no old cabins. So sparse was the soil that settlers shunned this area completely. Why should they settle here when the deep flat soils of the Distress Valley lay just a few kilometres east? Despite its "pioneer" condition, the road is passable, if slow.

After 18 km there appears a clearing and a white-frame house. This is the site of a one-time village, Mecunoma, and its famous hotel with the colourful name Bummers Roost. The original hotel burned in 1926 and today's house was built on the hotel foundations by T. R. Russel, son of the original hotelier.

For the next 2 km the Nipissing Road is impassable. So take the road right for 1.5 km and then the first road left, which again has no number. After 2 km you will rejoin the original alignment at the abandoned hamlet of Rye. Gone now are the store, post office, and log hotels—some sources say as many as four—and Rye today consists of a brick school (now a residence) and, 1.5 km north of that, an intersection full of old foundations. Its most picturesque building, a white-frame church, survived into the 1970s, but private owners then demolished it.

Four bush farms still guard the next kilometre of road, until once more the route becomes deserted and unusable. Follow a one-time concession road right for 6 km to a T-intersection with the Mandeville Road. Then turn left for 3 km to another T-intersection. Here you pass through an abandoned rural settlement, which was called Mandeville. The land is low and swampy, and a young forest closes in overhead. Bush barns, long abandoned, are collapsed, and their overgrown clearings are indiscernible from the road.

At the second intersection again turn left. Once more you emerge onto a rocky upland; the hills, however, are steeper. After winding through a mature forest and past a pair of marginal farms, you will suddenly come to the crest of a knoll. Below lies the Commanda Valley. As you descend the valley to Commanda village, the road merges imperceptibly with the Nipissing Road.

Commanda

Named for a local Ojibwa chief, Commanda is a small cluster of houses at the intersection of Highway 522. Here, in 1885, James Arthur built the area's first general store. It was larger than most for a pioneer village—two storeys high, with a double porch and extensions to each side. Arthur distinguished his store with elaborate flourishes to its fretwork. While most such buildings would have been replaced or severely altered, the Commanda store has survived five ownerships intact. In 1980 the Gurd Township and Area Historical Corporation purchased the building and refurbished it as a turn-of-the-century general store, and in 1982 opened it as a living museum. You may find it the single most photogenic building on this road trip and one of the most colourful in Ontario.

The unusual general store at Commanda is now a living museum.

Commanda to Nipissing

From the store follow Highway 522 east, and after less than 1 km turn left onto an unpaved road. Commanding a high, gravelly ridge is the Nipissing Road's only surviving farm community. Although stony, the soils here are deep and they have allowed the farmers to grow hay and to graze beef cattle. Most of the frame homes and plank barns have been little altered from pioneer days, though their occupants now supplement their incomes with off-farm jobs. At 5 km from Highway 522 your route swings east away from an abandoned Nipissing Road to pursue a concession road. After another 5 km turn left at Beatty Lake and continue 3 km to Highway 534. Turn right and follow the highway around a steep mountain and past modern rural residences into the road's final village, Nipissing.

Nipissing remains small, though modern cottages and retirement homes now mingle with the pioneer church, school, and houses. During the village's short-lived heyday as a busy stagecoach terminus, stores and hotels sprouted at each corner. Today they are gone. No longer does Nipissing provide liquid refreshment for the weary traveller. But then no longer does the journey from Rosseau take a full week as it did a century ago.

Nipissing marks the end of your route. From here you can follow Highway 534 east for 14 km to Highway 11 and then drive north 30 km to North Bay. This modern-day finish to your Nipissing Road trip has a number of restaurants, pubs, and, most important, a place to sleep.

213

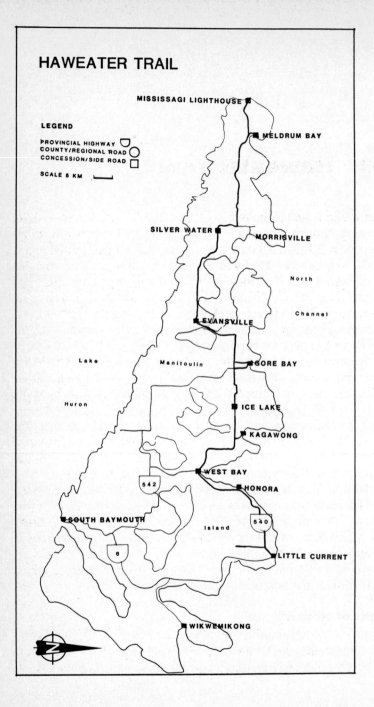

HAWEATER TRAIL

MISSISSAGI LIGHTHOUSE

MELDRUM BAY

LEGEND

PROVINCIAL HIGHWAY
COUNTY/REGIONAL ROAD
CONCESSION/SIDE ROAD

SCALE 5 KM

SILVER WATER

MORRISVILLE

North

Channel

EVANSVILLE

Lake

Manitoulin

GORE BAY

Huron

ICE LAKE

KAGAWONG

WEST BAY

542

HONORA

540

SOUTH BAYMOUTH

Island

6

LITTLE CURRENT

WIKWEMIKONG

20 Haweater Trail

Manitoulin Island is the world's largest freshwater island—80 km in length, though it narrows in places to just 2 km in width. It has more than 20 inland lakes, as well as one of Ontario's longest dead-end highways, Highway 540, which is the backroad for this trip. From Little Current at the island's eastern end, this road follows the cliffs and coves to Manitoulin's western tip. The route is 100 km long and paved, and passes towns and villages with gas stations, grocery stores, and restaurants.

There are only two approaches to Manitoulin Island. One is via Highway 6 south from the Trans-Canada Highway 17, 70 km west of Sudbury. This is a route noted for its high scenic passes across the ridge of rugged white quartzite which is known as the La Cloche Mountains.

The other approach is on Ontario's newest and largest ferry, the *Chi-Cheemaun*. It leaves Tobermory (300 km northwest of Toronto) four times daily during the summer and lands at South Baymouth on Highway 6, 65 km south of Little Current.

Here is a territory that the mainstream of Ontario has passed by. There are vanished sawmills and abandoned farmsteads. Many of the villages and towns have stagnated since Manitoulin's prosperity days of seventy years ago, and they provide rustic subject material for the photographer. High on Manitoulin's cliffs are hiking trails and picnic sites, while in their shadow lie inland lakes for fishing, boating, or camping.

A Bit of History

Centuries ago Manitoulin was an Indian stronghold that its aboriginal inhabitants, the Ottawa, called Ekantoten. However, during the seventeenth century, the Iroquois incursions forced the Ottawa people to flee to the shores of Lake Michigan, where they remained until 1836. In that year the lieutenant governor of Upper Canada, Sir Francis Bond Head, selected the large island as the centre of Indian relocation. The Indian people returned reluctantly at first, but by 1860 more than 1,300 Ottawa and Ojibwa were occupying a cluster of towns at the east end of the island.

But the haven was short-lived. Bowing to pressure from lumbermen and settlers, the Indian Branch sent William Bartlett and Charles Lindsay to take over the island. The Indians in return were to receive a paltry 10 ha each. Not surprisingly, they refused. The strongest opposition came from the large contingent who lived on the Wikwemikong Peninsula. The next year William McDougall, commissioner of Crown lands, tried again, but he too was rebuffed. Only when he arbitrarily excluded the Wikwemikongs from voting about whether they should cede their lands did the other smaller bands relent and move meekly to reserves. The Wikwemikongs, however, never yielded their land, and today the Wikwemikong Peninsula remains Ontario's only unceded Indian territory.

Between 1864 and 1879 the surveyors moved in, and by 1882 the government had sold 120,000 ha, much of it to absentee speculators who resold it at several times its original price.

The first white settlements were in sheltered coves. By 1881 fishermen and lumbermen had set up mills and fishing stations in Little Current, Honora, Kagawong, Gore Bay, Cooks Dock, and Michaels Bay. Only two roads linked the settlements—colonization trails from Michaels Bay, the main port of entry on the south coast, to Little Current and Gore Bay on the north coast. But by the turn of the century, farm concession roads were open throughout the island.

Farming, fishing, and forestry developed as mainstays of the island's economy but soon declined. Fire and overcutting combined to sweep the forests clean; overfishing and the dreaded predator, the sea lamprey eel, defeated the fishery; and the stony and infertile soils of land that should never have been settled in the first place drove away most of the farmers. Since 1900, Manitoulin's population has dropped from 10,000 to just over 8,000.

However, the picturesque vestiges of the early settlements and the natural beauty of the cliffs and waters combine to form the subject of the Haweater Trail. Haweater is the name Manitoulin

A young Wikwemikong Indian in ceremonial dress.

islanders give one another. It originates from early settlement times when the pioneers, often forced to rely for sustenance upon the berry of the hawthorn tree, became known as "haw-eaters."

Little Current

From the south, Highway 6 enters Little Current on Manitowaning Road, the island's first colonization road. As the highway bends east, continue straight on Manitowaning to Water Street, where the town's small business section lines the shore. Here, in a small park, you can watch the sleek American yachts glide to dockside, fresh from a battle with the turbulent North Channel. Along the street are grocery stores, gift shops, and also the bookstore and offices of the *Manitoulin Expositor*, which has been in publication since 1879. The Edgewater Restaurant beside the government dock offers a range of meals and a view over the water.

View from the top of the escarpment near Little Current on Manitoulin Island.

Little Current to Kagawong

The mighty rock ridge known as the Niagara Escarpment (the focus of two other routes in this book) dips beneath the waters of Georgian Bay at the northern tip of the Bruce Peninsula and re-emerges to form the backbone of Manitoulin Island. The escarpment's cliffs form the island's north shore, ring its fjordlike bays, and loom over its flat plains.

The first section of your trip follows the base of the escarpment and leads you to its highest lookouts and through its early ports. Your first lookout point, and one of the highest, lies close to Little Current. Follow Manitowaning Road to Highway 6 where Highway 540 begins its westerly alignment. Then follow Highway 540 west from Little Current for about 2 km to the foot of the escarpment. Turn left and follow a dirt road to the top of McLeans Mountain. The township has created a small picnic park with views that extend northward over the plain below, to the various channels that separate the island from the mainland and to the gleaming white La Cloche Mountains.

Resume your route west on Highway 540. Here, old farms mix with newer country homes until after 2 km the road enters the Sucker Creek Indian Reserve. Today, the band enjoys modern homes with a full range of services. After 3 km the road leaves the reserve, traverses another small farming community and then meets the shoreline. For the next 6 km it follows the shoreline, though for most of this stretch trees block the view. The road then bends south to Honora, where a handful of homes are all that remain of a once-busy fishing and sawmilling port.

At 3 km south of Honora, Highway 540 meets the Bidwell Road and your access to the Cup and Saucer Trail, a hiking trail to the island's highest lookout point. The Cup and Saucer (named for its appearance) is a rock formation that looms high above the road. The trail is about 2 km long and includes steps and rails to help you up the steeper portions. The views from the top are panoramic. Below, to the east, lie the waters of Lake Manitou, and beyond that the farmlands of the eastern end of the island. To the west lies West Bay and the North Channel of Lake Huron. Allow about three hours for the hike.

Continuing west from the trail for 6 km, the road brings you to the town of West Bay, which was an early Indian settlement called Mechecowedenong. It is the island's second most populous reserve (Wikwemikong is the largest) and, with its new secondary school and art gallery, one of its most modern. West of the reserve, the road swings inland for about 3 km and then turns straight north to cross a small agricultural plain. After 4 km it bends west to the historic village of Kagawong.

Kagawong

As the road signs indicate, Kagawong lies about 1 km north of the highway on the shores of Mudge Bay. Like most of the island's cove villages, Kagawong began as a milling, fishing, and shipping village, but it had one more feature that the others lacked—water power. Just 2 km inland lies Lake Kagawong, which a small river drains northward to the lip of a 20-m gorge. This drop in the river powered early sawmills, and later an electric powerhouse. Today, it provides the focus for a small park beside the highway. Though the powerhouse is no longer in use, it still stands on the beach at the foot of a 1-km flume.

The village—a string of buildings along the road by the bay—contains some of the island's earliest architecture. The former lighthouse, store, hotel, and an Anglican church (whose pulpit is made from the wreck of an old ship) all date from the 1890s when the village was rebuilt following a fire.

Kagawong to Gore Bay

From Kagawong, the road crosses the limestone plains of Allan township to the island's first leading town, Gore Bay. For the first 6 km a secondary growth of forest lines the road until a small farming community named Ice Lake comes into view. Then, 2 km farther on, the road bends to follow the shores of the small lake of the same name before entering the largest and most fertile agricultural plain of central Manitoulin. Cutting dramatically into the plain is the cliff-lined inlet called Gore Bay and the town of the same name that grew on its shore.

Gore Bay was once larger than Little Current, its future more promising. Today, it has slid to second place, but it is the only other place on this route where you will find grocery, hardware, and drug stores. To enter Gore Bay turn right from Highway 540 onto Highway 542 and drive 2 km into the town.

Gore Bay

One of Manitoulin's first white settlements, Gore Bay was the terminus of a colonization road from Michaels Bay on the south shore. By 1895 it had become not just a fishing and shipping port, but was the centre of a prosperous farming community and had been named the seat of the district court. But few buildings date from its early days, for in 1908 a fire razed most of the business district.

As Highway 542 enters the town it becomes Meredith Street, the business street where you will find most of the stores. Two blocks away on Phipps Street is the 1889 courthouse, which escaped the flames. Beside it stands the jail, built in 1895, which now houses the museum. Here you can look at a turn-of-the-century cell, as well as at early telephones and dental equipment. You will also find, on the grounds, a pioneer buggy and an antique fire engine, and the ruins of what may be the *Griffon*. The *Griffon* was built by the explorer La Salle in the 1670s and was the first ship to sail the Upper Great Lakes.

To leave Gore Bay and continue the trip, follow Highway 542 or 540 B south back to Highway 540.

Gore Bay to Silver Water

This section of the route traverses one of the island's most fertile

Much of Manitoulin Island proved unsuitable for agriculture, and abandoned farms are a common sight.

plains, crosses a long causeway, and includes watery lookouts and a pair of ghost ports.

Continue west on Highway 540. For 4.5 km the road crosses the fertile farming plains of Gordon township. Here you will pass Manitoulin's modern farms, with their fields wide and green, and their herds of beef cattle. As Highway 540 bends sharply south, Highway 540 A leads right to the island township of Barrie Island, a low limestone plateau with two dozen farms. But keep on Highway 540 and follow it south towards Lake Wolsey.

The road continues through farm country for about 4 km and then enters the narrow peninsula that divides Bayfield Sound, a wide indentation of the North Channel, from Lake Wolsey. This 2-km-long peninsula is separated from the south shore of the lake by a 1-km-wide channel, which Highway 540 crosses on a scenic causeway. Off to the side is a roadside park that offers picnic facilities and a chance to fish. The south end of Lake Wolsey lies only 2 km from Manitoulin's south shore and marks the narrowest point of the island.

Across the channel the road follows Indian Point to the Obigewong Indian Reserve, which is now abandoned, though portions are leased to farmers and resort operators. Then, 1 km from the causeway, Highway 540 meets a side road. If you turn left here and drive up the hill, you will come to a clifftop picnic park with views across the lake.

Continuing on your journey, Highway 540 takes you through a cottage community known as Evansville and then crosses another small farming plain with level, fertile soils. After the rocks and forests reappear, you will come upon small clearings that mark a one-time farming community called Elizabeth Bay. All that remain are wooden farm homes and a schoolhouse. Small clearings continue for the next 8 km as the road enters another fertile pocket of farmland, bringing you after a further 2 km to the partly abandoned village of Silver Water.

Silver Water

Silver Water was once western Manitoulin's most important village, the retail centre for a busy farming area and for two ports. But the ports have vanished, along with their fishermen, sawmills, and cabins, and most farms are now abandoned. Their decline affected the village, and many of its original buildings are now empty. Standing forlornly amid the inhabited buildings are a cabin and school at the village's eastern end, and a general store and large house at the main intersection. A few new homes have been added and a second general store, which sells soft drinks.

If you are a treasure hunter, you may want to visit the abandoned ports. Cooks Dock, tucked beneath a 100-m cliff, was at the turn of the century a fishing station and a lumber-shipping port. To reach it, return east on Highway 540, drive 3 km to the second side road on the left, and follow it a further 3 km to the dock site. No buildings have survived from the shipping and fishing days, but if you search the bush you may uncover an old bottle or kettle.

The other port lies north of Silver Water and was called Morrisville. To reach it, continue north from the main intersection for 4 km. As the road bends left, look for a green sign pointing to Sheshegwaning. Follow this road for 1.5 km down a hill and then look for a trail to the right. It is passable and you can follow it for 1 km to a wind-swept boulder beach. Like Cooks Dock, Morrisville has vanished. Only its name has survived on maps where the inlet is yet called Morrisville Bay.

Silver Water to Meldrum Bay

This, the last segment of the route, leads to Manitoulin's western extremity. It passes isolated pockets of farming, ventures into a tiny village of white homes on a green hillside, and ends at a curious lighthouse museum.

From the Sheshegwaning turnoff, continue west on Highway 540. For 16 km the road traverses a rugged land of rock and forest. Overgrown clearings tell of futile farming endeavours. Then, on the right, as the road makes a sharp swing left, the blue waters of Macrae Cove sparkle between the trees. A kilometre beyond that lies the village of Meldrum Bay. The bay from which the village derived its name is ringed with steep, forested hills. On the western shore are the church, hotel, stores, and houses.

Today, Meldrum Bay is home to fewer than 50 people, but at the turn of the century it contained a sawmill and a colony of fishermen. Now only the mill's foundations remain, and a solitary fisherman guides his white tug around the bay and into the North Channel. Sleek yachts and antennae-laden cruisers moor where the fishing boats once docked.

There is little traffic and the pace is leisurely. Here you can visit the Net Shed Museum, a former net-storage shed, that is operated by the small but active Meldrum Bay Historical Society. It is open daily on alternating mornings and afternoons throughout the summer months and displays early photographs and fishing equipment.

The village's two most prominent buildings are the hotel and the general store. Known as the Meldrum Bay Inn, the hotel still provides accommodation and meals. Arbours General Store is a traditional country store, while Meldrum Bay Outfitters caters to the many boaters that call. The drive has been long, and Meldrum Bay is a quiet place to stretch your legs before the final drive to the tip of the island and the Mississagi Lighthouse.

Meldrum Bay to Mississagi Lighthouse

From the village, return on Highway 540 for 1 km to a side road where a directional arrow points to the lighthouse. The dirt route crosses Manitoulin's remotest farming community and then, after 3 km, narrows and becomes a jolting, twisting trail through the bush. After a rugged 5 km it emerges into a small, rocky clearing. Ahead stands the Mississagi Lighthouse.

The Mississagi Lighthouse, on Manitoulin's western tip, is now a museum.

Built before the turn of the century to guide ships along the channel between Manitoulin and Cockburn Island, the lighthouse is a museum, another operation of the Meldrum Bay Historical Society. It is a squat, wooden structure, painted the mandatory red and white. The attached keeper's cabin is furnished in a turn-of-the-century style and contains equipment that the keeper of that period used. From the light level, you can view the rocky shoreline below you and the distant form of Cockburn Island. An automated beacon a few metres north has replaced the light.

Another building on the site is the former fog-horn house. Here, large boilers built up steam pressure which sounded the horn that warned ships far offshore in the waters of Lake Huron. Amid the boilers and old equipment, you can enjoy light lunches in a small restaurant. Adjacent to the lighthouse is a large area that has been cleared for a campground. Beside it a low limestone cliff winds along the shore and marks the submergence of the Niagara Escarpment, which dips once more below the waters of Lake Huron.

You can return to Little Current via Highway 540. However, if you are bound for the Tobermory ferry and want to traverse the southern portion of the island, return to Evansville (for up to that point 540 is the only road) and then turn south up Indian Hill. Farm concession roads lead through abandoned farmlands to active towns such as Mindemoya and to the fishing town of Providence Bay, where the limestone plateau dips gently under the waters of Lake Huron. On this route you end up at South Baymouth, where you can catch the *Chi-Cheemaun* to Tobermory or return north on Highway 6 to Little Current.

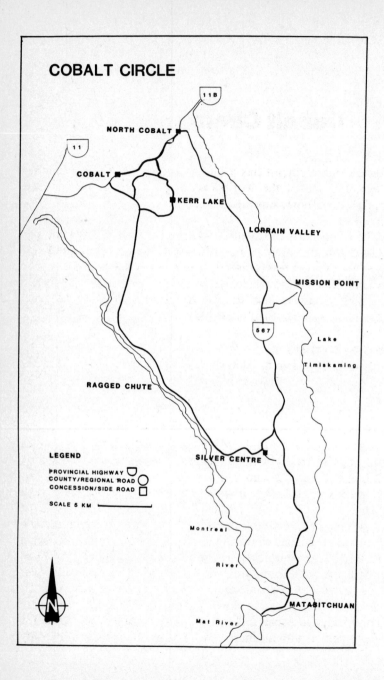

COBALT CIRCLE

11B

NORTH COBALT

11

COBALT

KERR LAKE

LORRAIN VALLEY

MISSION POINT

567

Lake

Timiskaming

RAGGED CHUTE

LEGEND

PROVINCIAL HIGHWAY
COUNTY/REGIONAL ROAD
CONCESSION/SIDE ROAD

SCALE 5 KM

SILVER CENTRE

Montreal

River

MATABITCHUAN

Mat River

N

21 Cobalt Circle

Ontario's old northeast has a bit of everything: hidden farming valleys, the site of the world's largest man-made geyser, and Canada's most notorious silver boomtown. This backroad takes them all in.

The route starts in Cobalt, 490 km northeast of Toronto, and follows a circular route of nearly 100 km, along which there are no gas stations or restaurants. So fill your tank and pack your lunch in Cobalt before you leave. Along the route, there are plenty of waterside picnic sites where you can spread your blanket. Cobalt can be approached via Highway 11.

A Bit of History

Northeastern Ontario in 1900 was touted for its farmland, not for its minerals. From the north end of Lake Timiskaming, a flat plain of fine clays spreads northwestward. This soon attracted settlers. Once the settlers had cleared their farms, they demanded a rail connection to the south, a request that was to have unexpected results. In 1903, while scouting the woods for timber appropriate for railway ties, the timber scouts James McKinley and Ernest Darragh found a glittering rock by the shore of Long Lake (now Cobalt Lake). It was analysed as silver—and the rush was on.

Within just five years, more than 50 mines clanged into the hills around the lake, while on the rocky shores boomed the town of Cobalt. It grew quickly, rising to a population of 10,000 as simple cabins and large stores vied for space on the steep hillsides. But as the deposits became exhausted and as silver prices plummeted, the mines began to close, and by 1940 Cobalt's population had plunged to less than 2,000. However, an improved market for silver, together with an increasing demand for cobalt in therapy treatments, stabilized the slide and today the town's population remains at 2,000.

As Cobalt boomed, prospectors tramped farther afield. Soon the hills around Kerr Lake south of Cobalt rang with new mines. By 1909—40 km south, at the remote mouth of the Montreal River—there grew another town, Silver Centre; it would become the ghost town that Cobalt did not.

Cobalt

Cobalt has retained the air of a boom camp. Although its drastic decline and a series of fires took many of the original buildings, others remain, and these you should explore on foot.

From Highway 11, the northern route of the Trans-Canada Highway, turn east onto Highway 11 B and drive the 4 km into the town. Even as you enter, gaunt, weathered headframes peer at you from bare, rocky hilltops. Start at the mining museum on Silver Street (as Highway 11 B is called). This is one of North America's most celebrated mining museums, containing ore samples, photos, rare mining equipment, and books on the romance of the Cobalt rush. It is open daily between May and September. The museum occupies the first office of the *Cobalt Nugget* newspaper, which during the peak of the boom had avid readers as far away as

During the silver boom, Cobalt had a population of 10,000. It is now a fraction of its former size.

England and California. Beside the museum, the present town hall is in the former YMCA building, while the original town hall across the road is home to the Cobalt pottery.

A few paces north of the museum, at the corner of Prospect and Silver streets, is Cobalt's most unusual group of buildings. On the northeast corner is the medieval Bank of Ottawa building, while across the street stand the present offices of the township of Coleman, which were prefabricated in British Columbia in 1903 and moved to Cobalt to serve as a Bank of Commerce. You will look twice at the former grocery store on the northwest corner, for it has a headframe protruding from its roof. Anthony Giachino, who built it in 1926, decided to recycle the cool air from the depths of the then-abandoned Coniagas shaft to cool his meat and vegetables. Now the offices of the Cobalt and Area Restoration Committee, it has become Cobalt's most photographed building.

On the southwest corner stands the Fraser Hotel, which was built as the Royal Exchange building. Although it seems massive in relation to its neighbours, several buildings of comparable scale once lined both Prospect and Silver streets. After the boom passed they burned down, one by one, and were never rebuilt.

Because there is so much to see in Cobalt, you should acquire the 16-page walking-tour guide. It will guide you along Lang Street, where a string of stores stretched more than half a kilometre and where illicit liquor and love could once be bought; it will lead you to the town's elegant railway station, a vanishing species in Ontario, and to Ontario's first provincial police cells.

The Kerr Lake Silver Fields

This first section of the route takes you on a short circular tour through the barren hills and ghosted headframes of the Kerr Lake silver fields.

To leave Cobalt, turn right from Silver Street onto Lang Street. As you climb the curving hill, look for the Gordon and Davies Meat Market. East of that store, every stick of early Cobalt was burnt in 1909 in what was called the Haileybury Road Fire. Continue to Ferland Street and turn right. As you cross the bridge you will see the weathered headframe from the long-closed Right-of-Way Mine, which looks across the bed of Cobalt Lake to the town on the opposite shore. Across the road from the headframe stands a simple log building, but one with a place in the

Cobalt legend. This was the blacksmith's shop of Fred Larose. According to legend, Larose threw a pick at a fox and literally struck one of Cobalt's richest veins of silver. For years this was taken to be the story of Cobalt's discovery. However, Larose's claim came well after Cobalt had become a busy camp.

Drive east from the shop for 1 km and then follow a fork in the road to the right. Here the road winds past empty cabins, abandoned headframes, and vacant mine buildings. On the hillsides, once scraped bare of vegetation and washed of earth so that no vein would remain hidden, a young forest is starting to regenerate. After 2.5 km you will come to another fork in the road and another cluster of buildings. This was the heart of the Kerr Lake camp. Most of the mines, homes, and facilities were located here and became the focus of the scattered village. But when the boom passed and the mines closed, the village died.

Follow the left fork where Kerr Lake, the water body, appears. Its hillsides are now wooded, but between 1905 and 1915 they were covered with headframes, mine buildings, and houses. In 1913 the lake itself was drained to investigate veins on the lake bed. Today, the cavity has refilled and a solitary headframe skeleton casts its reflection on the surface. For a further 3 km the road passes more abandoned headframes and houses, and then comes to a dead end.

Return to the Kerr Lake cluster of buildings and keep left. Here your road passes the University Mine bunkhouse on Giroux Lake and more silent headframes; then, about half a kilometre from a small bridge, it brings you back to the southern outskirts of Cobalt and to another fork in the road. Take the right branch, which leads along the south shore of Cobalt Lake to the site of the Nipissing Mine. This mine—shells, foundations, and all—has been converted to a municipal park, and it offers a panoramic view across the lake to Cobalt. Continue east from the park to Ferland Street, turn left, cross the bridge, and you will be back in the east end of Cobalt. From the junction with Highway 11 B, drive 2.5 km to the village of North Cobalt.

This village began as a miners' suburb. Because the rocky ridges of Cobalt itself were too steep for urban growth, a new townsite had to be found. So North Cobalt, an area of flat soils and reliable water, was surveyed into 400 town lots, with wide boulevards. Here the miners erected their simple frame cabins, many of which are still in use today.

North Cobalt to the Lorrain Valley

This section of the route leaves the scarred hillsides of Cobalt and leads you through a lush, hidden valley of high, wooded hillsides and a floor of pastures and fields. In the centre of North Cobalt turn right onto Highway 567 and follow this road southeast over a landscape of rolling rock and forest. After 7 km the road suddenly bends south and enters the Lorrain Valley.

The terrain southeast of Cobalt is marked by long bedrock ridges and valleys, the largest of which contains Lake Timiskaming. Paralleling the lake, separated only by a ridge of rock, is the Lorrain Valley. It is a much smaller fissure, 20 km long and less than 1 km wide. Within it lie deep soils which attracted settlers during the turn-of-the-century land boom.

The hidden Lorrain Valley is 20 km long but less than 1 km wide.

The road winds along the valley bottom. Above, on each side, the walls rise high and forested; along the narrow floor are the weathered barns and green pastures of the valley's farms. At 10 km from the turn into the valley, historic markers point down a side road to the Timiskaming Mission. Turn left and follow the signs 2 km to the shore of Lake Timiskaming. Here, where the lake narrows, a group of Oblate priests established a mission. The missionaries had originally been based in a fur-trading fort on the Quebec side of the lake, but they moved to the Ontario side in 1863. The mission closed just 24 years later and has left a mound of overgrown foundations. From the untended field on the Ontario side, you can see on the Quebec side a well-kept park and a white cross that marks the site of the fort.

To continue on your southerly route, return to Highway 567 and turn left. The road runs on through the scenic Lorrain Valley, passing farms and skirting the foot of the hills. Then, after 7 km, it climbs out of the valley onto a rocky plateau.

Lorrain Valley to Matabitchuan

This short section of the route takes you over the rugged plateau and into the spectacular twin valleys of the Montreal and Matabitchuan rivers.

For 9 km the road winds across a forested highland that to date has repulsed any efforts to settle it. Then it suddenly emerges from the woods and crosses a modern bridge. The lake to your right is the forebay for the Lower Notch Generating Station, completed in 1972. The dam and powerhouse lie to your left, but unless the gates are open you cannot drive to it. The pond created behind the dam backs 15 km up the Montreal River.

Across the bridge, the road winds another 1 km to the Notch—a dark rocky canyon on your right, which was the original channel carved by the Montreal River. A further 3 km lead you to the older dam, that on the Matabitchuan River. Built in 1910, this dam became the focus for a village of 70 residents, complete with church, store, and school. But after Ontario Hydro purchased it in 1945 and new roads made a hydro village unnecessary, most residents moved away. Only grassy fields remain where the village stood.

Matabitchuan to Silver Centre

The Matabitchuan dam marks the end of the road. You will need to retrace your route to get to your next point of interest, Silver Centre—a remote ghost town that was born and died on the silver boom. Drive back up Highway 567 for 10 km until you come to a small lake on the right. From the end of the lake count 1.5 km and look for a crushed-stone side road leading left, the former Silver Centre Road. This trail is steep and winding, but it is passable. Follow it for 2 km to a fork and branch left where headframes and mine buildings lurk behind young forests. These are the ghosts of Silver Centre.

As the Cobalt boom neared its peak in 1907, prospectors ventured far afield and in 1907 found silver in these remote hills. Other miners quickly moved in. At first, the only access was from Lake Timiskaming, and the first Silver Centre was on its shore. Then, when road and rail arrived from the north, the village moved to the site of the mines themselves.

Of the two dozen mines that worked the area, fewer than a half-dozen were profitable. Paramount among them were the Keeley and Frontier mines. It was from the Keeley that the famous "Keeley nugget" was taken. Of its weight of over 2 tonnes, half was pure silver. The nugget was so unusually rich that the Canadian government placed it on display at the 1924 British Empire Exhibition in Wembley.

By 1920 Silver Centre's population was 900 and the town could boast a school, church, store, and a winning hockey team. But by 1930 the silver boom had faded. Silver Centre faded too, for its only lifeblood was the mines. As these closed, the residents left; the rails were lifted and the road fell into disrepair. But as you proceed south from the branch, you can see in the bush former mine buildings and headframes. Near the junction lie the remains of the famous Keeley Mine, and a kilometre farther on are those of the Frontier Mine. Scattered between them, among overgrown bush, are the foundations of the houses.

The road comes to a dead end beyond the Frontier Mine. To continue to the valley of the Montreal River, you will need to return to the branch in the road at the Keeley site and turn left.

Silver Centre to Ragged Chute

This last segment leads you northwest along the widened Montreal River to the site of one of the world's most unusual power plants and then takes you back to Cobalt.

From Silver Centre the road continues to twist through the rocks and lakes of the highlands. After 5 km the Montreal River

This early power plant in the Lorrain Valley was once the centre of a busy village.

234

comes into view, but the placid pond that you see here is not the wild turbulent river of a decade ago. It is now part of the 15-km lake created by the monster dam of the Lower Notch Generating Station.

The road follows the shore, sometimes hugging it, sometimes ducking behind a buffer of trees. After 11 km it crosses a small bridge, rounds a bend, and enters a clearing. Ahead of you is the site of the Ragged Chute Compressed Air Plant, once a popular attraction and now, sadly, destroyed by fire.

The plant operated on an unusual principle. As the water fell through the plant, air was trapped in a chamber. Pressure built up and the air was released into pipes which ran across the ground to the mines. There, the force of the air was put to work operating the lifts that led down the shafts. When this pressure plant was built in 1909, it was one of only eight in the world. Until its recent demise, it was the only one of its kind left. It offered a spectacular sight at weekends when the mines were closed, for then the air had nowhere to go but up. When the pressure peaked, the air was released, and water and air would rush skyward in a mighty geyser that often reached 30 m in height. For decades, this was a popular spectacle for tourists.

Beyond the plant, your route swings away from the river and traverses a low, swampy terrain for 15 km before the buildings of Cobalt once more come into view. Having completed your trip, you may wish to stay the night in the area. There is ample accommodation. Within 15 km of Cobalt are the towns of Haileybury, New Liskeard, and Latchford. And 4 km west, the busy Trans-Canada Highway speeds its way northward, and it too has several motels where you can stay the night. However, your greatest choice of accommodation is in the city of North Bay, which lies 140 km south on Highway 11.

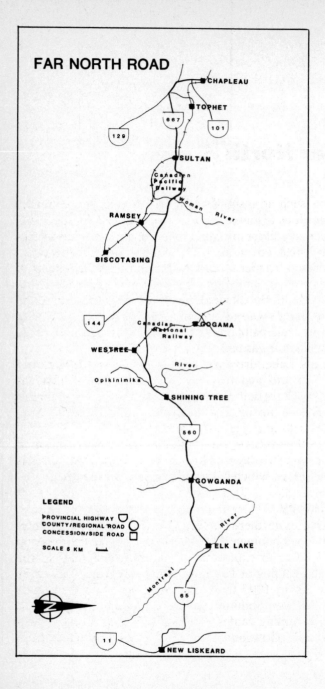

FAR NORTH ROAD

CHAPLEAU

TOPHET

667   101

129

SULTAN

Canadian
Pacific
Railway

Woman   River

RAMSEY

BISCOTASING

144   Canadian
National
Railway   GOGAMA

WESTREE

River

Opikinimika

SHINING TREE

560

GOWGANDA

River

LEGEND

PROVINCIAL HIGHWAY
COUNTY/REGIONAL ROAD
CONCESSION/SIDE ROAD

SCALE 5 KM

ELK LAKE

Montreal   65

11

NEW LISKEARD

22 Far North Road

No road gives such an insight into northern Ontario's colourful history and perilous resource economy as this road does. It visits turn-of-the-century silver mining camps, barren sand plains stripped of their forest cover, modern logging towns, and once-boisterous railway frontier towns. At 300 km, it is the longest of the backroads in this book. It begins in the town of Elk Lake, 80 km northwest of Cobalt, and ends near Chapleau far to the west. Portions of the route are unpaved, though they are of a good standard and are well maintained. Facilities are far apart, so make sure that you fill your gas tank whenever you can.

To reach Elk Lake, drive north from North Bay on Highway 11 to New Liskeard and turn west on Highway 65. This is Ontario's Little Clay Belt and it contains a farmscape that is surprisingly flat and fertile. Elk Lake lies at the head of the long, narrow lake of the same name, 60 km from the turnoff.

Although you can cover the route in a day, you may wish to spread the trip over two days. Conveniently at the halfway mark is the town of Gogama, which has motels and campgrounds.

A Bit of History

This route captures northern Ontario's history in capsule. Following the great Cobalt boom in 1903, prospectors made their way up the Montreal River to explore the promising rocklands to the west. From the landing at Elk Lake (then called Elk City) they struck westward. In 1907 they discovered silver on Gowganda Lake, and in 1909 on Shining Tree Lake. Both places grew into small but noisy mining camps. Although Shining Tree is now a partial ghost town, Gowganda's mines continue to produce from time to time.

The western section of the route recalls the romance of lumbering and the railway, for both went hand in hand. Although the lumbermen long knew of the pine stands far to the north of Sudbury, they had no means of hauling out the timber. But when the CPR eventually laid its rails through the woodlands, the lumbermen were close behind. Every 10 km the railway posted a section crew and built a small station, many of which became the focus for a mill and small town. While most such places vanished when the timber was gone, a few still cling to life. Today, lumbering continues to be the area's lifeblood, though most of the logs are shipped out by truck. Barren landscapes show that clear cutting is not a practice of the past.

Elk Lake to Gowganda

Although there were no mines at Elk Lake itself, the town grew out of the silver boom. It was as far up the Montreal River as steamers dared travel, so it became the jumping-off point for prospectors and miners on their way to the Gowganda finds. Soon a wagon road was built, connecting the Timiskaming and Northern Ontario Railway (now the Ontario Northland) with the town of Charlton, 35 km to the northeast. This was followed in 1913 by a branch line of the railway. Although most mines are now silent, Elk Lake village still exists, surviving on tourism and sawmilling.

You enter Elk Lake on Highway 65 and meet Highway 560 by the bridge in the centre of the village. Simple frame homes and boomtown stores line the small grid of streets. The lake stretches far to the southeast, and along its shores are the clearings of early bush farms now sprouting modern country homes. Elk Lake contains a fully computerized sawmill, where tours are available. There are stores and restaurants on both sides of the bridge and if you haven't already stocked up, you should do so here.

Follow Highway 65 through the village and then branch left onto Highway 560. The first section of your route traverses a rolling plateau of rock and sand laid down by the last glaciers. Forests mix with small lakes and rivers. After 35 km the road skirts the shores of Long Point Lake and enters the Gowganda silver fields. As the road twists around the rocky hillocks, empty mine buildings and gaunt headframes can be seen lurking in the bush.

After another 15 km the road enters the town of Gowganda. In

The town of Elk Lake was once the jumping-off point for miners on their way to Gowganda.

1907, as the prospectors and miners streamed in, Gowganda was surveyed into town lots and almost overnight grew into a town of log cabins and log stores with 5,000 residents. But mine closings and fires took their toll, and the population is now less than 200.

As Highway 560 enters the village and bends right, you will find a store and a gas station. Across the road, in what was once the miners' union hall, is the local museum. Here, through the summer, you can view old mining equipment and Indian and pioneer artifacts. Inside, you can buy postcards containing photographs of Gowganda's early days as a boisterous mining camp.

Gowganda to Shining Tree

This next section of the route follows the alignment of the first wagon road to the smaller mining town of Shining Tree. The road continues through a landscape much like that east of Gowganda, a forest broken only by rocky hills and small lakes. After 35 km the road crosses Michiwakenda Lake, the scene of much of the area's first flurry of mining. Here and there, beside the road and behind the trees, are the cabins and tailings of the early mines. Another 15 km leads you into the partial ghost town of Shining Tree.

A busy mining camp and jumping-off point in 1909, when silver was discovered, Shining Tree was linked to the outside by only a pair of crude wagon roads. One led east to Gowganda and the other southwest to what was then the Canadian Northern Railway's head of steel, Ruel, a village that has long since vanished. Shining Tree today has been reduced to a few scattered cabins. Although you will find a combined restaurant and store with a gas pump, many buildings lie empty.

Shining Tree to Gogama

This next section takes you down off the rocky plateau into the Ostrom sand flats where modern lumbering has created a barren desert. Here, too, is Gogama, your halfway point and a possible overnight stop.

Continue west from Shining Tree on Highway 560. The road continues to wind over the highlands. After 12 km it brings you to the bridge over the Opikinimika River, and 15 km after that to the junction with Highway 560 A and the fringe of the sand flats.

Highway 560 A is only 10 km long, and you can take a brief side trip down it to the partially ghosted town of Westree. This was once a railside sawmill town but most of the residents have left and the few remaining homes are used only seasonally. Displaying disdain for Canada's heritage, her railways demolish

False-fronted stores still line the dirt main street of Gogama.

every station they can, and only recently wiped the historic Westree station from the landscape. On its way to Westree, Highway 560 A passes Deschenes Creek, where you will find sandy and shaded campsites.

Continuing on your main route from the junction, Highway 560 descends onto the sand flat. Here the lumber companies have reduced the pine forests to a field of rubble that extends to a treeless horizon. After 40 km, Highway 560 ends at Highway 144. Completed in 1962, this is one of Ontario's newest roads, and it takes you 35 km north to Gogama.

Gogama began in 1912 when the Canadian Northern Railway laid its rails across the Minisinakwa River. It prospered on the lumber and fur trade, and today remains a neat village of 400 inhabitants. Its most interesting feature is its main street. False-fronted stores still line the dirt street as they did when the railway was built—a townscape legacy that few northern railway towns have retained, minus, of course, the station. In a Ministry of Natural Resources park on the wide river, you can stretch your legs beneath the pines or spread a blanket for a picnic lunch. If you plan to stay overnight in Gogama, you can choose from three motels.

Gogama to Biscotasing

This portion of the route leads you westward, through country where logging and railways have been a way of life for a century. Some of the towns are new, some old, and others are almost ghost towns.

From Gogama, return to the junction of Highway 560. This highway ends where it meets Highway 144, and your route continues west on a private logging road, which is open to public travel and is maintained in better condition than many a municipal road. Built in 1954–56 by a lumber company called the Kalamazoo Vegetable and Parchment Company, this road replaced the earlier wagon road that connected Gogama with Biscotasing. On weekdays, you should be prepared to share it with large logging trucks.

For a short distance the route continues past the sad spectacle of the deforested plain; then it enters a landscape of rock and water, a contrast to the barren plain you have left. After 40 km a road branches left to Ramsey. Follow it 10 km to another side

This Roman Catholic church sits neglected on its rocky perch overlooking Biscotasing.

road, where you turn left to Biscotasing. Narrow and winding, this road skirts several lakes where you can camp, fish, or picnic. After 40 km it enters Biscotasing, a one-time raucous railway town of bars and brothels.

Biscotasing

In 1882 the Canadian Pacific Railway's head of steel crossed Biscotasi Lake. Here was an ample water supply and level terrain suitable for a townsite. The CPR created a divisional town, which quickly became a rowdy and lawless frontier community. Then, in 1884, the CPR moved its facilities 100 km up the line to their new head of steel, Chapleau, and Biscotasing fell silent. In 1894 a mill was built, and despite two changes in ownership, it remained the town's lifeblood. After it closed in 1927, Biscotasing's population plummeted from 244 to 7.

Biscotasing later became noted for another legend. During its early years a young Englishman named Archie Belaney entered town, where he learned of trapping and the ways of the Indian. Later, he married an Indian girl and settled into a new life and a new identity as the "Indian" Grey Owl, under which guise he became an international celebrity as a lecturer and writer, and one of Canada's first conservationists.

Since 1931 Bisco has revived. Lumbering jobs with the E.B. Eddy Company have raised the winter population to more than 50, while the summer cottagers bring the number up to 200. After a disastrous fire destroyed most of the town in 1913, many hands went to work rebuilding homes and churches, most of which still stand, though they are used only seasonally. Among the more interesting is the Roman Catholic church, which stands now abandoned on a high rock cliff above the town. Many early houses still stand, perched randomly on hilltops or along narrow, dusty roads. Beside the track is the general store, which dispenses groceries and gas. For boaters, Biscotasing gives access to 200 km of channels and bays—waters which yield trophy muskies and pike, and which are bordered by shady and secluded campsites.

Biscotasing to Sultan

Along this last section of the route you traverse a rocky plateau covered with a young regenerating forest. At each end are lumber towns, one modern and prefabricated, the other a relic from the 1920s.

Return on the Biscotasing Road to the junction. Turn left and drive 2 km into Ramsey. After the railway went through in 1882, Ramsey remained a small section village, but when the Jerome Mine opened a few kilometres north in 1938, it suddenly became an important supply point for the mine. Then, after the mine closed in 1943, lumbering took over. Today, ten gleaming prefabricated homes, placed by the E.B. Eddy Company, contrast with the original railway homes. Other than a confectionery, the village's only facilities are those for employees.

Cross the tracks and drive 2 km to an intersection with another forest road. Keep right and drive 12 km to another intersection. Here you return to the bypass you left 10 km east of Ramsey. Turn left.

For the next 10 km the road resumes its straight course over a flat plain to Angus Creek, where a small meadow has been cleared for picnicking and camping. The terrain then changes markedly as you enter a rugged upland of rock and swamp. The road remains passable, but for the next 35 km it twists and winds until the trees part to reveal another large clearing and the 1920s lumber town of Sultan.

In the Biscotasing region, canoes are still transported by this age-old method.

Sultan, too, began life as a railway section village, with the usual assortment of insulbrick shacks, but it burst to life in 1927 when the McNaught Lumber Company erected the area's first sawmill. On the flat sands east of the track the company built a neat town of 30 houses as well as a store, a school, and a Catholic church. Soon there were 200 residents. When in 1956 the mill burned, the town failed to die. By then, the E.B. Eddy Company in Ramsey could offer jobs to many of Sultan's workers; others commuted to Chapleau.

The buildings that may interest you here include the church and houses of the 1927 planned townsite and the jumble of hilltop shacks by the tracks. Beside the store there is a gas pump, so you can fill up here if you need to.

Sultan to Chapleau

Highway 667 begins here and takes you the 36 km to Highway 129. From that intersection, Chapleau lies 32 km north.

Highway 667 crosses a flat lowland of swamp and tamarack. Half a kilometre before you reach the intersection with 129, look on your right for a side road to Nemegos. This leads on a side trip to a ghost town and a partial ghost town. Follow the road 10 km to a fork at the railway crossing; 6 km to the right lies an abandoned Indian village called Tophet. When the provincial highways replaced the railways as the main transportation system, the Indians negotiated for a new reserve near Chapleau and left Tophet to the wind and weeds. About 5 km to the left is Nemegos, a one-time mill town that is today half-abandoned and contains early examples of log cabins.

Once at Highway 129, you can choose your direction. In Chapleau, a busy railway and lumbering town, you will find an ample range of accommodation and stores. Highway 129 south leads to Thessalon on Highway 17, halfway between Sudbury and Sault Ste. Marie. The southern 80 km of the 190-km drive to Thessalon wind through the valley of the Mississagi River, a little-known canyon whose high, wooded slopes and fall foliage rival those of the more famous Agawa Canyon several kilometres west. There are, however, no stores or gas stations until you reach the vicinity of Highway 17.

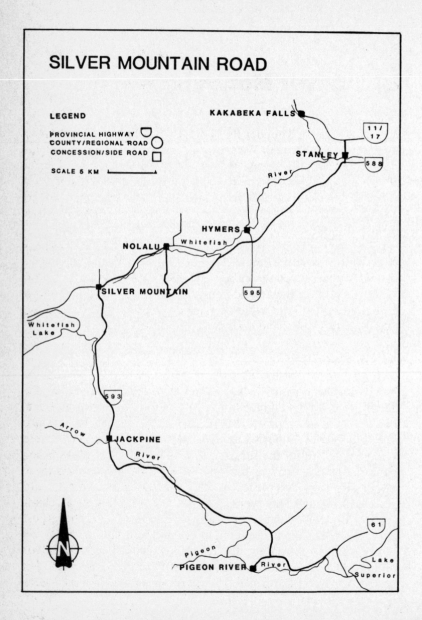

SILVER MOUNTAIN ROAD

LEGEND

PROVINCIAL HIGHWAY
COUNTY/REGIONAL ROAD
CONCESSION/SIDE ROAD

SCALE 5 KM

KAKABEKA FALLS

11/17

STANLEY

588

River

HYMERS

NOLALU

Whitefish

595

SILVER MOUNTAIN

Whitefish Lake

593

Arrow

JACKPINE

River

Pigeon River

61

Pigeon River

Lake Superior

N

23 Silver Mountain Road

West of the city of Thunder Bay lies a range of mountains that the Ojibwa call the Shuniah Weachu, the Silver Mountains. A series of soaring, flat-top mesas, they spawned one of Ontario's first silver rushes. This 80-km route winds beneath their looming cliffs, taking you not only to the early silver mines, but also to waterfalls and valley villages, and to northwestern Ontario's first Finnish settlements.

The route forms a 100-km semicircle. It starts at Kakabeka Falls, 30 km west of Thunder Bay on the Trans-Canada Highway 17, and follows paved secondary highways to Middle Falls, 50 km south of Thunder Bay. Once you get into the mountain country, there are few facilities other than general stores, and often these are far apart. Some have gas pumps, but many do not.

A Bit of History

The early history of the Thunder Bay area is one of fur trading. Fort William began as a North West Company fur post in the closing years of the eighteenth century and became one of Ontario's largest trading posts. Its neighbour on the shore of Lake Superior, Prince Arthur's Landing, grew into a small port where schooners called for the furs and fish. Not until the 1880s, when the Canadian Pacific was built north of Lake Superior, did these settlements grow into the towns of Fort William and Port Arthur. Nine decades later they were amalgamated into the city of Thunder Bay. With a population of 110,000, Thunder Bay is the largest city in the north and the seventh largest in Ontario.

As well as fur trading, this region also has a history of silver mining. In 1882 a local Ojibwa chief, Joseph L'Avocat, led prospector Oliver Daunais to the Silver Mountains west of Thunder Bay, and over the next twenty years nearly a dozen mining camps were built at their summits. The largest were the twin towns of Silver Mountain East End and Silver Mountain West End. To give access to them, the Silver Mountain Highway was built into the area, followed in 1891 by a railway called the Port Arthur and Duluth. But the deposits were meagre and production disappointing. By 1910 the mines were silent.

When the mines closed, many of the Finnish miners stayed on and cleared small bush farms along the Silver Mountain Road. Before the First World War, a wave of Finnish settlers swept along the railway and expanded the first clearings into farming communities, many of which had the distinctive Finnish barn and house styles. As recently as the 1920s, new land was being broken along the Pigeon River on the American border. It was one of Ontario's last true frontiers.

Kakabeka Falls to Hymers

This trip begins at a waterfall that has been called the Niagara of the North, and then follows the Silver Mountains to an early railway town. Well known to the early fur traders and Indians, Kakabeka Falls was the first difficult portage on the Kaministikwia River fur highway. Here, 30 km west of Lake Superior, the "Kam" River drops 20 m over a hard limestone brink. Erosion has carved a gorge 3 km from the original lip of the escarpment. Beside the falls is the Ontario Ministry of Natural Resources park and campground, which contains trails that follow ancient Indian and voyageur portages along the precipitous brink of the gorge and into its dark depths.

The village which took the name of the falls caters now to tourists, and gas stations and restaurants line the Trans-Canada Highway in the type of commercial sprawl that you would be more likely to encounter in the south. Nevertheless, this is a good place to have a snack and fill your tank before embarking on a route that has few gas pumps and no restaurants.

From the park, drive east on the Trans-Canada Highway for 4 km to Highway 588 and turn right. The next 2 km lead you down the wall of the Kam Valley to a hamlet called Stanley. Once a busy station stop on the Port Arthur and Duluth Railway, Stanley now has only a tavern and a closed store. By the river, the rails have long been lifted and a dirt road now follows the rail bed.

Kakabeka Falls—the Niagara of the North.

Cross the concrete bridge over the Kam River, where you will see prosperous farms on the silty soils of the river's flood plain. Across the bridge, at a T-intersection, Highway 588 turns right onto the Silver Mountain Highway. Although it bears no resemblance to the bush trail first carved into the forests in 1890, the Silver Mountain Highway still follows the route along the foot of the great mesas. After 3 km the peaks loom close on your left, while on your right are the small overgrown clearings of the area's first bush farmers.

At 8.5 km from the bridge, look on the left for a trail. This leads 1 km through the bush to the former Badger Mountain Mine, where you can still see the foundations of the few mine buildings. The trail is passable to most vehicles in dry weather.

Hymers is 3 km west of the mine. Originally a station on the Port Arthur and Duluth Railway, it grew into a busy service town for the pioneer community. But when the railway closed in 1934, and when better roads made Port Arthur and Fort William more accessible, many residents left. Today, without the newer homes of Thunder Bay commuters, Hymers would be a ghost town.

To enter Hymers, turn right onto Highway 595 and drive

The flood plain of the Kaministikwia River supports several farms.

down the wall of the Whitefish River Valley into the village. Many of the town's early frame buildings are unspoilt examples of turn-of-the-century architecture in wood. Before the bridge is the wooden St. Philip Church, as well as a wooden mansion—home to the family after whom the town was named. Across the small bridge is the village museum, housed in a wooden building that was originally the United Church. The museum has displays of early pioneer implements, along with photographs of the town in its heyday. A few metres beyond the museum Highway 595 turns right. This is the town's main intersection, where five stores, three blacksmith shops, and two boarding houses once stood. Today, only one closed and boarded store remains. Paralleling the road is the bed of the Port Arthur and Duluth, where a plaque commemorates the short-lived railway.

Hymers to Nolalu

This next section of the route leaves Highway 588 to trace the original Silver Mountain Highway beneath red cliffs and into northwestern Ontario's "little Finland."

From the centre of Hymers, return to Highway 588. If you

looked in vain in Hymers for a store, you will find one here at the junction of Highways 588 and 595. Turn right onto Highway 588 and drive 3.5 km. Here the highway turns sharply right, while the old Silver Mountain Highway follows a dirt road straight ahead. Follow the old road. This narrow trail winds past bush farms, many of which were started by unemployed miners on poor soils and are now abandoned. Then the road swings into the shadow of a high rocky mesa, which is called the Palisades because of its vertical columns of rock.

After 5 km you will come to a crossroads. Ahead of you, the old Silver Mountain Highway continues for another 1.5 km and then becomes a bush trail, passable only for four-wheel-drive vehicles. So you should turn right at the crossroads, crossing the bridge over the Silver Falls Creek. On this wide, sandy plain, a dozen Finnish farms once operated. Today, only three remain, some displaying the curving bell-cast roofs of the Finnish barn.

After travelling 4 km from the crossroads you will enter the valley of the Whitefish River and arrive at Nolalu, the heart of the Finnish settlement. Nolalu started as a station on the Port Arthur and Duluth Railway. Its odd name came not from a town in far-off Finland, as many have surmised, but from its first postmaster, who named it after his lumber company, Northland Lumber (No-La-Lu). The single village street, the store, and the houses were built beside the track. Trains at first called twice a week, later thrice, and the village became the focus for the Finnish farm community that surrounded it. Despite a decrease in the rural population after the closing of the railway, the village has remained almost purely Finnish. It is the most picturesque village on this trip, surrounded by the steep wooded walls of the river valley.

On your left as you cross the bridge is the former main street, the railbed, and the now-closed general store. Ahead of you is the stop sign marking Highway 588. Here too are some newer houses and a general store with gas pumps.

Nolalu to Silver Mountain

The next stretch of the route follows the railbed of the Port Arthur and Duluth, winding along the valley of the Whitefish River to the Shuniah Weachu, the Mountain of Silver.

From Nolalu, turn left onto Highway 588 and drive west out

of the village. Here, more small bush farms peer from the young woodlots, though new country homes of commuters to Thunder Bay have replaced some of the early farm homes. After 5 km you will come to a sample of an early twentieth-century Finnish farmhouse. Distinguished by its receding gables, this two-storey wooden building stands in a field on your left, framed by Silver Mountain.

The junction of Highway 593 is the site of Silver Mountain station. It is the only Port Arthur and Duluth station to survive, though its walls have been altered. Highway 588 continues for another 30 km, passing through the Finnish settlement of Suomi and into Crown forests, a land of mountains and lakes. The shoreline is public, so if you have a canoe or fishing gear, this is a side trip worth a day or more. Otherwise turn left onto Highway 593. Looming above the plain on the southeastern horizon is Silver Mountain. It was on this peak, between 1890 and 1910, that the twin silver towns of Silver Mountain East End and Silver Mountain West End grew. Each contained not only mines and mills, but hotels, stores, and two dozen log cabins. But the mining activity was only sporadic; by 1910 it had ceased, and the villages vanished.

West of Silver Mountain lies a land of unspoilt lakes.

Silver Mountain to Jackpine

Your route now ventures into a remote part of Ontario that was one of the province's last frontiers. Over the next 5 km, Highway 593 crosses a flat, rocky plain toward the high mesa, skirts the west end of the mountain, and then enters the canyon of the Little Whitefish River. After 8 km the river tumbles beside the road, and here you can stop and stroll in Devon Park, a small picnic site. The river meanders along the roadside for another 5 km until the first of the bush farms appears, marking the northern fringe of Jackpine.

Jackpine

Until the First World War, the valley of the Arrow River was a mystery to all but a few trappers and lumbermen. But surveys showed a wide, apparently fertile, valley floor that could become a new farming community. Then, in the late 1920s and the early 1930s, with the Depression in full gear and bread lines growing, the Ontario government threw open the flat soils of Devon township to settlers. Many of the settlers were Finns, attracted by the proximity of the Finnish colonies of Suomi and Nolalu to the north. Others were simply trying to escape the Depression.

Roads were cleared along both sides of the river, and of the 200 lots surveyed more than 50 were quickly taken. No town ever grew here, but the store and school were focal points for the rural community. Then, during the postwar boom, many of the settlers left the harsh life of the pioneer bush farm for the new jobs in Port Arthur and Fort William. Fewer than a half-dozen of the farms have retained their barns, and none operate commercially. Yet, through this valley, the remains of the community are there for you to see.

Jackpine to Pigeon River

The last section of your route continues down the valley of the Arrow River and ends amid the spectacular mountains and waterfalls that mark the mouth of the Pigeon River.

From Jackpine's community centre, cross the bridge and continue on Highway 593. For 5 km the road crosses the flat flood plain of the valley. Abandoned cabins and overgrown clearings dot the roadside and peer from a young, regenerating forest. The road then crosses the river once more and traverses a rolling,

The waters of the Pigeon River plunge over Middle Falls.

rocky countryside, where the clearings of the bush farms become farther apart. After 10 km, at a T-intersection, Highway 593 turns left, and the road to Pigeon River right. Turn right and drive 2 km to the abandoned border crossing of Pigeon River.

The recorded history of the Pigeon River dates from the fur-trading days, when it was the highway to the west. Fur seekers, both French and Indian, paddled upstream to the fur grounds and returned laden with beaver skins. But after the American Revolution, the Pigeon River became the new international border. Threats of customs duties forced the fur traders to the Kam River, a more difficult route but one that was free of international wrangling. There, the North West Company built Ontario's largest fur fort, Fort William, a fort which gave its name to a city. It has been carefully reconstructed as a living museum.

Just as the Pigeon River route was abandoned, so eventually was the border crossing at the end of the road. The area's first road had been built in the 1880s to bring mail from Duluth to the silver mines, but once the railways assumed this function the road fell into disrepair. It took until 1913, with angry petitions from area settlers, to improve the road. Rotary clubs in the Lakehead cities collected funds to bridge the river; but because they failed to complete an international agreement for the crossing, the bridge was dubbed the Outlaw Bridge.

During the late 1950s and early 1960s, when highways across Ontario were widened and improved, the westerly crossing of the Pigeon River was abandoned in favour of a new alignment 10 km east. The customs buildings and most of the homes were dismantled and moved. Among the foundations and vacant lots, fewer than a half-dozen remain. And the Outlaw Bridge has vanished forever.

Return to Highway 593 and follow it east. The highway crosses another rocky plain and then for 6 km follows the north bank of the Pigeon River to Middle Falls. Although the falls are only 15 m high, they are wide, and the water plunges furiously into the eddies below. Here you can park and follow a short trail to the lip of the falls, or you can fish in the river below them. Portions of an early timber chute, one of the few such structures to survive, lie beside the falls.

Highway 593 ends 2 km from Middle Falls at Highway 61. To the right is the entrance to Middle Falls Provincial Park, with its hiking trails to the spectacular 40-metre-high Pigeon Falls. Thunder Bay lies 55 km north on Highway 61.

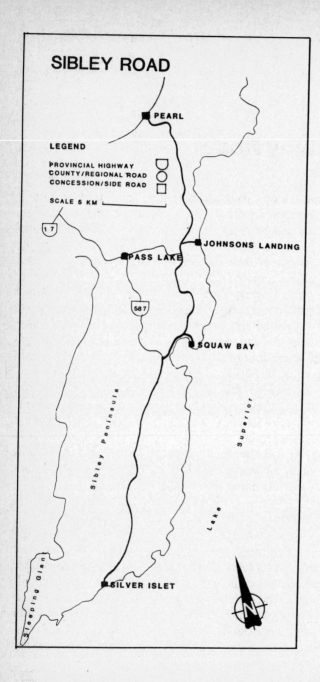

24 Sibley Road

Ontario's most famous rock formation is the Sleeping Giant. Arms folded across its chest, the figure consists of ancient limestone mesas that mark the tip of the Sibley Peninsula southeast of Thunder Bay. This trip uncovers the mysteries of the Sleeping Giant and probes the forgotten farming and fishing communities of this remote finger of land.

The route starts at Pearl on the Trans-Canada Highway, 50 km east of Thunder Bay, and runs south down the Sibley Peninsula on about 100 km of paved and dirt roads. While the Trans-Canada abounds in gas stations and restaurants, the peninsula has only one gas station and no restaurants. There are, however, many picnic areas, especially in the 320-km² Sibley Provincial Park.

This journey is for the hiker, the photographer, and the historian. Tiny fishing villages (reminiscent of the much-photographed Peggy's Cove in Nova Scotia) indent the east coast of the peninsula. Through Sibley Park, the authorities have cut hiking trails to the lofty head and chest of the Sleeping Giant; and at the remote tip of the peninsula sits Canada's oldest, richest, and best-preserved silver-mining town, Silver Islet.

A Bit of History

In 1845 silver was discovered on a small rocky islet 2 km off the tip of the Sibley Peninsula, and it became the focus for the first white settlement, Silver Islet. Then, in 1882, the Canadian Pacific Railway hammered its rails across the neck of the peninsula. It was followed in 1913 by the Canadian Northern Railway, which ran a few kilometres south. From the station villages of Pearl and Pass Lake, bush trails extended down the peninsula. Commercial fishing had been in full swing along the American shore since the fur-trading days of the 1820s and 1830s, but now the railways provided a means of shipping out the local catch. Soon most of the coves that could harbour a tug or a few skiffs had a small fishing station.

Farm settlement was much slower. Bush farms along the roads to the railway stations gave way after the First World War to a settlement scheme to open the Sibley's fertile postglacial sea deposits near Pass Lake. It was to this plain in 1924 that the Ontario government invited 65 Danish settlers.

Although there were fewer farmers than fishermen, their activities are still evident on much of the Sibley's landscape. Tourism, however, has surpassed both farming and fishing as travellers pick through the amethyst mines near Pearl, hike the trails of the Sibley Park, or settle for the summer into the miners' cabins of Silver Islet.

Pearl to Johnsons Landing

This first portion of the route follows a one-time bush trail from Pearl, passes some of the bush farms, and then leads into Johnsons Landing, the Peggy's Cove of the peninsula.

From Pearl drive south on Road 5. After less than a kilometre the road crosses the CNR tracks and then for 1 km follows the Pearl River—more a creek than a river. Along its banks one of the larger

The tiny fishing village of Johnsons Landing on the Sibley Peninsula.

of the early bush farms still operates, though the barn is now a sagging shell. The road then swings south and traverses a low, rolling landscape of young forest and overgrown clearings. Here, the pockets of soil were small and infertile, and the bush farms were soon abandoned.

After 9 km you will come to a T-intersection. Your route lies to the right, but first turn left for a short trip to Johnsons Landing. Reminiscent of east coast fishing villages, the wooden cabins and sheds of Johnsons Landing perch upon the smooth, pink rocks that ring the small bay. Beyond the wooded inlet are the waters of Black Bay, a wide indentation of Lake Superior that contains some of the lake's best fishing. A few paces north of the cove are the Kemp Fisheries. Although there is no public shoreline, you can take photographs from the road.

Johnsons Landing to Silver Islet

This next section of the route leads through the prospering Danish farm settlement to the Squaw Bay fishing colony, then through Sibley Provincial Park to the legendary Silver Islet and the land of the Sleeping Giant.

From the dead end at Johnsons Landing, return the way you came and then turn left at the intersection. Suddenly the wide, level plain of the Danish farming community appears from the bush. A few metres west of the first crossroads, in a clump of bushes on the north side of the road, is a log cabin built by the twentieth-century pioneers. Around it are the new homes and modern aluminum barns that replaced most of those log buildings. Farm enlargement and abandonment of the fringe area has reduced the dozen and a half original farms to the half-dozen that carry on today.

Continue south from the crossroads. The road now traverses the fertile plain and after 2 km crosses a narrow wooden bridge. Look for a side road 1 km beyond the bridge. This side road leads west to Highway 587, the route you will take on your return. For the present, continue straight ahead. After 1 km the road leaves the last of the farms and returns to Crown land; 3 km farther on you will come to a side road on the left. It is a dead-end road, leading 1 km to the fishing colony at Squaw Bay. Here you can see the drying racks, the log cabins and plank sheds and white tugs of the cove's fishermen.

Back on your main route, the road continues to follow the bay. Summer cottages mingle with fishermen's cabins and even with the clearings of an early farm. Another 2 km bring you to the boundary of Sibley Provincial Park and, after a further 1 km, to a stop sign at Highway 587. Turn left to the campgrounds and trails for which the park has become famous.

At 3 km from the turn you will see on your right the starting point of a scenic drive through the park. Remember this point, for it provides you with a spectacular return drive from the tip of the peninsula.

The park's most famous feature is the Sleeping Giant. Ojibwa legend says that it is the form of an early chief named Nanabozho, who was the son of the west wind. Nanabozho had led his people to the peninsula to keep them safe from their traditional enemy, the Sioux, and it was here on a tiny rock shoal that they uncovered silver. But to reveal its location, especially to white men, meant retribution from the Great Spirit, so Nanabozho swore his followers to secrecy. However, one of his subchiefs had secretly made jewellery from the metal, and after the Sioux had captured this subchief in battle, they led a group of whites to the islet. When Nanabozho saw them coming, he called up a storm to send the canoes and their travellers to the cold depths of the lake. In punishment, the Great Spirit turned Nanabozho to stone, the Sleeping Giant.

The geologists' less colourful theory is that the rocky mesa is the remnant of a great limestone plateau, whose sediments were laid down by an ancient sea. Ontario's most spectacular hiking trails lead to its lofty summits. To reach them, continue 12 km south on Highway 587 and ask for route maps in the park office.

You should allow at least half a day for a hike and wear sturdy hiking boots, for the trails are a 10-km round trip. From the peak, 140 m above the waters of the lake, you can watch grain ships gliding in and out of Thunder Bay harbour and see the ribbon of sulphurous smoke from the pulp mill extending to the horizon. And you can look down far below you to the restless waters of the lake as they roll and crash against the massive mesa.

Silver Islet

From the park office, continue south along Highway 587. After 3 km the road leaves the woods and enters a clearing. Then, in a

The miners' village at Silver Islet has survived almost unchanged for more than a century.

long row, the cabins of the 100-year-old village of Silver Islet appear.

This was the site of Canada's richest silver strike. It all began in 1845 when Joseph Woods, who was exploring for copper, discovered an unusually rich silver vein on a rocky shoal 2 km from the tip of the peninsula. But there was no economical means of transporting the ore, and it lay idle until 1870 when Major William Sibley of Detroit bought the claim for what would be the bargain price of $250,000. He hired an engineer named William Frue to build retaining walls and to bring the mine into production. But the spirit of Nanabozho grew restless and sent storms, tidal waves, and ice to destroy Frue's efforts. However, by 1873 Frue had constructed a breakwater that withstood all that the Sleeping Giant could hurl at it, and production began.

On the islet were the mine buildings and bunkhouses; on the shore a stamping mill with 50 stamps; and extending over an area of 2 km were 40 houses, a hotel, two churches, a store, and a log jail. Within ten years production exceeded $3 million. But as the shafts edged farther under the floor of the lake, the boilers had to pump ever harder to keep out the perpetual leaks.

By 1884 the peninsula had been stripped of its forest and as winter drew near all eyes looked for the coal boat. But, unknown to the townspeople, the boat was stuck fast in the ice on the south shore of the lake. There would be no coal. By March the boilers had consumed the last of the wood. As the flames died, water began to fill the shafts; the days of Silver Islet were finished.

Miraculously, the town survived. Soon after the miners left, residents of the growing towns of Port Arthur and Fort William (today amalgamated as Thunder Bay) began to buy the sturdy cabins as summer homes. In an unusual display of pride in local heritage, successive owners have preserved the town. The only buildings to have disappeared are the mill, the mine buildings on the islet, the Catholic church, and the mansion of the owner, Major Sibley. The rest remain. Thus, visitors can explore a miners' village that is a century old.

As you enter the village, the first building you see (on your left in a field by the water) is the log jail. It is Ontario's only surviving log jail and is privately preserved. Then the road enters the village proper and leads straight to the massive wooden store, which is now closed and is used in part as a summer home. Stretching in both directions are the miners' homes. Except for fresh coats of paint or new windows, they too are unchanged.

The road to the right is a dead end and although the sign declares it a private road, it is public. Highway 587 follows the shore to the left. Because it is still the narrow road that the miners built, the highway is a one-way road during the summer. A few paces east of the store is a log home which houses artifacts and silver samples from the mining days. Here you can buy local handicrafts, as well as books that recount the many stories that Silver Islet can tell.

Follow the road east along the shore. Lake Superior laps at your right, while the miners' cabins line the road on your left. As the road swings inland, the miners' graveyard lies about 100 m in the bush to your left. To your right, far off the shore, you will be able to discern the low form of the shoal that produced Canada's richest silver mine.

Silver Islet to Pass Lake

The last segment of the route returns up the peninsula along a clifftop drive to the hamlet of Pass Lake. From there you can continue to the deep Ouimet Canyon and to some of Canada's best amethyst-gathering sites.

Danish colony at Pass Lake. Despite its wilderness image, northern Ontario has pockets of fertile farmland.

The lake that gave the village of Pass Lake its name.

263

Ouimet Canyon, the main attraction of one of Ontario's most spectacular parks.

About 1 km after the one-way road leaves the shore, it reconnects with the two-way Highway 587. To return north, turn right and travel 15 km to the scenic drive on your left. If you wish to pass it by, you can continue 15 km to Pass Lake on 587.

The scenic route twists across a rough and rocky terrain to the clifftops. Here, 150 m above the lake, it follows the cliffs. At three locations there are specially cleared viewpoints. From them you can see the wooded Caribou Island and the coastline of Lake Superior as it curves towards the city of Thunder Bay. After the road reconnects with Highway 587, Pass Lake village lies 1 km to your right.

Pass Lake was originally a station on the Canadian Northern Railway, and it became the focus for the Danish farm colony to its east. Many of the people from the colony have relocated in the village. One, Petersen, operates the general store; another, Sorensen, sells wooden furniture and carvings. The squat white Lutheran church dates from the Danish migration.

More to See

Follow Highway 587 west from the store. Boegh Park lies about 1.5 km from the store and contains a plaque to commemorate the prehistoric Aqua Plano Indians who occupied the area shortly after the last ice age. From here, a drive of 5 km north brings you to the Trans-Canada Highway.

Canada's best amethyst deposits lie a few kilometres east. Most are in private hands and the owners, for a fee, will allow you to collect on your own. The best pieces, however, usually make their way to the on-site gift shops and sales tables.

The Thunder Bay Amethyst Mine lies 5 km east of the intersection and a further 7 km on the East Loon Lake Road. At the 5-km mark there is a steep hill and switchbacks which are too hazardous for trailers and campers. However, the mine owners have constructed a parking lot here for large vehicles. The fee for collecting is $1.

In addition, there is the Dorion Amethyst Mine Road, which is located 6 km east of Pearl and 16 km east of the intersection. Three collecting sites lie on this dirt road, all easily accessible. One, the Ontario Gem Amethyst Mine, lies 3.2 km from the highway. (Fork onto a road that branches left about the 1.5-km mark.) The second is a small private pit, to be found a short distance after you branch right. And 2 km beyond that is the Dorion Amethyst Mine with a gift shop and a parking lot for trailers.

Ouimet Canyon is a 5-km-long fissure that plunges 100 m into the ancient bedrock. So little sunlight reaches the bottom that arctic vegetation can grow there. To reach the canyon, drive 10 km east from Pearl and follow the Ouimet Canyon Provincial Park signs for another 10 km. This free park contains several kilometres of hiking trails—but be careful, for there are no guard rails and the footing is at times slippery.

Few people visit the north shore of Lake Superior without spending several days. You will find ample accommodation in Thunder Bay and another cluster of motels at Nipigon, 50 km east of the canyon. Private campgrounds abound in the area, and the several provincial parks along the Superior shore contain some of the province's most scenic campsites.

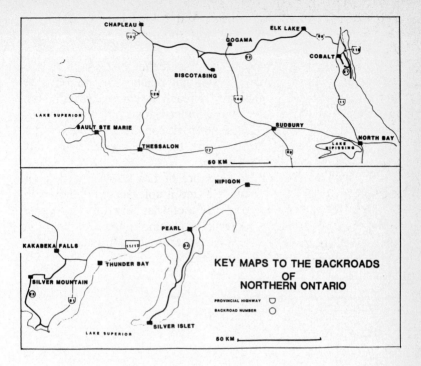

KEY MAPS TO THE BACKROADS
OF
NORTHERN ONTARIO

PROVINCIAL HIGHWAY
BACKROAD NUMBER

50 KM

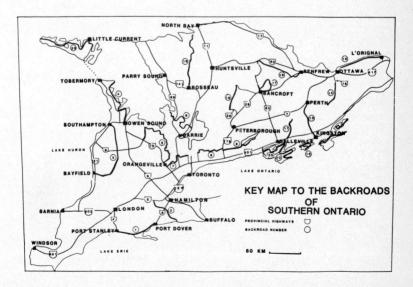

KEY MAP TO THE BACKROADS
OF
SOUTHERN ONTARIO

PROVINCIAL HIGHWAYS
BACKROAD NUMBER

50 KM

Index

Printed in Canada